JUST FOR FUN

Just for Fun

The Story of AAU Women's Basketball

ROBERT W. IKARD

The University of Arkansas Press
Fayetteville
2005

08   07   06   05   5   4   3   2   1

Designed by Liz Lester

☉   The paper used in this publication meets the minimum requirements of the American National Standard for Permanence of Paper for Printed Library Materials Z39.48–1984.

LIBRARY OF CONGRESS CATALOGING-IN-PUBLICATION DATA

Ikard, Robert W.
    Just for fun : the story of AAU women's basketball / Robert W. Ikard.
        p.   cm.
    Includes bibliographical references and index.
    ISBN 1-55728-783-X (cloth : alk. paper)
        1. Basketball for women—United States—History. 2. Amateur Athletic Union of the United States—History. I. Title.
    GV886.I43 2005
    796.323'8—dc22

                                                            2004021104

To the women who played AAU basketball
in historic obscurity
but always, for the love of the game,
with exuberant excellence

CONTENTS

Introduction   ix

CHAPTER ONE
A Forgotten Era   1

CHAPTER TWO
Basketball in the Oil Patch   21

CHAPTER THREE
Beer Distributors, Business Schools, and Hosiery Girls   51

CHAPTER FOUR
Expansion and Consolidation   95

CHAPTER FIVE
NBC, "The Greatest"   121

CHAPTER SIX
Looking Back and Ahead   155

APPENDIX A
AAU Women's Basketball All-Americans   201

APPENDIX B
Top-Four Finishers in AAU Tournaments   215

APPENDIX C
The Mythical All-Star Teams   219

Notes   223
Bibliography   239
Index   247

INTRODUCTION

Small-town living and loyalty traditionally center on the local high school. In addition to seeking education of their progeny there, townsfolk have enjoyed quilting bees, theatricals, political debates, raffles, and sundry other social activities at the schoolhouse. The most unifying and important school-related activity though has always been interscholastic athletics. Students and parents, saints and sinners, old maids and bachelors, moguls and ne'er-do-wells—all rooting for the locals, "us," to prevail over the odious others, "them." Because it is more affordable and there are usually enough students to make a team, basketball is played more than any other sport in small towns. The quality of their team often determines a town's place in the regional or state pecking order. "Ours are better'n yours!" Besides, in a pre-television era, what better entertainment during a cheerless winter could one get than a courtside seat purchased for way less than a buck among friends in a bright, toasty gym?

Such a place is Hampshire, which nestles snugly in the hilly western section of fertile Maury County, Tennessee. Though established in 1837, this unincorporated, middle Tennessee burg never got big enough to be called a town. Hampshire has been "not so much a place as a state of mind."[1] Yet it has survived despite relentless urbanization and has remained a very strong "state of mind" to its daughters and sons.

Much of that devotion is attributable to its basketball history. In the late nineteenth century within the decade after the sport was invented, a secondary school teacher named Mr. Hays supposedly built the first basketball court in Maury County—an outdoor one in back of the nearby Cathey's Creek Church of Christ. The high school gym, built in the 1920s, was one of the best around. Two pot-bellied stoves inset into the sidewalls at mid-court heated the glistening hardwood floor and the bellicose fans that filled the bleachers and balconies at the ends of the court. Madison Square Garden paled in comparison.[2]

The high school's traditional red uniforms were appropriately symbolic of the passion invested in Hampshire basketball. Local folklore included tales about how newborns were assessed for basketball potential. If, when offered a bottle or a basketball, a baby chose the bottle, the parent hit the offspring over the head with it. In a direr version of this testing of instincts, the baby's demeanor was closely watched when it was first presented a basketball. If its face lit up and it grabbed for the athletic icon, the kid was a keeper. If the infant showed any disfavor toward the big orb, its Hampshire parentage would certainly be questioned and, unfortunately, it might have to be drowned in the creek like some useless cat.[3]

Unlike fable though, Goliath usually whips up on David; and Hampshire was rarely a state basketball power. Still, Hampshire's teams (known variously as Reds, Red Devils, and Hawks) consistently gave the locals much to cheer. Fortified by pregame meals of baloney sandwiches and Moon Pies®, the boy's team began a seven-year home-undefeated streak in 1940. In 1943, the seven-member squad made it to the state tournament. When the lads from their school of seventy-five students were pitted against Chattanooga Central, a school of two thousand, the coach reassured that, "They will play 5 and we will play 5, that makes it dead even." Despite a good tussle, they lost to the eventual champions.[4]

The girls' teams received just as much loyalty and were more consistently successful. Led by the "best player in the state," Neva Thompson, the Hampshire girls in 1927 lost 26–24 in the state finals to Nashville's Peabody Demonstration School. Though struggling with the handicap of playing in the winner's gymnasium, the Hampshire folks were just happy to be there, enjoyed visiting the city, and gave the champions all the competition they wanted.[5]

Girls' basketball remained important in Hampshire, and such success continued into later generations. Betty Booker scored 3,329 points for the team in the mid-1970s and became the first woman to score over 1,000 points at Memphis State University. Leslie Travis notched over 2,000 points in a Hawk career that ended in 1998.[6]

In places such as Hampshire, the team coach may be a bigger wheel than the mayor, the principal, or the Baptist preacher. The pressure, though, may exceed the prestige of the position. My father, Robert Edwin (Bob) Ikard, was on the Hampshire hot seat during most of the 1930s. In addition to being the science teacher on the four-person faculty, he coached the girls' basketball team from 1934 to 1939 and the boys' squad from 1937 to 1939. Though certainly not getting rich teaching at a country school during the depression, he allegedly made more money than the other faculty members.[7]

Coach Bob Ikard and the 1935 Hampshire (Tennessee) High School girls' basketball team. As an eighth grader, Tennie Cathey is the player on the left, front row. In a time of fewer rules, Tennie played five years of varsity basketball. *Photograph courtesy of Tennie Cathey Chaffin.*

His teams did real well. Though Tennessee girls did not have the opportunity of state tournament competition during the thirties, the Hampshire lasses were highly competitive in their area, winning county and district tournaments (invariably against bigger schools) and occasionally advancing to regional competition.[8] Coach Ikard's round-ball empire was short-lived, though. To the chagrin of his adoring players, he left the teaching profession in 1939.

So I learned early at my daddy's knee that girls' basketball was interesting and could be important in a little southern town. He had enjoyed coaching girls and thought that in the "touch" aspects of athletics, girls were probably better than boys. For instance, he thought that with practice they could be better foul or outside (then usually a two-handed set shot) shooters than boys. This impression about girls' basketball excellence was almost squelched by the game I saw played in my mid-1950s high school years. The six-player game of three guards and three forwards, neither of which could cross the center line, was stiflingly dull. There was no full-court running, little dribbling, and a frequent traffic jam at the midcourt. In games between less athletic teams, there seemed to be an endless series of tie balls. The charm eluded me.

Though not recognizing it at the time, my youthful observations also planted the subliminal seed that big athletic accomplishments, especially in basketball, can come from small and unlikely sources. That impression solidified when I saw some really good basketball coming from tiny, usually rural schools. Year after year, small schools were successful in the Tennessee State High School Tournament. Characterized by good coaching and year-round dedication, teams from schools with student bodies numbering fewer than three figures were highly competitive and often won the tourney.

As an avid sports page reader, I saw the occasional article on the fringes of Nashville papers' sports sections about the NBC women's team. No, those initials did not refer to the National Broadcasting Company. Rather, they stood for some obscure educational institution called the Nashville Business College. Those articles kept coming for the better part of a decade. Yet I never saw this team play, and I did not know anyone who had. Who were they?

There was recurring allusion in these articles to NBC's star, one Nera White. In the twentieth-century-ending explosion of seemingly innumerable rankings, newspaper pieces about this player referred to her as someone really important in Tennessee sports history. Could she have any importance beyond the state's borders—or generally to the sport of basketball?

Preliminary research into the NBC team revealed that they had Nashville progenitors, teams with exotic names such as the Vultee (or Convair) Bomberettes and Cook's Goldblume. What is a Bomberette?

What is a Cook's Goldblume? Some of these NBC ancestors had won *national championships* of some sort. I could not recall a national championship team of any sport from Nashville.

These Nashville teams that aroused my interest in this book's topic competed in schedules and tournaments sponsored by the Amateur Athletic Union (AAU).[9] Their opponents were little-known college teams such as Wayland Baptist and Iowa Wesleyan and industrial teams sponsored by diverse companies such as Hanes Hosiery, Lion Oil, and the American Institute of Business (AIB). They featured stars unknown to today's supposedly sophisticated fan of women's basketball: Alline Banks, Lurlyne Greer, Hazel Walker, and the great Nera White. A contemporary aficionado of athletic trivia might recall at least one player from the league. Mildred (Babe) Didrikson (Zaharias), whom some designate the greatest athlete of all time, received her first national fame through AAU basketball.

Though numerous women's professional leagues have failed, the contemporary pro game may yet survive due to the munificence of the (men's) National Basketball Association (NBA). However, the college game currently dominates the popular market for women's basketball. Millions of dollars springing from television, donors, and profitable intercollegiate men's sports are lavished on "programs" characterized by huge coaches' salaries, plush facilities, and lavish travel, all ending each year with a television rite and Eldorado, the Final Four. Blinded by the modern malady of short historic attention span, various individuals and colleges have taken credit for launching this bonanza sometime within the last couple of decades.

Those doing so seem oblivious to a four decades' precedent of superb AAU women's basketball. As Harley Redin, the great coach of a great AAU team, the Wayland Flying Queens, noted, the AAU "got dumped" on the trash heap of history. From the AAU player pool, the United States formed several successful international teams. Due to a dearth of publicity and public interest, gifted players on those teams sometimes enjoyed fame abroad but realized only anonymity at home. Until nearly the last quarter of the twentieth century, AAU ball was the only route that the most skilled women players could pursue after high school. The history of that era has been merely sketched.

So many questions quickly arose about the women who played that game. Why did they labor in such obscurity? Or was it really labor? Who were they? From where did they hail? What kind of people were they? Could they compete today? Now when writers actually cover women's sports, why do we not read about AAU basketball? Why were Nashville teams so successful?

While writing about the spectrum of AAU women's basketball, the emphasis may seem greater on those Nashville teams. Because that is my home, I had better access to people and materials relevant to the topic. The Nashville teams' experiences were representative of how those from other places played the AAU game. Certainly that was the case for the very successful squads. The teams from Nashville were special. Of forty-two AAU tournaments contested until 1970 when the five-player game was adopted, Nashville teams won sixteen (38 percent). A 1952 article in a Nashville paper's rotogravure section called the city the "World Capital of Woman's Basketball." During the dominant AAU era, other places such as Winston-Salem, North Carolina, and (especially) Plainview, Texas, would make the same claim. Time and records, however, substantiated the writer's claim.[10]

Seeking answers led me to interesting friendships with many people, mainly women. Most were generous with their time, recollections, and materials. Whether or not discussants felt their AAU experience beneficial or fun, they all retained a noticeable edge of competitive spirit— sometimes in sport, invariably in life. Their stories are richly redolent of a vanishing phenomenon, amateur athletics. In an environment of little public support, they played sport for its own sake. In the process, they did important things that need to be lauded by modern fans, who have no concept of truly amateur athletics and thus often have a jaded perspective on sport. Such fans need to appreciate these pioneers of women's basketball in the United States.

Though the story is much more than just data, it is important that results be collated. As accurately and fully as possible, I have recorded wins and losses, champions, and honors. These cumulative facts noted in approximate chronological order will substantiate the accomplishments of AAU players, coaches, teams, and sponsors. Profiles of some of the most important players will substantiate the high quality of athlete and person who played AAU basketball.

The field of women's sports history is a relatively new one. There are, therefore, many fertile and only preliminarily tapped facets of a big subject. AAU women's basketball is one of those. Though some analysis of demographics, economics, sexuality, and other characteristics of participants will be presented, my principal goal is to provide a comprehensive overview of the great game of AAU women's basketball, thereby honoring those who perpetuated it and providing accurate material for future researchers. There is plenty to tell.

It's tip-off time. Let's play!

CHAPTER ONE

A Forgotten Era

"Who left out chapter two?"

—Carolyn Miller

The Current Game

The 2003 National Collegiate Athletic Association (NCAA) Division One women's basketball championship in Atlanta, Georgia, was a big event. The University of Connecticut Huskies, coached by Geno Auriemma, won their fourth NCAA championship, beating the six-time-winner University of Tennessee Volunteers, coached by Pat Summitt, the winningest coach in women's basketball. Played in the Georgia Dome, a closed stadium more suited for football than basketball, the two sessions on April 6 and 8 were each attended by 56,420 fans. The two telecasts on ESPN (formerly Entertainment Sports Programming Network) averaged 2.3 million household impressions, the first time the network had more than two million for this tournament. The championship game was the fourth most watched basketball game in ESPN history.

A week later, those big numbers paled somewhat against those posted for the men's NCAA championship, an invariably more popular affray. The men also played in a mega-gym, the New Orleans Superdome, where 54,500 fans attended each session. The most telling data reflecting disparate public interest between the men's and women's finals were in television viewership and broadcast rights prices. The 2003 men's championship game was viewed in thirteen and one-half million homes, six times more than turned on the women's final. In 2004 CBS paid $389 million to broadcast the men's tournament, while ESPN paid a relatively paltry $11 million for the women's tournament. Still, women's collegiate basketball was now a big, important operation.[1]

In addition to the team excellence shown by Connecticut in winning their fourth NCAA tournament in 2003, the dominant play of their star, Diana Taurasi, was conspicuous. The strong, smooth, tough, six-foot tall forward towered over all others in scoring fifty-four points in two games. Her consistent brilliance led to knowledgeable fans opining that she surely ranked among the best women players of all time in the United States, such as past collegiate stars Chamique Holdsclaw of the University of Tennessee, Cheryl Miller of the University of Southern California, and Sheryl Swoopes of Texas Tech University. Taurasi won the Naismith Award as the Player of the Year; Auriemma was Coach of the Year. Surely this was women's basketball at its best—now or ever.

As the twenty-first century began, girls and women were also playing the game in record volume. In the United States, high school girls played basketball more than any other organized sport. Between 1971 and 2001, girls' participation in high school sports increased almost tenfold, from 294,015 to 2,784,154. In 2002 over 450,000 girls played high school basketball. In 1999–2000, 14,445 women played NCAA basketball at all levels, a growth of 151 percent since 1981–1982.[2]

Thus a big chunk of the American public was obviously interested in women's basketball. Fans were attending games and following their favorites as enthusiastically portrayed by broadcast and print journalists. The sport was riding the crest of a steadily rising wave of popularity. Was it always thus? How did it get that way? What were the historic landmarks leading to such a lofty status?

A Forgotten Era

Women's Sports before Basketball

Depending on the historic era, women's participation in sport has usually been sparse at most. Most ancient cultures forbade it. Spartan women were encouraged to be athletic in order to produce stronger mothers and children, and in the Roman Republican society there was the occasional woman gladiator. The Greeks and Romans also recognized some athletic goddesses (Artemis, Diana) but generally consigned women to roles as matrons. There was no leisure time, money, or adequate health for women to pursue sport during the Dark and Middle Ages. Beginning in the Renaissance, upper-class European women began participating in golf, archery, and falconry. Their lower-class peers occasionally pursued team sports, sailed, ran foot races, or even boxed. Performing the latter two events sans blouses reflected a prevalent pandering of a lascivious public (i.e., fans) attitude toward the activities. In North America, unmarried Indian women of various tribes participated in ball throwing (usually an animal bladder), lacrosse, running, and double ball, a team sport often taking place over miles of territory.[3]

Sport for women became more plausible and popular in the post–Civil War United States. This interest was abetted by a critical change in costume created before the war. In 1851 Amelia Bloomer, an early advocate for women's rights, recommended a loose dress worn over baggy trousers to replace the corseted fashion of previous centuries, thus alleviating a principal physical impediment to female athletic participation. Among other activities, the "bloomers" allowed pedaling of affordable bicycles that were introduced to the American public at the 1876 Philadelphia Exposition.

Commercial team sports for women tentatively emerged in the late nineteenth century. While a few women's cricket teams were being displayed in Britain, American sponsors organized traveling baseball teams. Promoters used a proven marketing technique, emphasizing the players' sex rather than their athletic skills. Nonetheless, teams such as the "Blondes" and the "Brunettes" were short-lived business failures.[4]

In that same time, middle- and upper-class European women athletes got instruction and competition through well-established athletic clubs. In addition to the individual sports, they enjoyed team competitions in boating, tennis, cricket, and racing (on land or ice). In the

United States an abiding movement toward women's team sports arose from a new environment, the physical education departments of colleges and universities.

Despite the prevalence of Victorian concepts of femininity (woman as frail), some schools had recognized since the early nineteenth century the value of athletic training for the health of their young female charges. This did not mean competitive sports. Conscientiously eschewing the perceived crude activities of their male counterparts, women physical educators emphasized an amalgam of gymnastics and strength training, all initially performed in bulky gowns and later in the barely less voluminous but certainly more comfortable bloomers. Advocates of the Swedish System employed gymnastics, dance, and a few accoutrements such as Indian clubs and bar bells, aiming to develop grace and strength in the whole body. Though some still moaned that muscles were unattractive on women, educators, students, and parents increasingly recognized the importance of such nonacademic physical activities.

A persistent problem with these obviously beneficial, esthetically correct exercises was student boredom. Drill did not motivate; sports did. The athletes and the pedagogues finally concluded that in order to enjoy exercise, they might have to accept some of the ostensibly odious aspects of men's sports—competition, scorekeeping, and aggressiveness.[5] For women at the academies that offered physical education, having a goal of winning made exercise more fun. Thence came basketball.

The Rise of Women's Basketball

Several milestones leading to the current elevated level of interest in women's basketball are generally recognized. True aficionados quickly recall the fundamental contributions of James Naismith (1861–1939) and, especially, Senda Berenson (1868–1954), the respective founders of men's and women's basketball.

When considering the twenty-first century's most powerful U.S. women's basketball schools, usually from big universities known for their athletic eminence, it is ironic that foremost among the pioneering colleges in getting collegiate basketball started were the so-called Seven Sisters, Barnard, Bryn Mawr, Mt. Holyoke, Radcliffe, Smith, Vassar, and Wellesley. The spark that inflamed collegiate interest came from a very academic milieu. These small, elite, private women's schools of the Northeast were enlightened about physical education and made student participation mandatory during the last quarter of the nineteenth century. They recognized the spirit engendered by team sports and early on offered baseball for the young women.[6]

In 1875 at age seven Senda Berenson (nee Valvrojenski) immigrated to Boston from Vilna, Lithuania. The childhood of the Jewish girl with her harsh peddler father in the city's West End was compounded by physical weakness that supposedly plagued her throughout her formative years. She did not finish the Girl's Latin School and failed at her music studies at the Boston Conservatory of Music. To combat a persistent, historically undefined malady, she enrolled in the Boston Normal School of Gymnastics (BNSG). This fortuitous choice turned her life and fundamentally affected women's sports in the United States.

The success of the BNSG was possible because society, especially educators, were leaving behind the popular nineteenth-century concept that if women were not fragile, they at least should act so. It was far more than an academy to teach stretching and tumbling. Representative of a growing number of schools that taught only physical education, its curriculum included anatomy and physiology, the teaching of which was enhanced by the BNSG's association with Harvard during Berenson's second year there.

Senda thrived at BNSG and lost her mysterious debilitating weakness. She was recommended in 1892 to fill a teaching vacancy in gymnastics at Smith College in Northampton, Massachusetts. When she took the job as director of the gymnasium and instructor of physical culture, she moved to the central part of the state, away from her unpleasant Boston childhood, and into an academic environment receptive to her interest in teaching the joys and benefits of physical fitness. Founded in 1875, the year Berenson immigrated, the young college had just opened a new gymnasium featuring all the modern amenities, including a swimming pool.[7]

The energetic, innovative Berenson quickly decided that the plethora of individual sports available to the Smith women needed to be amplified by team sports requiring close physical competition. Almost commensurate with her new employment, a new game that would solve her problem, basket ball,[8] was being invented nearby.

James Naismith was a thirty-year-old Canadian who had, like Berenson, embraced the rapidly evolving field of physical education. Naismith was an orphan who grew up in rural Ontario. An intelligent lad and an exceptional athlete (gymnastics, boxing, wrestling, rugby football), he had graduated from McGill University in Montreal, Canada, with a philosophy degree in 1885. He followed that with studies in theology at Presbyterian College, an affiliate of McGill. During his time there, Naismith continued to play sports and became acquainted with the Young Men's Christian Association (YMCA). Though finishing near the top of his class in 1890, he confounded his family and associates by rejecting the ministry and pursuing a career in physical education, a field in which he hoped to use his proclivity for sport to ". . . lead young men to a good end." In 1891 Naismith matriculated at the School for Christian Workers, soon known as the "International Y.M.C.A. Training School," in Springfield, Massachusetts. There he learned about his calling with enthusiastic friends such as Amos Alonzo Stagg, also a former theology student, a prodigious Yale athlete, and soon to become one of the great football coaches.[9]

Naismith was an instructor during the last of his two years at Springfield. As part of a seminar on the psychology of play, Dr. Luther Gulick Jr. assigned Naismith the daunting task of inventing a new team game. The successful completion of that assignment would solve a nagging problem for physical educators, interesting competition for students between the football and baseball seasons. Even as a beginning teacher, Naismith recognized that though independent American students might concede the benefits of exercise, they would much rather attain that with competition than via stilted European gymnastic drills or children's games.

If it were to be generally accepted, the game had to be played indoors since it was to be contested during winter in a northern clime. Limitations of both the athletes' bodies and the gymnasium structure prohibited the rougher features of games such as soccer and lacrosse. Gym walls and floors are not as resilient as turf, and windows are not immune to flying balls. Roughness should not, therefore, be a primary characteristic of the new game. Naismith's musings on the problem finally coalesced into four principles: (1) no running with the ball; (2) no tackling or other rough contact; (3) a horizontal goal above the players' heads; (4) the opportunity for any player to score with the ball. Based on these fundamentals, Naismith composed thirteen guiding game rules.

The first basketball game took place in the Springfield YMCA gymnasium just before Christmas vacation in 1891. The requisite equipment consisted of a soccer ball and two peach baskets (provided at the last moment by the school janitor), one nailed to the balcony at each end of the court. Because there were eighteen men in Naismith's class, each team had nine players. Division of players was approximately equivalent in modern terms to three guards, three centers, and three forwards. No one memorialized the game score.

The Training School faculty provided physical training for the school's secretarial staff as well as its students. Naismith claimed that the first women's basketball game was in early 1892, the teams composed of those secretaries (among whom was Naismith's future wife) and teachers from the Buckingham School in Northampton. At first Naismith was unhappy with women's reactions to team competition. Though he changed his mind in later years, he initially concluded that women and preachers showed the worst sportsmanship of all.

Enthusiastic word-of-mouth tidings about basketball spread immediately after its introduction. The college students disseminated the news on their Christmas vacations and even organized holiday games back home. Naismith published an article in his school's newspaper, the *Triangle,* in January 1892, entitled "A New Game." The first organized basketball team was a group of nine students from his school that played exhibition games around the eastern states during the spring 1892 term. The team was led by a rough and recalcitrant student named Mahan, who, after early skepticism, had enthusiastically adopted the game and suggested Naismith call the immediately popular sport basketball.[10]

It is uncertain when or how Senda Berenson learned about basketball. Naismith asserted that she was introduced to it during a conversation between them at a physical education meeting at Yale in 1893, yet Berenson had already introduced the game at Smith in 1892. Since Northampton was only ninety miles from Springfield, she obviously had learned about it earlier, perhaps from Naismith's article in the *Triangle.* At any rate, she was immediately intrigued, recognizing the answer to her quest for an appropriate team sport.[11]

Berenson employed the game to solve the same problem Naismith had faced, the provision of interesting indoor exercise spiced by competition. However, she believed the women's game should be different from the men's. In order to protect the players, she divided the court into three sections and required players to stay in them. Staying with Naismith's team size precedent, she used nine players per side, three in each section of her tripartite court. Going even beyond Naismith in eliminating roughness, she forbade players to grab the ball from an opponent's grasp.

Both physical educators were riding an unexpectedly popular tiger that attracted spectators as well as thrilling the athletes. Berenson organized the first women's collegiate basketball game between the Smith College freshmen and sophomores, the classes of '96 and '95. Before an excited capacity crowd of women (no men other than college president Seelye allowed) chanting team songs and waving banners in Smith's Alumnae Gymnasium bedecked with the competing classes' colors of violet and yellow, the game was played on March 22, 1893. Two nine-member teams clad in costumes of dark stockings, middy blouses, and bloomers had at it with gusto. Berenson must have wondered if her efforts to protect the players were for naught when a freshman center dislocated her shoulder on the opening tip, a mishap sardonically publicized in a local newspaper story entitled "Gladiators Appear, One Dying." The game was joyously joined thereafter though, much to the delight of the teams and their rooters. The freshmen prevailed over the sophomores, 19–18.

Throughout her career, Berenson felt the same way as Naismith about the competitive aspects of basketball. It might be intense, but it should be friendly and supportive of relationships that would prevail after the game. Sportsmanship and team play were more important than victory won at the sacrifice of these principles. After her introduction of the game to women, the Smithies were peppered with challenges from other college teams. Berenson demurred, establishing an athletics philosophy that would prevail at Smith—the engagement of all women, regardless their skill level, in the benefits of exercise through intrascholastic sport.[12]

Basketball was just too popular though; and, contrary to Berenson's philosophy, intercollegiate competition was inevitable. Dramatizing the rapid and far-flung spread of the game, many competitive milestones soon

The Smith College freshman and sophomore classes line up to begin a basketball skirmish before a packed gymnasium in 1901. Senda Berenson is the woman in a dark skirt and *chignon* on the left side of the gym. *Photographer unknown. Reproduced by permission of Smith College Archives.*

occurred on the West Coast. The University of California, Berkeley team played a series of games with Miss Head's School, a local preparatory school, in November 1892. The first two intercollegiate games occurred within two weeks in California and Washington. On April 4, 1896, California, Berkeley played Stanford, an early contest in an abiding, fierce rivalry. Stanford won 2–1! Up the coast in Seattle on April 17, the University of Washington women prevailed over those from Ellensburg State Normal School in a higher scoring game, 6–3.[13]

All the early games were played with rules largely communicated by word of mouth and liberally adapted to local preferences. The Washington-State Normal game for instance was played with each of nine players per side occupying only her *one-ninth* of the court. Clara Baer formalized this concept of multiple court sections in 1893 with the unveiling of *Basquette* (her sectional term for basketball) to the South and her physical education pupils at New Orleans' Sophie Newcomb College, yet another private school contributing to the early development of basketball. In order to avoid roughness and overexertion by her developing ladies, Baer employed seven to eleven sections of the gymnasium floor. The State-Normal worthies in the initial Pacific Northwest intercollegiate contest were also frustrated by a University of Washington rule that allowed players to knock the ball from opponents' hands. Senda Berenson had strictly forbidden this rough practice of "snatching," a recommendation followed in most women's games.

Berenson felt that "true womanhood" required the development of both body and mind. She decried the late-nineteenth-century perception of a woman as ". . . small waisted, small footed, small brained damsel, who prided herself on her delicate health, who thought fainting interesting, and hysterics fascinating." Her delight with basketball arose from the development of physical (quickness, coordination) and mental (self-denial, self-reliance) skills her students gained from playing the game. Like Baer, however, she was influenced by contemporary ideas about the different physiology of the sexes and an emphasis on gentility in women. That is to say, ladies were presumed to be a physically weaker vessel and behaviorally should strive for decorum rather than strife. It is unclear how she reconciled the latter philosophy with the observation that much of the pleasure of basketball arose from its competitive flavor, a classical masculine characteristic. *La difference* prevailed in her attitude toward basketball; ergo, the women's game should be different from the men's.[14]

Development and codification of rules occurred quickly because of the prompt general acceptance of the game. Because of her role in rules making, Berenson's influence on basketball extended far beyond her pioneering introduction of the game to collegians. Although Clara Baer is correctly awarded kudos for first publishing a set of women's basketball rules in 1895, the ultimately prevalent rules sprang from Berenson. She edited *Spalding's Official Women's Basket Ball Guide* in which they first appeared in 1901 and were published annually thereafter. These first generally accepted guidelines were called "Berenson's rules." In addition to the division of the court into three parts[15] and the prohibition against snatching, the rules included a time limit of three seconds for holding the ball (anticipating a current collegiate rule), a limit of three dribbles, and a range of from five to ten players per team. Arising from an 1899 Physical Training meeting in Springfield, the Women's Basketball Committee that promulgated these rules became a part of the American Physical Education Association (APEA) in 1905, thus acquiring the political status to assure its influence.

Many of the rules guiding the modern game were developed by 1918. These included awarding of an out-of-bounds ball to the opponent of the team that caused the infraction, personal foul limitations, introduction of the bounce-pass, liberalization of substitution rules, and the breakthrough acceptance of the open-bottomed basket. Team sizes were changed to a range of six to nine. As a harbinger of the most definitive rule change in women's basketball later in the century, five players could be used on a smaller, two-division court. Though the center could run the entire court in this new hybrid, only forwards were allowed to score. There was ambivalence about the dribble. Theoretically that technique promoted dominance by the more skilled players and de-emphasized team play. However, the brief time the ball was not in a player's hands was the only opportunity for an opponent to steal it. Rule makers vacillated between allowing three dribbles, no dribbles, and one dribble (by 1913).

Between World Wars, there were few significant rule changes. One allowed guarding in planes other than the vertical. This finally made possible the performance of truly aggressive defense, thus pressuring offensive players to become more inventive. In 1938 the previously experimental two-division court, six-player game became official for women, a rule status that would prevail for over thirty years. Ball size was set at twenty to twenty-two ounces and approximately thirty inches in circumference, the same size as that used by men, a standard not to be broached until rules changes by the NCAA in the last quarter of the twentieth century.

So women began playing basketball around the same time as men and seemed to enjoy it as much. From its inception though, its female propagators wanted a different game. By the time she ceased editing the *Spalding Women's Basketball Guides* in 1918, Berenson and her pioneering ilk had codified the philosophy that women's rules were necessary for the women's game.[16]

Latter-Day Developments

Casual basketball fans might believe that the sport really began for women in the last quarter of the twentieth century. A couple of events are usually posited as bases for this incomplete understanding of the history. In the annual buildup for the NCAA Women's Final Four, commentators invariably recall the groundbreaking work of Carol Eckman. As coach of the West Chester State (Pennsylvania) Ramettes, Eckman became frustrated with playing AAU basketball. Disregarding the great success of several college teams in such competition for thirty years and believing it only fair for college teams to compete against each other, she promoted a sixteen-team tournament at her school in spring 1969. West Chester won this first national women's tournament exclusively for collegians, a forerunner of such competition under different auspices that has burgeoned since then.[17]

Title IX though is conceded to be the greatest sociopolitical impetus to the recent development of elite women's basketball in the United States. The provision was only part of the 1972 Educational Amendment to the Civil Rights Act. Passed to eliminate sexual discrimination at schools receiving federal funds, its varying interpretations came to interest the general public only in their application to sports.

Adjudications of the act have been in a constant state of flux since its inception. The prevalent interpretation of it is that educational institutions must show balanced sports expenditures for both sexes. This has not been easy or inexpensive. Acceptable methods for accomplishing this have included fielding the same proportion of male and female athletes as are in the student body, showing increased opportunities for female athletes, and by merely satisfying the interests of women athletes in the student population. Title IX implementation has often meant sacrificing nonrevenue, usually men's, sports so that larger, more prestigious, revenue-generating men's sports such as football could be maintained. In invoking mandates, rule makers continued to confuse "equal participation rates with equal opportunity rates."

However the legislative mandates have been fulfilled, more money has flowed to women's athletics. Advocates unanimously point to Title IX passage as the seminal event in the participation and popularity booms of women's sports in the late twentieth century. No interviewed former AAU player, few of whom enjoyed adequate funding, ever had anything other than praise for the changes wrought by Title IX. Its almost universal approval by female athletes even resulted in a commercial sportswear firm named after the legislation, TITLE NINE SPORTS©. More than that commercial attestation though, Title IX spurred a revolution in women's sports, one of which was basketball.[18]

The Second Chapter—AAU Basketball

After recognizing these fundamental individual and political stimuli to the evolution of U.S. women's basketball, there is an obvious historic gap between Senda Berenson and her physical education students in bloomers and the tidal wave of Title IX. That gap was largely filled by Amateur Athletic Union basketball. Though the interval extended from 1926 (date of the first AAU women's tournament) to 1979 (date of the last), the era of AAU's greatest import was approximately 1930 to 1970.

Because basketball provided such pleasurable, healthful recreation for women, it quickly escaped the confines of academic gyms and became popular with the general public. Industrialists recognized the morale value of competitive sport for their employees and claimed that active athletes were better workers. They provided equipment and leagues for tennis, golf, and track and field; but the team sports of softball and basketball drew the most interest and participation. Municipal and industrial leagues arose to supplement the basketball participation opportunities already available in schools, Young Women's and Men's Christian and Hebrew Associations ("Y's"), and church leagues, particularly the Catholic Youth Organization (CYO). Since its early role in spreading the game around the world by the graduates of the Springfield Training School, the Y's had continued to beget basketball. The organization now worked with company recreation planners, providing facility time for their competition and building branch divisions near large employers.[19]

In the last quarter of the nineteenth century, numerous athletics' advocates, mainly eastern sports clubs, had worked to rationalize competition, concentrating on rules and eligibility. Among these were the Caledonian Society of New York, the New York Athletic Club, and the North American Amateur Athletic Association. After its founding in 1888, the Amateur Athletic Union achieved consolidation of all these and control over amateur sports in the United States. This included alliances with the main individual sports organizations and the national Olympic Committee. The AAU was continually guided by the precept that amateurism in sports was both desirable and achievable in the United States and worked with the YMCA and the Intercollegiate Athletic Association in promulgating rules to assure that.

Initially, boxing and track and field were the most popular and regulated sports. Early diverging from the prevalent philosophy of physical educators, the AAU in 1914 deemed swimming an acceptable competitive sport for women. After World War I, the union endorsed elite female competition in track and field (1922), then all generally recognized sports (1923), including basketball. In doing so, it turned 180 degrees from the attitude expressed by its president, James E. Sullivan, in 1910. Invoking an increasingly dated outlook, Sullivan had said his organization would not "register a female competitor and its registration committee refuses sanction for . . . a set of games where an event for women is scheduled."

The AAU thus brought important opportunity and organization to the enlarging pool of women athletes in the 1920s. The times were rapidly changing, and the AAU showed flexibility in responding to American women's increasing interest in sport, a movement harmonious with the prosperous and pleasurable decade. They urged employers to provide recreation opportunities for their employees. They reasonably perceived the evolution of amateur sports, their bailiwick, to have occurred in three phases: (1) through private athletic clubs; (2) through colleges and schools; and (3) now through industrial athletic clubs. Of course it helped the organization to encourage a big crop of potential sponsors for teams that might participate in AAU competitions.

In so doing, the AAU prompted quick opposition from groups that believed highly competitive sports were, both physically and morally, deleterious to women. Prominent among this opposition was the National Amateur Athletic Federation (NAAF), whose women's division was headed by Herbert Hoover's wife, Lou. The strongest and most prevalent opponents of the movement toward public competition were the physical educators, represented by the ever altruistic Women's Division of the National Amateur Athletic Federation (WDNAAF). This philosophic struggle to avoid the pitfalls of cheating and commercialization already apparent in men's sports would continue for decades.[20]

The masses of interested women and the excellence of their performances were overwhelming, however; and no amount of theoretical disapproval would stifle the rapid growth of women's sports in the twenties. The AAU would provide the stage on which elite athletes, women and men, could display their talent nationally and worldwide. Women's basketball was on that stage.

Though the AAU had conducted numerous more-or-less national men's tournaments since 1897, the first such women's "basket ball" tournament was played in the Los Angeles (California) Athletic Club gymnasium in 1926. The AAU worked hard to give the tournament true national representation, even delaying the initial planned date of early March till early April in order to try and entice more teams. "Girl teams" from as far as Kansas City, Salt Lake, Nevada (Churchill County High School), and Chicago (Tri-Chi) said they were coming; but they ultimately did not. The tourney became a small (six teams) West Coast meet. The AAU also boldly used 1926 men's, five-player, full-court rules in order to make the game more interesting for fans, a one-time circumstance deemed so radical that it was thereafter quickly discarded from U.S. women's basketball. The only concession they made for the players' gender was a longer halftime intermission.

The champions of the six-team field were the Pasadena Athletic & Country Club ("P.A.A.C."), under whose auspices the tournament was held. The pace-setting "Flying Rings" basketball team was ahead of their time because of the aggressive general support of women's athletics by the PAAC. The club had previously sponsored a national championship track and field team. That sport was popular and widely covered in the newspapers of always sunny southern California. Such was not the case with women's basketball, and the PAAC chafed at the lack of available competition for their fine team that had compiled a 24–0 pretournament record in 1926.

In the run-up to the "first Girls' National Basketball tournament," articles in local papers extolled the excitement of women's basketball. "Ask any coach; he will say that woman's instinctive determination makes her rougher than the ordinary man when playing basketball." Coached at different times by Eddie Laurenson and Allean Allen and led by speedy center Ethel Nichols and Captain Alice Ryden, the Rings upset the favored Anaheim team on April 9 to win the tourney. The event was obscure, little noticed locally and not at all nationally. Nevertheless, the AAU national women's tournament had been launched, and the Pasadena Athletic & Country Club Flying Rings were its first champs.[21]

Babe and Other Working Women

Basketball was now firmly established as the most popular club or company sport for women in the United States. Uninhibited by staid mores of other social classes, "working girls" romped and ran, deriving physical pleasure impermissible to their ostensible social betters. Basketball was available to them; some of them were pretty good at the game; and it was just great fun. Some colleges were recruiting in a haphazard manner; but there was no formal structure, and intercollegiate sports for women would be sparse until the latter half of the twentieth century. The AAU women champions, therefore, were immediately recognized as the best team in the country.

Intercompany competition in industrial leagues, yet another relatively new and blooming phenomenon of the prosperous twenties, was growing. Businessmen financed off-hours recreation for their employees and took pride in company teams composed of the best athlete-workers. Not surprisingly, the bosses also latched onto a bonus benefit of all this largesse—publicity. Newspaper depictions of successful company teams on frequently read sports pages were free and more interesting than advertisements in other sections. The company name on the back of gaudy uniform shirts worn by successful teams was a marketing motive for industrial leagues to succeed.

Yet women's basketball still was rarely on the front sports page. The AAU may have instituted a national tournament, but women's basketball had not captured the public fancy as a sport. One reason for this was the absence of any known spectator entertainment value. Most leagues (Y, church, whatever) had a small, discrete audience; and results

A Forgotten Era

were of no moment to most sportswriters or readers. There was also no well-recognized woman basketball star for sports-worshipping, Jazz Age fans to follow—no hoops equivalent of Sonja Henie, Eleanor Holm, or Helen Wills.

Women's AAU basketball rarely dominated communities' sports menus, even their own. However, in one U.S. region in the late 1920s it would surmount public apathy and become a frequent topic of breakfast table conversation as the morning sports pages were perused. Though women's basketball began in the cloistered academic gymnasiums of the Northeast, by the late twenties the center of its excellence was in the plains states of the Southwest. Teams from Dallas, Texas, in particular would dominate the first few years of AAU competition; and the attention-grabbing star the sport needed, Mildred (Babe) Didrikson, would emerge from that league.[22]

Business leagues in the Southwest were increasingly competitive, and players were aggressively recruited far afield, usually before they finished school. Texas girls' high school basketball was an early breeding ground of the sport. Babe Didrikson had been a hotshot at Beaumont High School, where she attracted the attention of M. J. McCombs, who had developed the Dallas, Texas, Employer's Casualty Company (ECC) Golden Cyclones. A five and one-half foot, 125-pound dynamo, Didrikson signed on with ECC in 1929 before her high school class graduated. She was crude, outspoken, rough, and hugely talented. Her coarseness and masculinity made her controversial. Loved by some, hated by others, she was always outstanding, colorful, and reportable. ECC and other teams in the terrific Dallas city league soon became so popular that they regularly played before several thousand fans. Babe, herself, surely was not solely responsible for this success; but among scores of outstanding players, she was the most conspicuous.

One of McCombs's promotional innovations was to clothe his players in scandalously skimpy, vivid, bright orange, satiny uniforms. Though certainly beneficial to movement, their main attribute to the sponsor was to attract ogling fans. As in the past, the public was more likely to view an athletic contest between women if more of the women could be seen. This sensational evolution of uniforms in the decade after World War I was arguably a bigger innovation than that promoted by Amelia Bloomer. Almost overnight players went from coverage of all skin save, at most, the face and forearms to shiny briefs covering only the torso. Fans marveled at more epidermis draped with less fabric than they were accustomed to.

Business/industrial leagues came to be characterized as "independent" or "semiprofessional," with the emphasis on the "semi." None of the women was making a financial killing at sports, but employers were known to fudge on their salaries and work requirements. Whether players worked for a sponsor after being tapped for their athletic skills varied according to local practice. Continually draping themselves in the pristine cloak of amateurism (much to the AAU's approval), employers such as ECC insisted that their prime athletes were highly qualified to do their jobs and pulled their share of the workload. Babe was probably representative of the rest of the Cyclones. She was paid more ($75–$90 per month) than the average employee and, despite many myths she propagated about her clerical abilities, was probably marginally qualified for whatever work she did at the insurance company.

Hazel Walker, one of the most experienced and important AAU players, put all this alleged altruism into perspective. "There is a fine line in amateur ranks and being a professional. You would draw a salary for working on a real job with the company, but you might be out of the office playing basketball on the road three weeks out of a month. It was all advertising for companies, and you might be handed money under the table."[23]

The basketball experience of Babe Didrikson and her teammates was also illustrative of some other consistent social facets of semipro basketball for women. Most of the players were, euphemistically, economically underclass. They were poor. There were no debutantes on these teams. Their relative poverty assured their appreciation of whatever the income from their jobs. Babe, herself, sent a big portion of her salary back home to Beaumont.

ECC's All-Americans also played on the company's baseball and track teams. The players pleasurably filled their basketball off-season hours on the diamond and cinders as ECC concomitantly reaped publicity. While competing for ECC, Didrikson got some of her first coaching in track and field prior to her sensational 1932 Olympics performance in that sport.

Recognizing that her talents went far beyond the limitations of

Babe Didrikson's Dallas Employer's Casualty Company Golden Cyclones basketball team. Arrow depicts Didrikson. *Reproduced by permission of Mary and John Gray Library, Special Collections, Lamar University, Doct. 11.2.22.8.*

AAU basketball and yearning to shed the restrictions of amateurism, Didrikson quit the sport. After making All–American for two years and leading the Cyclones to the national championship in 1931, she dropped it for the Olympics and a subsequent career as a professional athlete. Never a good team player, she recognized her financial future lay in exploiting her individual athletic talents. After dominating the 1932 Olympics by being the first female to win three medals in track and field, she became a barnstormer in various sports. Beginning in the late 1930s, she concentrated on golf, becoming the best in the world and a spearhead for the founding the Ladies Professional Golf Association (LPGA).

Didrikson was far from the best women's AAU basketball player. Had she concentrated on basketball, she might have become that. However, the early popularity enjoyed by teams such as the Cyclones and Didrikson's subsequent success in sports helped establish women's AAU ball in the United States. In most current, cursory journalistic discussions of the four-decade AAU preeminence in women's basketball, the player most often featured is Babe Didrikson.[24]

Thus the AAU had launched its women's national tournament and reaped the publicity of its first sports page personality. These events did not, however, presage consistent publicity or growth of the sport. Other women basketball stars would emerge before the post–Title IX era but none with the panache and historic impact, mainly in other sports, of Didrikson. As the economic gloom of the 1930s descended, American women felt less inclined and were less able to play games, basketball or otherwise. The AAU tournament would continue but would do so without much general notice as the populace concentrated more on survival than sport, whether as a participant or a spectator.

The best U.S. women players continued perpetuating and improving the game within the AAU format for more than four decades, with pleasure but, despite the promising start, in obscurity. While playing basketball and certainly afterwards as they observed the changes springing from the feminist movement and the collegiate women's basketball boom, they wondered why their accomplishments went so unnoticed. Carolyn Miller, a star of the great Wayland Baptist teams of the late 1950s, succinctly summarized that frustration about their era's lack of current notoriety. Though both fans and historians recognized innovators such as Senda Berenson and the exploits of players after Title IX, there had been some overlooked major women's basketball between those eras, causing Miller to wonder, "Who left out chapter two?"[25]

CHAPTER TWO

Basketball in the Oil Patch

"I've never lived the life of a normal human being."

—Hazel Walker

The AAU players marched to their own drummers. They did not mind straying from the bell-shaped curve of normality to live full lives different from those of their women peers. Hazel Walker was one of the best and most interesting of the great AAU women basketball players. Her life and long basketball career represented the antithesis of normality for women of her time. Not only was she in a tiny minority of women who participated in sport during most of their adult lives, she was one of the very few of her time who made a living at it.

The decade in which she emerged onto the athletic scene was also abnormal, a unique and dangerous time in her nation's history. From 1929, the year of the New York Stock Market crash, until 1941, the year when the Japanese bombed Pearl Harbor, the United States went from the giddy, prosperous 1920s through the Great Depression to the nation's entrance into World War II. This was a time of uncertainty for most and fear for many. Because of the distressed economy, the

1930s were years of limited horizons and relative obscurity for those participating in sport—as for many institutions and individuals, a time of simply hangin' on.

Unlike the twenties when the opportunity to recreate seemed inevitable and infinite, there were no such limitless possibilities in this darker decade. If people had salaries, they were decreasing; and many fans chose to listen to their sports heroes' exploits over affordable radios rather than going to the venues. Baseball, college football, and boxing were increasingly heard over those airways. There were some milestones in basketball. The first National Invitation Tournament (NIT) was held in Madison Square Garden in 1938. The following year, the first NCAA tournament, then a second fiddle to the NIT, invited eight teams to Evanston, Illinois. All this was little noted in newspapers, and there was nil national coverage of women's basketball.

Forty-four percent of the American population was still rural in the 1930s. Over half of those were members of farm families. The communities they lived in or around were conspicuously calm in comparison to the urban centers. In rural communities, agriculture economies had been only sporadically prosperous even during the Roaring Twenties and before. Commodity prices gradually fell between the World Wars. Uncertainty, even penury, was common in these people's lives. Relying on traditional values of thrift and self-sufficiency, country folks muddled through the hard times without significant outcry, much less revolution, a possibility often discussed in U.S. cities during the troubled 1930s. They relied on the institutions they had always respected and supported —family, church, and community.

By the 1930s, basketball was a big part of those communities and a wonderful escape from hard times. There was no social stigma whatsoever associated with girls and women participating in a physical team sport such as basketball. This was not croquet or polo country. Basketball was often a big part of those folks' social life, and females enjoyed approval as well as pleasure in playing it. There was never any doubt that strong farm girls could muster the physical capability to do so. For women playing organized basketball in the thirties, the Great Depression may have been as bad as it was for others; but, if one can judge from the joy they got from playing ball, it probably did not seem so.[1]

From such a rural, poor milieu in Arkansas came Hazel Walker. Her quest for publicity became as tenacious as that of Babe Didrikson's. She was perhaps even more marketable than Babe but, because of her obscure sport, never garnered Didrikson's plaudits or riches. Nevertheless, Walker's long career would be productive and pioneering for women's basketball.

Hazel

Just as later generations would have no difficulty knowing certain sports and entertainment stars when they were called by their first names—Babe, Bing, Ella, Elvis, Michael, Frank—anyone knowledgeable about AAU women's basketball knew instantly about whom one was speaking when she said "Hazel." Hazel Walker was to that sport what Helen Wills or Chris Evert was to tennis—a longtime, classy champion. She played basketball for more than four decades. Beginning her AAU career in the 1930s, she may have been a better player in the forties. She was not as individually overwhelming as a few later AAU players but must be recognized as one of the most talented and important people in the entire history of basketball.

Most AAU players had rural upbringings, and Hazel was no exception. She was a country girl. As Doris Rogers, a later NBC star, said of herself and other AAU country women, they were "as country as pump water."[2] Born in 1914, Hazel grew up outside Ashdown, 1930 population 1,607, in southwestern Arkansas near the Red River border with Texas. A tomboy, she learned sports, especially basketball, by playing with her two brothers. "I just ran around with my brothers and some neighbor boys." She enjoyed basketball enough to work at it, shooting year round on outdoor courts. If the weather were cold, she just "put on another petticoat."

A forward in the old three-court-division game, the 5' 9½" Hazel was a four-year starter and regional star in high school. Arkansas schools at that time did not sanction a state tournament for high schoolers; the AAU did. In 1932, after her team lost in the finals of the first AAU Arkansas state girls' championship (several of the girls on her team were recovering from measles), she was selected All-State.

She received another honor at that tournament, being named "the most beautiful girl in the tournament." Hazel claimed to have Cherokee

Indian heritage from both her parents, genetic markers supposedly responsible for her dark, natural good looks. It seemed both Hazel and those using it considered her resultant nickname, "Squaw," to be distinctive and not demeaning. Those looks would abet great talent and moxie to open many doors for the initially unsophisticated but savvy farm girl.

Walker and a teammate were recruited out of high school to play basketball for the Tulsa Business College. They chose in the pit of the Great Depression to move the almost three hundred miles west to begin for Hazel a peripatetic life's adventure in basketball that would wend over hundreds of thousands of miles.[3]

Led by Hazel's durability and multiple skills, especially free-throw shooting, the Tulsa Stenographers ("Stenos") began to succeed. The team was eliminated early from the 1933 national tournament in Wichita but won the championship in 1934, the first of four Walker-led teams to be recognized as America's best. Returning to her home state, Hazel played for the El Dorado Lion Oil team for two seasons. Her former team, the Tulsa Stenos, won the championship both years, beating the powerful Lions by one point in Hazel's last year in El Dorado.

During the remainder of Hazel's notable amateur career, she played for Little Rock squads. Her initial Little Rock team, the Flyers, included several of the now disbanded El Dorado Oilers and was sponsored by the Lewis-Norwood Insurance Company. The Flyers won three AAU championships, 1937, 1940, and 1941. The Little Rock team would get close but win no more AAU championships after 1941, losing in the finals twice (1942, 1945) under different sponsors. In 1946 the Dr. Pepper team was defeated in the semis by the American Institute of Business (AIB) of Des Moines, Iowa; and Hazel Walker's AAU competition ended. She had played for a gamut of typical AAU team sponsors—a business school, and oil, insurance, bottling, and transportation companies.

In her fourteen-year AAU career, Walker was first or second team All-American eleven times. She was an almost automatic free-throw shooter, winning the AAU championship six times and hitting a record forty-nine out of fifty in 1940. Her all-round skills were exceeded only by her reputation as a team player. She was a James E. Sullivan Award nominee in 1942 when pole-vaulter Cornelius Warmerdam won.[4]

When she quit AAU basketball, Hazel Walker was thirty-two years

The stylish off-court Hazel Walker, March 1937. *Photograph courtesy of Margaret M. Dunaway.*

old but far from finished with basketball. Her unique contributions to her sport, now vocation, would continue for two and one-half more decades. Instead of playing basketball part time, she turned professional and broke new ground for women in sport.

From an entertainment standpoint, Olson's All-American Red Heads were the most successful touring women's basketball team ever. Presenting a combination of basketball skills (they were good players), pulchritude (sex sells), and comedic schlock (as pioneered by the Harlem Globetrotters), they toured the country for most of a half century.

Organized in 1936 by C. M. (Ollie) Olson of Cassville, Missouri, the team was originally called the All-American World's Champion Girls Basketball Club. With an emphasis on femininity, Olson and subsequent owners consciously contrasted the Red Heads with the masculinity of athletes such as Babe Didrikson.

Willing to use almost any shtick to amplify the entertainment aspects of their performances, Olson's team perfected various trick routines, including the Referee Chase and the Old Pinch Act. He also invoked the skills of his wife, a beautician. Mrs. Olson dyed all the players' hair red, matching the shade naturally displayed by the tall Langerman twins on the team. Whether with tint or wig, all subsequent "Red Heads," the name by which the team came to be known, suited up with henna hair.

By 1947, the team was traveling 30,000 miles per year to play 180 games in thirty-eight states. Games were played against local men's teams using full-court men's rules. By ruse, skill, and conditioning, they won more than half of them. Hazel Walker turned pro by joining the Red Heads in 1946. Rejecting chemical pollution of her raven locks, she wore a red wig onto the court. In addition to her established playing skills, her looks were considered a big business bonus to Mr. Olson. Describing herself to a *Colliers* writer as "part Arkansas, part Cherokee," Hazel was now comfortably into showbiz.[5]

After three years with the Red Heads, Walker was the floor and off-court leader of the operation. She was, however, unhappy. She missed the unalloyed competition she had enjoyed in AAU ball and scoffed at the "setup" rules the club wanted against men's teams, for example, no fast breaks for the men and referee leniency on the Red Heads' fouls. Walker believed that a women's professional team could present a product that had showmanship but still featured basketball—something between the much criticized masculinity of Babe Didrikson's various athletic tours and the emphasis on silly sexiness of the Red Heads. She decided to form her own touring team. According to Gary Newton, she thus became the first woman to own a professional basketball team.

Hazel Walker's Arkansas Travelers took to the road, via station wagon, in 1949. The team was originally financed from her own savings and money loaned by Henry Levy, a Little Rock boxing promoter, alleged head of the city's underground gambling, and longtime companion of the new team's owner. Though subsisting mostly on receipts, the team had various business sponsors over the years.

Basketball in the Oil Patch

Hazel Walker as a professional basketball player. *Photograph courtesy of Diane Hall.*

Hazel insisted her players always dress well, use makeup, and conduct themselves as ladies. This behavior was necessary to overcome the perception that such a touring group of bachelorettes must be "trash." Though behaving off-court like women, they bragged about playing on-court like men. From inception to disbanding in 1965, the team averaged an amazing 220 games over a September-to-May season against men's teams often consisting of prideful, local coaches and former hard-court heroes. More amazing, they won over 80 percent of those contests. The Travelers did not out-muscle the men's teams to overcome a big rebound disadvantage. They were in peak condition, though, and would eventually wear their opponents down. If they did not get a rebound, they had the quick hands to steal the ball once the carom had been garnered by an opponent. Their ultimate advantage was to easily outshoot the men.

From the foul line, Hazel Walker was still money-in-the-bank. In harking back to her early expertise at this skill, she recalled shooting at a booth in a county fair as a teenager and "busting" the establishment, winning all the prizes despite aiming at a crooked goal. Walker allegedly never lost as a pro in over 3,500 such contests. Hazel put on halftime free-throw exhibitions at Travelers games in which she hit consistently while standing, kneeling, or sitting down. According to longtime teammate, Francies (Goose) Garroute, Hazel Walker could "go strong" until she was way into her forties. She seldom toured with the team the last ten years before it disbanded in 1965 when Hazel was fifty-one years old.

Hazel Walker was an unpretentious, outgoing, personable, clever woman. She was attractive to men and popular with women, including her employees. Because the Tulsa Stenos then forbade their players to marry, she secretly wed Gene Crutcher, an Ashdown man, in 1934. Crutcher was killed in a railroad accident in 1940. Though she had another brief marriage in 1944–1945, she considered her first husband to be the love of her life. Preferring to remain an independent woman, Hazel never married again.[6]

Honors continued to come to Walker after retirement. Selected for her overall contributions to sport by the Helms Athletic Hall of Fame in 1954, she was in the first class of women basketball players inducted into the Helms Basketball Hall for Women in 1967. She is Arkansas's most famous female athlete. Kermit Smith, another Arkansan and former coach of Martin Junior College in Pulaski, Tennessee, called her "the toast of Arkansas." She was the only woman inducted with the first class into the Arkansas Sports Hall of Fame in 1959. Listed sixteenth, Walker was only one of three women on a 1999 *Sports Illustrated* list of the fifty greatest twentieth-century Arkansas athletic figures.

Typical of the way AAU players have been historically regarded, the important national "halls" have not ranked Walker all that highly. Despite all her pioneering accomplishments and well-documented nominations, her place in the pantheon of U.S. women's basketball is little recognized. Walker is not in the Naismith Hall of Fame despite well-organized and enthusiastic campaigns for her induction. She was not selected to the Women's Basketball Hall of Fame (WBHOF) until its third class in 2001, behind thirty-nine others.

Hazel Walker retired to Little Rock and died in 1990, age seventy-six. She is buried with her family in Ashdown. Those who knew her fondly recall a woman with the combined characteristics of Babe Didrikson, Elizabeth Taylor, and P. T. Barnum—an athlete, a beauty, a businesswoman, and a friend. She used all these attributes to pave some important yet unlauded paths.[7]

The Dallas Teams

The teams that dominated during the first decade of AAU competition were from the Southwest, a part of the country that seemingly always had been associated with uncertainty, whether from the vagaries and dangers of weather, war, pioneering, or the Great Depression. Because of drought, much of the area was known as the Dust Bowl in the 1930s.

Even though petroleum prices, like most others, were down then, the liquid gold was still flowing and was a reliable source of money in the Southwest for most of the first half of the twentieth century. Oil-related businesses naturally were prominent sponsors of AAU women's basketball. From 1929 to 1941 every championship team came from Arkansas (3), Oklahoma (5), or Texas (5). By decade's end, it would be clear from tournament participants that AAU basketball was expanding north and east from this epicenter of U.S. women's basketball, most obviously to Iowa, Kansas, and Tennessee. Until after the start of World War II though, the best AAU basketball came from the so-called oil patch.

Through the early years of AAU-sanctioned competition, the organization was still somewhat ambivalent about women in sports. Mr. J. Lyman Bingham in 1931 reassured worried readers of *Amateur Athlete,* the AAU's official magazine, that basketball was not harmful to women. What's more, pep and enthusiasm prevailed amongst the competitors instead of the dreaded and anticipated hysteria, fainting, and melancholia.

To spice up the proceedings, a beauty contest became a featured sideshow at national tournaments. A queen and some princesses were chosen and publicized—the queen often photographed in an incongruous outfit of basketball uniform embellished with fur-lined cape, crown, and scepter. She was usually not one of the star players. Those women tended to focus on basketball rather than beauty competition and rarely competed in pulchritude. Through the beauty contest, the AAU reminded an American public still equivocal about women in rough team sports that femininity remained foremost, though the basketball was pretty good too.

Another early addition to the competition was the free-throw shooting championship. The winner usually made forty-five or more shots out of fifty in the final round. The women enthusiastically took to this skill contest, usually completed a couple of days before the finals.[8]

Except for the years 1931 and 1932, the national tournament was held until 1940 in Wichita, Kansas. A town of around 100,000 people, Wichita was noted for its cattle trade, agriculture, and airline industry. Wichita and most subsequent tournament sites were national cultural and journalistic backwaters, reflecting the standing of AAU women's basketball and hampering marketing of the sport. Since the principal teams were from middle America and the game was most popular in those parts, the affordability of traveling to host cities influenced what teams attended the AAU national tournament during the depression and even afterward.

Wichita was obviously interested in and capable of putting on national tournaments. In March 1927, the city had hosted a girls' high school national championship, with teams coming from as far as Idaho and Pennsylvania. The final game of that competition was emblematic of the state of girls' and women's basketball for the imminent future.

Nashville Business College student Patsy Epps, 1958 AAU Tournament Queen.
Photograph courtesy of Mrs. John L. Head.

The finalists, teams from Lawton, Oklahoma, and Cockerill, Kansas, were from the Midwest, the geographic center of the nation as well as where the best basketball by females was then played. Cockerill was also representative of the tiny towns from which women's basketball would spring. That little community in the coal-mining section of Kansas had only thirty houses. Its high school had only twenty-five girls, twelve of whom played good enough basketball that their team was a national runner-up. Lawton won the final, 27–23.

In 1928 Wichita hosted the men's AAU final tournament, a fifty-three-team competition played before crowds as large as eight thousand. The Wichita Elks later that same month sponsored an invitational "two-division girls' tournament" for independent teams. Most of the sixteen squads in that tourney came from Kansas, Oklahoma, and Texas. Dallas Trezevant & Cochran beat the Cockerill Robins of Pittsburgh, Kansas, in the finals. Wichita had thus shown it was quite capable of hosting the planned resumption of the AAU women's tournament in 1929.[9]

The first three champions after the institution of a regular annual AAU women's tournament in 1929 came from Dallas, Texas, a state with an early enthusiasm for basketball at all levels—secondary school, college, and industrial leagues. The 1929 finals were an all-Dallas contest between teams sponsored by insurance companies, the Schepp's Aces and the Employer's Casualty Life Insurance Company Golden Cyclones. The Aces beat the Cyclones, that year's Dallas City Champion, 28–27. The Sparkman (Arkansas) Sparks beat Wichita Wallenstein-Raffman for third place. The AAU designated three teams of six players each on their first All-American team. Dallas players dominated the first team. (See Appendix A.)

In addition to businesses, colleges early on sent a few teams as well. The collegiate teams came from small, obscure schools. Except for a very few exceptions, that would be the case throughout the duration of AAU women's basketball. West State (Tennessee) Teachers College (later Memphis State) sent a team to the Wichita tournament in 1928. In 1929 the Middle Tennessee (Murfreesboro) Teachers, Ada (Oklahoma) Teachers, and Randolph (Chico, Texas) College Kittens came to the competition. Some strong, usually regional high school teams were in the fields as well.

Three of the same four teams made the semifinals in 1930. The early strong Dallas teams consisted of the same people with different sponsors, the players going where their jobs were most liberally remunerated. Beginning with the Trezevant & Cochran team that won in Wichita in 1928, the same names—Alford, Haden, McElroy, McElvey, Williams, and others—populated newspaper box scores. The coach migrated too. Howard Allen coached the 1928 Trezevant & Cochran, the 1929 Schepp's Aces, and the 1930 Sun Oil teams. The 1929 Aces were the Sunoco Oilers of 1930.

In another close one, the Aces/Oilers again defeated the Golden Cyclones in the 1930 semifinals by the same score as the previous year, 28–27—this despite the presence of the insurance company's new star, Babe Didrikson. In another close final, Sonoco beat Sparkman, 27–24. Even with a lineup loaded with some of the nation's best athletes, the Cyclones could not seem to win the championship. The Randolph College Kittens beat them for third place. Unable to decide on just how many all-stars to honor, the AAU awarded All-American honors to two teams of ten. (See Appendix A.)

The Golden Cyclones finally won it all in 1931. They had the advantage of playing at home that year as the tournament was held in the Fair Park Automobile Building in Dallas. In an upset, the Wichita Thurstons (a garment manufacturer), one of the consistent winners in the thirties, beat the Sunoco Oilers in the semifinals. This was Babe Didrikson's tournament. She scored thirty points in two games (a total she tended to inflate by multiples in the retelling) and hit a late shot to beat Wichita in the finals, 28–26. The Oilers beat Crescent College of Eureka Springs, Arkansas for third place.

Perhaps anticipating modern, nonelitist award attitudes, the AAU had yet another formula for its 1931 All-American team. They designated twenty-four players, divided between the guards and forwards. Four players came from each of the four semifinal teams. Who did not make All-American?[10]

Those Amazing Cardinals

The Dallas clamp on the championship was dislodged in 1932, and a pattern of strong teams dominating for consecutive years continued. Oklahoma's era began with a most unlikely champion.

All Sooners were not migrant Okies as portrayed by John Steinbeck in *Grapes of Wrath*. Some stayed home and played basketball. The championship team was the Cardinals of the Oklahoma Presbyterian College (OPC) for Girls, of Durant. Located in southeastern Oklahoma less than one hundred miles from Dallas, Durant was a trading town of fewer than eight thousand people in 1932. It was incorporated in 1898, after the first basketball games far away in Massachusetts but nine years before Oklahoma became a state.

Founded in 1894 and supported by wealthy Choctaw Indians and the Presbyterian Church, OPC had initially been a school for poor, mainly Indian children. After briefly evolving into a coed, degree-awarding college, financial straits necessitated that it retrench to a junior college for girls. With a student body of fewer than three hundred, its basketball program grew strong, and OPC became the first college to win an AAU women's basketball championship. Their story is one of tenacity—of a small town, its school, and a team that became champions round the world.

More than anyone else, Sam F. Babb was responsible for the seemingly miraculous, worldwide success of the Cardinals. He was the first AAU coach to cast a long historical basketball shadow. The stout fellow had lost a leg in a tractor accident and after the injury had turned from playing athletics to the profession of teaching. The OPC had established a strong regional women's basketball tradition by the mid-1920s, but only after the arrival of Babb did they begin to make a national splash. Beginning in the 1927–1928 season, they were a threat in the AAU tournament and only got better thereafter.

Babb's accomplishments were not miraculous. They were due to hard work on his and his players' parts. Babb applied his master's degree in education from the University of Oklahoma to his administrative work in the state's school system. That experience provided him statewide contacts that he used in his later recruitment efforts for OPC. Enticing recruits with the opportunity for economic relief through education during the depression, Babb offered college educations to good players from rural schools in a basketball-enamored state. There was no scholarship money, and making the team was not a given. The girls had to earn spots on the squad from among the multitudes Babb brought to Durant. He enjoyed a great advantage in teaching a bunch of well-motivated women. Both they and their families appreciated the opportunity to earn a college degree during hard times. Most of them graduated, many enjoying long careers in education.

Though not harsh, Babb's rule was firm. He stressed conditioning and created a supportive, disciplined, instructive atmosphere. The players ran a mile every day and shot one hundred free throws at practice. Lahoma Lassiter Carlton, a former Cardinal, felt Babb's strongest forte was the psychology of game preparation, not in teaching the proverbial "x's and o's." Working without a history of honed and publicized coaching or player techniques, both Babb and his charges were feeling their ways along in the basketball backwoods. Their improvisational approach produced some remarkable results.

The team was stocked with women recruited from small Oklahoma towns—Cement, Randlett, Cache, Broken Bow, Union Valley, to name a few. Several of the players had Indian heritage though none was full-blooded. The Durant Young Men's Business Alliance supported the team's travels. During tight times, everything was make-do. After uniform shorts became *de rigueur,* the mother of the three Hamilton sisters on the team made them for the players out of their old, pleated bloomers. The team had to practice from four to six-thirty in the morning in their nonregulation, fourth-floor gym or bus across town at that dark hour to Southeastern Oklahoma College. They all had part-time jobs, including chores such as sweeping pigeon dung out of the gym, to pay their school expenses. Yet from these primitive conditions, a regional emphasis on basketball, and good coaching came one of the AAU's longest winning streaks and its first international success.[11]

The 1932 AAU tournament was played in Shreveport, Louisiana, the only time it would be held there. Locals packed the Coliseum to see the games. Among the nineteen-team field were the perennially strong Mesquite (Texas) High School team and another strong Wichita team led by an enduring All-American, Correne Jaax. The girls from Durant enjoyed their trip. As Coach Babb looked the other way, a couple of them sneaked out of their hotel to attend a dance held for the visiting players, violating a stricture of their religious school while kicking up their heels.

Despite the OPC Cardinals having beaten Dallas ECC twice during the regular season, the smart money was on the defending champ

Cyclones. Those bettors were dead wrong. Doll Harris led the Cardinals throughout the tournament, netting nineteen points in the final upset win over the Golden Cyclones, 35–32.

Shreveport got some competitive consolation when Susie Tugwell, a local player, won the free-throw championship. The two finalists dominated the All-American team. (See Appendix A.) This tournament was Babe Didrikson's farewell to basketball, as she turned to track for the 1932 Olympics and subsequently to other sports in order to, of all things, make a living.

Durant shut down to welcome back the victorious OPC Cardinals. A parade of cars carrying the players preceded bands that played "Boomer Sooner" and "A Hot Time in the Old Town Tonight." The team's success was just beginning.[12]

The Cardinals repeated as champions in 1933. This tournament, back in Wichita, followed form as the top two seeds met again in a colorful final—the vivid orange-clad ECC Cyclones and the vivid cardinal-red-clad Cardinals. The insurance company team had three former Cardinals on its squad. Once more the junior collegians won in a game more closely contested than indicated by the final score, 49–39. The winners had to overcome playing most of the game without their star, Doll Harris, who was injured during the fray. Alberta Williams, the Cyclone star and a former Wichita player, could not get untracked. Even the presence of their former teammate, Babe Didrikson, rooting for them on the bench did not help the Dallas team. As in most athletic struggles, the best team won.

Yet another formula for awarding All-American status was coined in 1933. Because the AAU was still using the two-division game, honors were bestowed separately on first and second teams of forwards, guards, and centers. The two finalists, Dallas and OPC, dominated the squad.[13] (See Appendix A.)

Responding to economic vagaries with energy and ingenuity, the Cardinals' great run continued for two more years. In summer 1933, they played the Edmonton Grads in Canada for the mythical North American championship, partially financing the trip by playing games against men's teams along the 2,100-mile travel route. The format was to play a five-game series alternating the five- (international rules) and six- (U.S. rules) player games. The Southeastern Teachers College "Savages" men's team in Durant taught the Cardinals the full-court game. Regardless the rules used, the Cardinals waxed the Canadians, winning three straight and ending the Grads 112-game winning streak. This time they were welcomed home to Durant as conquerors of their hemisphere, not just the United States.

The OPC continued to struggle for funds and ended its shaky but sensational basketball program the next year. Briefly in the 1933–1934 season they played as the Cardinals of Southeastern, the state-supported college cross town. After only a semester there, most of the team moved

The 1933 OPC Cardinals, North American champions. This picture was originally in Doll Harris's scrapbook. *Photograph courtesy of Lee Reeder.*

to Oklahoma City to become the Oklahoma City University Cardinals. Due to the absence of any rules regarding player transfers and subsidization of college athletic teams, the Oklahoma City Chamber of Commerce supported the women with jobs. Representing their new school, the Cardinals, after eighty-nine consecutive victories, finally lost their first game—to the Tulsa Business College.

By beating the Edmonton team the previous year, the Cardinals had qualified to compete in the so-called World Championship Tournament in London, England, in 1934. Despite losing to Tulsa in the AAU finals, they intended to go. With support from the Chamber of Commerce and by raising money by playing exhibitions in the players' hometowns, they eked out enough money to make the trip. After losing to France that August in a frustrating final contest, the Cardinals returned to persistent money problems back home.

Coach Sam Babb sadly had to disband the team, as financial support in the midst of the depression had finally run out. Even the Chamber of Commerce could not get enough jobs for the women. The improbable history of the Cardinals as a team was over. Yet this was not the end of the program's influence. Many of the players disseminated among other teams in the oil patch and won championships. Former Cardinals would be featured on teams in El Dorado, Galveston, Holdenville, Little Rock, and Tulsa. Lera Dunford and Hazel Vickers were charter members of Olson's Red Heads in 1936. Lera's twin, Vera, later joined the team.

Babb would successfully surface again in AAU basketball. After the Cardinals disbanded, Babb coached in Shreveport and in Galveston. In the 1937 finals, his Galveston Anicos lost to Little Rock, a team led by Lucille Thurman, his star at OPC. He became ill, perhaps with peritonitis, while coaching the Galveston softball team in Chicago that summer. Instead of seeking medical care there, he wended his slow way home to Chickasha, Oklahoma, where he died at age forty-five. Lucille Thurman Berry called him "a good coach and a wonderful man who helped a lot of girls have a richer and fuller life."

The rural Oklahoma women had produced several All-Americans and in Doll Harris and Lucille Thurman two of the best AAU players ever. They had won two AAU national championships, finished second in another, won a North American championship, and traveled the world. Basketball was not only fun; it occasionally opened unimagi-

Coach Sam F.
Babb. *Photograph
courtesy of Lee
Reeder.*

nable vistas. Though neither Sam Babb nor the OPC Cardinals are well
known nationally, Oklahomans appreciate their accomplishments. Sam
Babb was posthumously inducted into the Jim Thorpe Memorial
Oklahoma Athletic Hall of Fame in 1979. His team, the Cardinals, were
inducted as a Team of Legend in 2003.[14]

Tulsa's Turn

The year 1934 was one of experimentation at the AAU tournament
and marked the introduction of another powerful team, the Tulsa
(Oklahoma) Business College Stenos. Led by the center-forward, Alberta
Williams, the Stenos upset the still-tough Oklahoma City Cardinals in

the final, 32–22, thus winning the Oklahoma championship, which was becoming synonymous with the AAU championship. The Cardinals had apparently not yet recognized Hazel Walker's prowess as a free-throw automaton. They foolishly kept fouling the deadeye Steno from Arkansas, allowing her to can fourteen of sixteen underhanded tosses.

The final result was mildly surprising, but the big news in 1934 was the AAU's nervous fiddling with the rules. The AAU recognized that their women's games were dull relative to those played by men and began flirting with men's rules, particularly the full-court game. Early in the tournament, Lambuth College of Jackson, Tennessee, and the Wichita Thurstons played such an exhibition game. There were actually two parallel tournaments, one for the standard six-player game and one for the few teams that played full court. The Chicago Spencer Coals won the latter tourney. Teams stayed in Wichita an extra day after the finals for a playoff between the Stenos, champions of the "softie" (i.e., regulation half court) tournament, and the Coals, champions of the "tomboy" tournament. In a game modified to allow closer guarding, it was irrelevant that the "softies" won. More important, the women's game was haltingly but surely changing to a faster format.[15]

The 1935 final AAU competition in Wichita drew big crowds and thirty-two teams, mostly from the Midwest. For the first time in many years, there were no teams from Dallas. Again led by Alberta Williams, the talented Tulsa Stenos once more won the championship. Their closest scrape was an overtime semifinal victory over a Shreveport team coached by the ever-successful Sam Babb. In the final before five thousand fans they defeated the Holdenville Flyers, yet another Oklahoma team loaded with former OPC Cardinals, 28–16. The four semifinal teams dominated the large All-American team that was awarded the best players at three positions, forward, center, and guard.[16] (See Appendix A.)

Few disagreed with the dictum that women's and men's basketball competition should be different. Dr. Naismith himself legitimized this attitude. After viewing the exhibition games of women playing men's rules at the 1934 national tournament, he recoiled in horror. He liked many features of the extant women's game, including the one "bound" (dribble) rule, the requirement to pass the ball within three seconds, and the lack of congestion around the basket. The latter circumstance derived from the two-division game with three guards and three for-wards on each end. He regretted, however, a couple of emerging fea-tures. Because players were defensive or offensive specialists, they could not develop all-round skills; and, in the two-division game, tall women were beginning to dominate on the offensive end. His proposed solu-tion to this was altruistic and not necessarily conducive to winning games. In order to balance the pleasure and skills of players, he sug-gested the guards and forwards exchange positions after the halftime. Not too many coaches bit on that one.

The big crowds that attended championships in the thirties were about to get a lot more for their money because of a rule change that would characterize AAU basketball until 1970, the "running" or "shoot-ing" guard, ultimately known as the "rover." This ingenious change added full-court transit and the potential for fast-break offense. It also eliminated a two-division, stolid game of limited excitement. No other segment of the women's game at any level ever used the rover rule on a prolonged basis; and, in one form or another, it remained unique to AAU basketball.

The rover rule evolved from a 1920s five-player game in which the center alone was allowed to run the entire court. This older crossbreed game retained the exclusive guard and forward skills and required one player, the center, to be in mighty good condition. The new rule, intro-duced in the 1936 tournament at Wichita, permitted one guard to cross the centerline and participate in her team's offense. The guard crossing the heretofore sacrosanct Rubicon had to be the one who passed the ball into the offensive end. An opposition forward would follow the guard in order to defend her, putting eight players on the end of the court where the ball was.

Fans unused to the rule were often perplexed. Once recognizing the flow though, sophisticated fans saw a much faster game that was more challenging to the contestants. When combined with the limited dribble and the three-second rule, the rover or "running guard" innovation made for a game with more passing and outside shooting. First used in the 1936 national tournament, the rule was embraced by AAU players.[17]

The 1936 tourney had teams from twelve states, mostly from the South and the Midwest. The balance of power still tilted toward the Southwest, but more southern teams were showing up and winning games. This was the fourth year their sponsor, Mr. H. O. Balls, had brought his NBC team to the national tournament. From 1933, NBC publicists would claim thirty-nine years of consecutive appearances. Lambuth College of Jackson, Tennessee, another obscure school but one of the first four-year college participants, strongly competed in tourneys throughout the late thirties.

The two-time defending champion Tulsa Stenos were seeded first in the 1936 tournament, but most observers favored the El Dorado (Arkansas) Lions. Tulsa had lost several games during the season, and El Dorado, known also as the Oilers, was undefeated. Now in her second year on that team, Hazel Walker considered the Lions to be "the greatest AAU team ever assembled." Several of the women had moved to Arkansas from another Oiler team, Holdenville (Oklahoma). In addition to Hazel, there were other AAU All-Americans on the team: Ernestine Lampson, Lucille Thurman, Hazel Vickers, and Frances Williams. El Dorado had beaten the Stenos four times during the regular season.

The Lions awesomely showed that firepower in an early mismatch, beating the Wichita Centrals 103–2, not surprisingly an AAU record. There was the usual smattering of early round upsets, but the top four seeds emerged into the semis. Ranking held there, too, as El Dorado beat AIB, and the Stenos easily dispatched the Wichita Thurstons. Before five thousand fans the Tulsa Stenos became the first team to win three consecutive AAU championships and garnered the Wichita Beacon Trophy by edging the supposedly better El Dorado Lions, 23–22. Always strong but never winning the big one, the Lions/Oilers thus became one of the really good runners-up of AAU history. All but one of the first team All-Americans came from the two finalists.[18] (See Appendix A.)

The 1937 champion was another southwestern team, the Little Rock Lewis & Norwood Flyers. Among other women from rural Arkansas and Oklahoma, the ubiquitous Hazel Walker led the Flyers. Her eastward migration from Tulsa through El Dorado exemplified a persistent pattern of movement by the best players among teams, as they pursued more money through better jobs and greater opportunity to win championships. The Flyers were loaded with experienced players, who had represented the Tulsa Stenos, Durant and Oklahoma City Cardinals, and El Dorado Oilers in AAU tournaments. Walker, Leota Barham, and Lucille Thurman had been All-American multiple times. (See Appendix A.)

Though this migratory method of team formation certainly led to the suspicion of "undercover professionalism," Little Rock coach Bill Dunaway argued the contrary. Only Barham and Thurman worked for the insurance company, the others doing mostly clerical work in the Little Rock region. Noting that the players had to use vacation time to attend the annual AAU tournament, Dunaway felt that to deny them the opportunity to change teams during their brief athletic careers was unfair. The players enjoyed team hopping, and annual tournaments became cordial old-home weeks to renew acquaintances with former teammates.

Powerful, first-seeded Galveston, now coached by Sam Babb, ended the Tulsa Stenos' great run, eliminating them in the 1937 semifinal contest. The best game of the tournament was the Little Rock Flyers' thrilling double-overtime, come-from-behind, 30–28 victory over the Wichita Thurstons in the other semifinal. After scoring the winning goal with a blind heave, Lucille Thurman, who had been conked on the head in the game, supposedly fainted in disbelief or exhaustion. The final 17–10 upset win over Galveston to complete an undefeated season for the Little Rock team must have seemed a breather.

Either women were in better shape, or losing consciousness, despite Thurman's collapse, was going out of vogue. Mrs. Irvin Van Blarcom, the AAU basketball chairman, noted that there had been no fainting for the last several tournaments even though the organization had carefully provided stretchers ". . . to care for the comely fainters." Perhaps the officials had not been watching the evolution of fast, tough women's basketball that was far removed from any previous century concept that women were prone to faint because of exertion or excitement. These women were sweating, not perspiring.

This year the AAU designated first and second All-American teams of six players each. They were close to settling on a consistent method for distributing tournament honors.[19] (See Appendix A.)

Apparently discounting the premier national tournament in Pasadena in 1926, the AAU presented its so-called tenth national tournament in 1938, again at the Municipal Forum in Wichita. Thirty-two teams from seventeen states came to contest over six nights, the finalists needing to play five games over that span. Teams came from as far away as Pennsylvania, Florida, and Washington; but the bulk of participants were still from the plains states—seven from Kansas and four from Texas.

The Little Rock Flyers, 1937 AAU champions. *Front row:* Lucille Thurman, Hazel Walker, Vera Dunford, Leota Barham, June Kirtley; *top row:* Bernice Goelzer, Anne Prause, Elizabeth Osterloh, Chloe McCrary, Virginia Russell, Coach Bill Dunaway. *Photograph courtesy of Margaret Dunaway.*

The NBC team, coached by Leo Long, was pictured in the program with a new school motto—"Appealing to Those Who Want the Best." Lambuth College was back and considered a contender.

This tournament was anticipated not only by the AAU but by the Federation Internationale de Basketball Amateur (FIBA) as well. Men's basketball had been introduced into the official competition in the 1936

Olympics, and there was strong consideration of introducing the women's game at the 1940 Tokyo Olympics. From where else but the AAU ranks could a U.S. team be selected?

Though the Little Rock Travelers were the defending champions, the most feared team was the Galveston Anicos (an acronym for the American National Insurance Company). Because of their strength and their snug black uniforms, they were known as the "black threat." The Anicos were yet another power from the Southwest consisting of remixed, proven ingredients. Most of the players had worn the red of the Oklahoma City Cardinals. There were supposedly no Galveston players on the squad. The star, 5' 11" Frances Williams, had played for teams from Fort Worth, Oklahoma City, Holdenville, and El Dorado. Other players in their loaded lineup had suited up for teams from Nashville, Tulsa, and Wichita. Itinerancy was an accepted way of life in AAU women's basketball. Mr. William L. Moody III, mogul of the sponsoring insurance company and a big contributor to amateur athletics in Galveston, had assembled a very experienced team.

The semifinals were a mid- and southwestern affair. The Wichita Thurstons defeated the defending champion Little Rock Flyers, and the Anicos defeated the perennially strong Tulsa Stenos. If scoring were critical for selection of any national U.S. team, this tournament was a disappointment. In the finals, Galveston beat the Wichita Thurstons by the barnburner tally of 13–8. Someone must have missed an extra point! Wichita scored one point in the first half. Nevertheless, the 29–0 Anicos were obviously the best team in America. Their average season game score of 26–12 reflected the emphasis on defense by this tough, tall squad.

NBC was proud to finish fifth in the tournament; they were climbing the ranks in the AAU. Hazel Walker reclaimed the free-throw championship from Lambuth College's Mildred Spivey, who had beaten her in 1937. Anicos and Flyers dominated the All-Star team.[20] (See Appendix A.)

Prevalent power teams of the 1930s again met in the 1939 semifinals. The still undefeated Anicos defeated Des Moines AIB, and the Little Rock Travelers beat Wichita. With another score resembling that of a gridiron rather than hardwood contest, Galveston repeated as champion by beating Little Rock 21–8; defense was still the Texans' forte.

The featured player in a deep, talented, '39 Galveston lineup was

Lottie Jackson, a Nashville Tennessean, said to be "America's greatest girl basketball player." Hazel Walker and her fans may have disputed that, as Hazel again won the free-throw championship, hitting 45/50 tosses. For the third consecutive year, NBC finished fifth.

The stars seemed aligned in U.S. women's basketball as Texas once more ruled the roost, the fifth time during eleven years the AAU tournament had been regularly held. That state's players had saturated All-American teams throughout the 1930s, and Galveston was in the midst of a winning streak. During the next decade, Texas power would fade, and another section of the country would come to the fore in the women's game. For the moment, however, most women's basketball eyes were on Texas.[21]

In 1940 the women's AAU national basketball tournament moved to St. Joseph, Missouri, yet another obscure site far from the madding crowd and anything resembling national publicity. Known mainly as a cattle market, as the eastern terminus of the Pony Express, and as a jumping-off place from the shore of the Missouri River for nineteenth-century western pioneers, "St. Joe" had a population of fewer than ninety thousand people in 1940. That population would remain essentially static during the subsequent twenty-five years when the midwestern town hosted most of the AAU tourneys. As AAU women's basketball evolved, host city populations were getting smaller.

Regardless the town's relative obscurity, its civic groups and citizens provided enthusiastic support, crowding the city auditorium with up to four thousand fans for late tournament games. There was usually a local team in the tournament—the St. Joseph Welders, St. Joseph Goetz (a beer distributor), or Platt College (another business school). The tournament itself did not make much on gate receipts. In 1944, the St. Joseph Junior Chamber of Commerce netted $1,612.[22]

In 1940 the epicenter of AAU women's basketball power also moved. Champions during the forties would come mostly from the Southeast, Nashville in particular. Teams from as far afield as California and New York came to the tournaments, usually consisting of twenty-six to thirty-two teams; and some good teams from Iowa would spring from that state's powerful high school basketball programs. Most champions though from 1940 to 1970 would come from Arkansas eastward and below the Mason-Dixon Line.

Basketball in the Oil Patch

An AAU women's basketball championship opening ceremony at the St. Joseph Civic Auditorium. *Photograph courtesy of Anne Paradise Hansford Langston.*

Led by Coach Bill Dunaway and player Hazel Walker Crutcher, the Little Rock Travelers were the 1940 and 1941 champions. In both championship contests, the Travelers bested NBC. These games also featured the first head-to-head confrontations between Hazel and the dominant player of the new decade, Alline Banks. It was hard to determine whether sports writers' interest in Banks was because of her looks or her game. When pointing out that she was accurate in the post from whichever direction she pivoted, they always appended such evaluations with a comment about her red hair and long legs.

The teenaged Banks led the Nabucos, a moniker given NBC by Nashville sportswriters, to a big upset of the defending champion and top-seeded Galveston Anicos in the 1940 semifinals. Crutcher's more experienced Travelers prevailed in the final, 23–13, as Hazel outscored Alline, 15–10. Seeding was accurate that year, as Little Rock had been ranked first and NBC second. However, the baton of player supremacy had been passed; and Banks won her first Tournament MVP award.[23] (See Appendix A.)

Hazel Walker cemented her reputation as a clutch player and AAU great in the semifinals of the 1941 tournament. The Flyers were down one point to Des Moines AIB with two seconds remaining. After intercepting a pass, a Little Rock teammate hurled the ball to Hazel at the half-court. Whirling instantly and flinging the ball, she swished the winning hoop, causing AIB's coach Rueben Bechtel to faint dead away. Apparently passing out at AAU tournaments was not exclusive to women. Hazel, herself, was shook up by the improbable drama. "I was rather weak in the knees, too."[24]

The outcome was the same in 1941, though by a lower and closer score, 16–15. This final was a sore loss for the Nashvillians. Had they won, they would have been the first national championship team of any kind from Nashville; and they were proudly aware of that. Just as Banks had joined NBC as a ringer in her senior year of high school, Mary Jane Marshall of nearby Joelton, Tennessee, joined the team after her senior tournaments in 1941. She was not cowed by the experience of playing in the AAU tournament. The tough, multitalented forward could shoot, assist, and play defense. In addition to her talent, she was a hustler, leading the team in a coach-pleasing category—floor burns. After her frustration at not being able to play the full-court, five-player game, nothing bothered her more about 1940s AAU rules than not being able to steal ("snatch") the ball.

Flyers defensive specialist Loretta Blann held the very hot Alline Banks to one field goal in the championship game. Near the end of the game, the teenager Marshall made a shot that would have put NBC up 16–15; but the referee, after some vacillation, said she was fouled before the shot. She made the one awarded free throw to tie the game, which was promptly lost when an NBC player made a technical foul and Little Rock converted.

The result put NBC coach Leo Long into a prolonged funk. He bemoaned the officiating (not an unusual response for a losing coach) and the lack of Nashville support for his team. He claimed that the Little

Mary Jane Marshall of Cook's Goldblumes (*right*) is fouled in 1947 AAU tourney. *Photograph courtesy of Jane Marshall Ingram.*

Rock women had received approximately five hundred telegrams from their boosters, while the Nabucos got only five from theirs—a strange contemporaneous barometer of fan support. He was a busy enough man coaching prep football and basketball at Father Ryan High School, and the galling lack of hometown support fueled his anger. On return to Nashville, he resigned from coaching the NBC team. (He obviously reconsidered when winter rolled around, for he coached the Nabucos several more years.) As for the competitive, grim-jawed Marshall, in the twenty-first century she still burned over the loss. "They stole that away from us."

This was not a good tournament for Hazel Walker. Suffering from shin splints on her "pretty legs" (male sportswriters always alluded to physiognomy whenever possible in their coverage of women's sport), she was left off the All-American team and did not win the free-throw championship, a victory she perpetually enjoyed. The Most Valuable Player award again went to the younger, very talented, increasingly dominant Banks. The two finals teams garnered eight of the ten All-American slots.[25] (See Appendix A.)

Coach Long's and player Marshall's disappointments would after December 1941 seem petty in perspective. The Japanese bombing of Pearl Harbor was a tragic and shocking catalyst for what had seemed inevitable anyway, the entrance of the United States into what would now be called World War II. Organized athletic leagues from sandlots to the majors would de-emphasize, as players were lost to the military, money and materiel were allocated to the war effort, and thoughts were usually elsewhere than the playing field or court.

The AAU women's basketball had survived the Great Depression, and it would continue throughout the war. Considering that the circumstances were not propitious for basketball of any kind to claim great public interest, the continuation of the women's game was fortunate. The game could have faded away. In that unilluminated effort by the AAU women's teams, however, it would get better, new stars would emerge, and, along with other hopeful segments of a war-obsessed society, the players would look forward to better times for their sport.

CHAPTER THREE

Beer Distributors, Business Schools, and Hosiery Girls

"We blazed the trail."

—Mary Jane Marshall Ingram

So Long to the Oil Patch

With the onset of World War II, the center of AAU women's basketball power drifted away from the Southwest. Another Texas team, Wayland Baptist College of Plainview, would emerge a decade later as the most important AAU college program and longtime rival of Nashville Business College. From 1942 through 1953 though, the best teams would come mostly from the Southeast. Before women's basketball preeminence settled into that region, there would be some Iowa champions.

The losing semifinalists in 1941 were two Iowa business school teams that were important AAU forces for years, the American Institute of Business (AIB) of Des Moines and the American Institute of Commerce (AIC) of Davenport. The schools were a family affair. Everett O. Fenton, a co-founder of AIB in 1921, founded AIC in the late 1930s with his brother, Stephen. In 1934 AIB was the first Iowa team to play in the AAU tournament. Des Moines was an insurance center, and the AIB team honed its skills in the tough Women's

Insurance League in that city. Because their players in the 1930s had played only the three-division floor game in high school, they were handicapped by the relatively greater speed of the two-division AAU competition. That deficiency was corrected when the AIB team supported the introduction of the two-division game, sans rover, into Iowa high schools in 1936.

The AIC Stenos were more aggressive in recruiting, traveled internationally, and were a more potent AAU team than their numerous Iowa semipro sisters. The Stenos won the AAU title in 1942 and 1943. In 1942 they narrowly defeated number-one-seeded NBC in the semis. Led by the long-range shooting of Ruth Campbell and Margaret Macomber throughout the tournament, Coach Leo Schultz's Stenos walloped Hazel Walker's Little Rock Motor Coaches (new sponsor, same team) in the finals, 42–25. The AIC team was a testament to the tremendous strength of Iowa high school girls' basketball. All its players were graduates of Iowa schools, and the team was the youngest of AAU champions. Its players averaged only seventeen and one-half years of age. That teenage mean was in part due to the youth of the women attending the business school. As pointed out by a contemporary AIB opponent, it was also due to the several outstanding "ringers" AIC brought in each year after the players had finished their high school careers.[1]

It was small consolation to Hazel Walker that she was the 1942 Tournament MVP and All-American for the ninth time, more than any other before her. Similarly the previously petulant Leo Long was probably not placated by a lengthy telegram from Nashville mayor Thomas L. Cummings extolling NBC's successful season and wishing them well in the tournament. Increased attention by the folks back home could not get his team into the finals.

The consolation tournament, in which first-round losers kept playing, was often a harbinger of future AAU champions. Another Nashville team, the Vultee Bomberettes in their first year of competition, won that prize in 1942. This time the harbinger was quite accurate, as Vultee and its postwar incarnation would be one of the truly important AAU sextettes.[2]

In 1943 the Iowa alphabet competition continued as AIC won their second championship by beating fellow Iowans AIB in the finals, 41–31. This was a last hurrah for the Corn Belt queens. Hazel Walker did not make All–American, though she yet again won the free-throw competition, hitting forty-five of fifty. NBC never got their act together that year and did not organize a team until a fortnight before the tournament. Players were introducing themselves to each other as the competition began, and the lack of practice showed. As a salve to their mediocre performance and in spite of All-American Jimmie Vaughn breaking her leg, the Nabucos did win the consolation championship; and, garnering the ultimate kissing-your-brother award, brunet (sic) Margaret Turrentine was chosen Beauty Queen.[3]

From 1940, Nashville, as represented by NBC, had recorded two seconds and one third-place finish at the tournament—hardly a dynastic record. Anyone paying attention to performances of the team's star, Alline Banks, though must have realized that whatever team she represented would be potent. Unlike Hazel Walker, she had not yet acquired the ultimate credential of an individual champion, a team championship. Walker had been on four such teams—one in Tulsa (1934) and three in Little Rock (1937, 1940, and 1941). Though they had been close, none of Banks's teams had won a national championship. In the midst of the war, that was about to change. In addition to Alline Banks's supremacy as a player, Nashville was to emerge as the paramount city in AAU basketball competition for the rest of the 1940s. (See Appendices A and B.)

Consolidated Vultee Aircraft was the largest manufacturing employer of U.S. women during World War II, and 30 percent of workers at the big Nashville plant were women. Making such craft as the P-38 Lightning fighter and the Vengeance dive-bomber, its busy assembly lines offered lots of opportunities for regional Rosies to be Riviters and earn a hefty eighty cents to one dollar hourly, plus overtime. Like most prosperous factories of the time, they also had sports teams. Representing Vultee Aircraft and called variously the Vulcans, Vulcanettes, Convairs, or Bomberettes, the women's factory team and its later postwar version would dominate AAU women's basketball for several years. The Bomberettes also verified the ascension of middle Tennessee as a center of girls' and women's basketball, rivaling Iowa, Oklahoma, and Texas.[4]

Vultee gave Billy Hudson, a longtime Nashville athlete, referee, and municipal league coach, the job of coaching a new women's team at the aircraft factory. Janie Marshall played only a handful of games with NBC during her decade-spanning career. After the disheartening loss to Little Rock in the 1941 AAU finals and the apparent retirement of Leo Long, a coach universally respected by his players, Marshall changed teams. According to Marshall, Hudson "collected six or seven of us" to play for Vultee. Most of the women joined up because of the good wages at the plant. Probably because of their well-known athletic skills, the players usually had clerical or inventory jobs, none on the assembly line where injury was always a threat. Including the coach's wife, Pollye, almost all sprang from middle Tennessee high schools.

The Bomberettes were good from the git-go. After winning the consolation championship in 1942, they acquired a couple of new players for the 1942–1943 season, both of whom much preferred winning to losing. The best player in the country, Alline Banks, joined up. The second addition was a gifted, pure guard, Margaret Sexton. Margaret was a precise peer of Alline, having graduated from Bellevue High School west of Nashville in 1938 and immediately joining the NBC team. She was a slender, fast, tall (5' 10"), extremely aggressive player, who was said to "bounce other players around like ping-pong balls." She had no ego problems about not being a scorer. She just loved defending and was among the best ever at it. When these All-Americans joined a core of middle Tennesseans, Doris Weems, Margie Cooper, and the Marshall sisters (Mary Jane and Kathryn), Coach Hudson surely realized he was leading a special team.

The Bomberettes almost won the AAU championship in 1943. Led by Alline's fifteen points per game (ppg) average, they ripped through an undefeated season. In the tournament quarterfinals Vultee faced the AIB Secretaries, a team they had beaten twice in the regular campaign. Both Alline Banks and Mary Jane Marshall had nagging injuries as they approached the game. That impediment plus a double-team defense the Iowans put on Banks led to an unexpected 30–26 loss for the top-seeded Bomberettes. In the words of faithful Brooklyn Dodger fans, "wait'll next year . . ."[5]

Nashville won its first national championship in 1944 and established Alline Banks as the premier women's basketball player in the United States. Teams led by her would win five national championships over a seven-year span. She had plenty of help. Another sister act, Blanche and Doris McPherson of College Grove, Tennessee, had

Beer Distributors, Business Schools, and Hosiery Girls

joined the Vultee team, continuing a seemingly endless infusion of talented middle Tennessee players.

After losing their opening game in 1944, the Bomberettes won thirty straight. They made a shambles of the national tournament and dupes of the seeders in Hudson's seventh trip to the AAU tournament. The Bomberettes polished off number-two-seeded Little Rock Motor Coach in the quarterfinals, then allowed only three field goals and destroyed a strong Dallas team, 31–8, in the semis. AIB, the first seed and their nemesis in 1943, was dispatched, 23–16 in the finals.

Vultee's emergence was a surprise to AAU women's basketball buffs. An Associated Press writer told his readers that this April first outcome was not an April fool's joke. Had he been paying attention to the Bomberettes' rise, he might also have recognized that this was the debut of a basketball dynasty. Alline Banks Pate (she was now married) scored fifty-eight points in the tourney, more than the combined totals of her team's opponents. Several hundred hometown fans of what remained an obscure sport to the general public welcomed back to Union (railroad) Station in Nashville the triumphal "Basket Queens."

Vultee had become Nashville's first national champion before a now less prominent NBC squad could do so. Mr. Balls's team was hanging around though and picked up several honors at the 1944 tournament. While Pate and Margaret Sexton Petty made All-American for Vultee, NBC also had an All-American, Mary Hoffay. NBC's Jimmie Maxine Vaughn was selected queen of the tournament. The 5' 8" twenty-year-old was a proven player, having made All-American in 1942. In an upset of sorts, Nell Seagraves of NBC won the free-throw championship, hitting forty-six of fifty and beating the seemingly perennial champ, Hazel Walker.[6]

As the Bomberettes got more experience, they were unbeatable. The 1944–1945 season was a breeze, though they did have some close games against Hazel Walker's persistent Little Rock team. Vultee beat Little Rock in Nashville by one point and won their forty-ninth straight game in the AAU finals by beating the Dr. Pepper-sponsored squad, 22–20. Banks was overwhelming, scoring sixty-five points in the tournament, again more than all the teams playing against Vultee in the competition.

The emergence of the Nashville area as a center of women's basketball power was exemplified by the 1945 All-American team, most of

The AAU 1945 Champion Vultee Bomberettes. *Front row:* Coach Billy Hudson, Margaret Sexton Petty, Alline Banks Pate, Doris Weems, Lucille Gentry; *middle row:* Margie Cooper, unknown, Catherine Marshall, Lorene Linville; *back row:* Mary Jane Marshall, Virginia Hamlen. *Photograph courtesy of Jane Marshall Ingram.*

whom hailed from little Tennessee towns. If you wanted to create a strong team, come to the Volunteer State.[7]

As World War II ended in the summer of 1945, defense plants geared down. An aircraft plant would be at the Vultee site for decades, but it became less prominent in Nashville industry. Its athletic teams also dwindled. Would Nashville's first championship team, the Bomberettes, be recalled only as a passing phenomenon, a bizarre byproduct of the wartime when people were otherwise occupied than in sport? Well, maybe not . . .

The team was determined to stay together and solidify their dominance. The women were still young, mostly unmarried, and loved playing ball as much as ever. All they needed was a sponsor. The AAU teams had been subsidized by business schools, hard industries, insurance companies, bottling companies, oil companies, and colleges. Surely a backer could be found in prosperous postwar Nashville.

John Wesley Little was a country boy who came to Nashville to make good. In 1945, the fifty-five-year-old gentleman was established as a livestock dealer, a Tennessee walking horse aficionado, a Methodist Church activist, and a dabbler in local Democrat politics. He also owned the Southern Beer Company. Little had bought the distributorship in 1933, the same year Herman Balls began taking his NBC teams to the AAU national tournament. The company distributed both prominent (Budweiser) and obscure brands. One of the latter was Cook's Goldblume, a less-than-premium brew manufactured by the F. W. Cook Company of Evansville, Indiana.

Though not an athlete and definitely unsophisticated about basketball, Little, known as "Mr. Johnny" or "Captain Johnny," enjoyed sports. Southern Beer's general manager was his niece, Mrs. Angie (Robert) Ball, who was interested in women's basketball. It was probably through her that the request was made that Southern Beer sponsor the now-adrift national championship women's basketball team. Perhaps Mr. Little felt some sense of competition with Herman Balls and his decade of success with the NBC program. Whatever his motivation, he hired many of the former Vultee players, whether they were needed for the company or not, and instantly had a winner.

The sexual/athletic pecking order had not changed. Then and into the indefinite future, women's basketball teams would play second fiddle to men's. While Southern Beer's cheaper brand, Cook's Goldlume, sponsored the women's team, their more prestigious Budweiser product sponsored the men's team.[8]

Relying on close-in shooting, tough rebounding, and vicious defense, the Cook's Goldblumes became the best. Alline Pate was the star; but, unlike some of her earlier squads, this was not a one-woman show. Certified All-Americans Mary Jane Marshall and Margaret

Sexton would be joined by other proven players such as Doris Weems and Margie Cooper to create a team with several All-American starters and a long, capable bench.

Alline and Margaret Sexton felt the 1945–1946 Cook's team was the strongest of the three consecutive champion Nashville teams on which they played. It solidified these teams as among the best in AAU history. A Nashville sportswriter would rhapsodize that they became "the most feared and formidable girls' independent basketball team of modern times." The Blumes lost one game that year, 16–12, in a slow-down contest won by the Chatham Mills (Elkin, North Carolina) Blanketeers. That aberration was avenged during a remarkable championship tournament.

In 1946, the Cook's team showcased their defense at the St. Joseph's competition, playing five games in six nights against the best extant women's teams. In beating an Omaha team 45–10, they gave up only two field goals. In the semifinals against third-seeded Chatham, they gave up *one* basket while prevailing 36–10. By beating a tough Dr. Swett's (a root beer distributor) team of Des Moines in the final before four thousand fans, they became the second team to win three straight AAU women's basketball championships. They thereby retired the AAU "traveling trophy," an icon annually awarded to the champion. The Cook's team was recognized as the Vultee team with new uniforms, and the AAU treated them as such for purposes of competitive continuity. The women who ended the circulation of that "beautiful gold" trophy were proud of the accomplishment. In the 1980s Margaret Sexton Gleaves gave the totem to the Naismith Hall of Fame where in 2001 in sadly tarnished condition it resided in an obscure AAU corner of that Hall.

Alline Banks Pate and the Blumes now dominated AAU competition. Pate scored eighty points in the 1946 tourney, exceeding opposing teams' totals for the third consecutive year. Pate, Gleaves (the best guard in the tournament), Marshall, and Weems were All-Americans. The Des Moines Dr. Swett's team also had four All-Americans, one of whom would migrate to Nashville as part of the annual merry-go-round of players.[9] (See Appendix A.)

The AAU teams from Atlanta had sporadically shown up at the championships for years, though not succeeding with the consistency of

Beer Distributors, Business Schools, and Hosiery Girls

teams from cities such as Dallas, Nashville, and Tulsa. The Atlanta Sports Arena was a privately owned basketball and entertainment venue. Owner L. D. ("Pop") Warren held square dances several times a week in order to subsidize the money-losing women's basketball team he sponsored, the Atlanta Blues. The Blues had been a mediocre AAU team representing the arena since 1942. That changed dramatically in 1946.

Alline Banks Pate was getting out of a bad marriage and wanted to leave Nashville. Hearing that she and her Goldblume teammate, Doris Weems, were foot loose, team manager Lamar Wells and Coach John McCarley did some big-time recruiting from Nashville. In addition to Banks and Weems, they persuaded Jimmie Vaughn, Pat Carney, and the McPherson sisters to come play for the Sports Arena Blues. Over half the looming powerhouse's players were middle Tennessee imports. Anne Paradise, a Georgia woman who had been playing for NBC, was also persuaded to come back home to Atlanta.

The AAU was still "semipro" ball, but inducements to players were available when necessary. The most frequent and reputable of these was a job with the sponsoring company or another employer in the town. There were others. The Atlanta Sports Arena built "a little house" for Banks, Paradise, and Weems adjacent to the arena. Alline and Doris both worked for oil companies. Anne Paradise was subsidized by her father and preferred to remain unemployed at anything other than basketball at this time.[10]

Back in Nashville, the Goldblumes appeared decimated, especially following the loss of the scoring machine Banks. Such was not the case; they were still very potent. The team promptly acquired the services of two young, outstanding players. Pauline Lunn from Sheldahl, Iowa, had been an All-American for Dr. Swett's, the Goldblumes' opponent in the recent AAU finals. Lurlyne Greer of Des Arc, Arkansas, and last on the Little Rock team, was a player with big potential. They were not scorers like Banks; but, at just under six feet in height, these women could maintain Cook's rebounding excellence. They would be important AAU players for several years. The experienced Mary Jane Marshall and Margaret Sexton provided excellent leadership for the defending champions.[11]

By mid-January of 1947, Cook's Goldblumes had won 100 of their previous 101 games. They would lose a game that year to Hanes Hosiery

The Atlanta Blues' "big three" in practice: Anne Paradise with the ball flanked by Doris Weems (*left*) and Alline Banks (*right*). *Photograph courtesy of Anne Paradise Hansford Langston.*

of Winston-Salem, North Carolina, an emerging team with which to be reckoned, and were again seeded first in the national tournament. Despite that, most sportswriters favored the undefeated Atlanta Blues because of Alline Banks (she had regained her maiden name). Said sportswriters still competed in phraseology to describe her hair. "Titian tressed" probably won out over "comely redhead." Regardless the color of her hair, Banks quickly reinforced her reputation on a new squad as the surest key to victory in the 1940s. Since 1942 she had played in one losing game. In 1947 everyone at the St. Joseph tourney called her "Miss Basketball."

1946–1947 Cook's Goldblumes. *Left to right:* Pauline Lunn, Lurlyne Greer, Mary Jane Marshall, Dot Bruce, Margaret Gleaves Sexton. *Photograph courtesy of Jane Marshall Ingram.*

The four semifinalists were led by their pivot players: Lurlyne Greer for Cook's Goldblume, Joy Crowell for Des Moines Home Federal, Alline Banks for the Blues, and Mary Link for AIB. When the two Des Moines teams fell in the semis, Iowa fans bemoaned another near miss. Despite the continual flow of well-coached Iowa high school players, the state's strong AAU teams usually fell into the runners-up category. (See Appendix B.)

The 1947 final was a corker. Cook's appeared to have won their fourth straight championship until Banks wriggled free for a layup to tie the game in its last seconds. In overtime, she led Atlanta to a 26–22 victory, having scored fifteen of her team's points. Since they had both played as teenagers on the NBC team and through their great years on the Vultee and Goldblume teams, Margaret Sexton had been guarding Alline Banks in practice. Now in crunch time, the best defensive player could not stop the best offensive player. The unshakably assured Alline summarized her good friend's performance, "Margaret couldn't hold me."[12]

The 1946–1947 AAU Champion Atlanta Blues. *Front row:* Anne Paradise, Doris Weems; *middle row:* Macile Wilson, Julie Hartness, Alline Banks, Genevieve Rainey, Margaret Richardson; *top row:* Madge Moon, Kathryn Williams, Jimmie Vaughn, Mildred Wilson. *Photograph courtesy of Jane Marshall Ingram.*

Prior to the Goldblumes losing in the finals, it had seemed to be a Tennessee-dominated tournament. There were four Nashville teams in the competition. The Parisi Dreamettes, a one-year wonder sponsored by a Nashville tailor, won the consolation championship. Six of the ten All-Americans were from the state: Banks and Weems of the Atlanta Blues; Marshall, Greer, and Sexton of Cook's Goldblume; Mary Hoffay of NBC; and Lottie Jackson (from DuPont, Tennessee) of New Orleans Jax Beer. Jimmie Vaughn won the free-throw championship, hitting eighty-five of one hundred in the two rounds of competition, thus completing a trifecta of AAU basketball honors. Over the years Vaughn was AAU All-American, Beauty Queen, and free-throw champion.

There was another obscure Tennessee event at St. Joe's that year. John Head had his AAU tournament coaching debut. No one could have imagined he would rack up more victories and championships than any other coach in AAU history. Because of Head's success in regional high school basketball, H. O. Balls asked him to take the NBC team to the 1947 tournament. His young team included a couple of players, Bea Baldwin and Fern Gregory, who had just completed their high school competition for him at Cross Plains, a town of no stoplights but many basketball players. NBC was no factor at the tournament. Baldwin and Gregory were beginning successful, globetrotting AAU careers.

AAU officials gradually liberalized rules, speeding up the game and edging perilously closer to men's rules. Beginning in the 1947–1948 season they passed a rule allowing *two* dribbles before the ball must be passed or shot. Billy Hudson urged the AAU to adopt the men's rule for bringing the ball inbounds after a made basket. The women were still being coddled by bringing the ball in at the free-throw line in order to diminish court running.[13]

The rivalry between Atlanta and the Goldblumes continued another year, 1948, Alline's last with the Sports Arena team. Hudson, the Blumes' feisty coach, attempted a little gamesmanship against Banks at the national tournament. Because her picture had been displayed on the front of a game program, he claimed she was a professional and was, therefore, ineligible for the pristine AAU competition. Well, she did not have her best tournament; but Hudson's mischief did not bother her.

Perhaps the Blumes were especially loose and eager after an incident the afternoon of the final game at the hotel where all the teams stayed. Pauline Lunn, Mary Jane Marshall, and Margaret Sexton on returning from shopping observed the Blues team being photographed in the hotel lobby with the championship trophy, still in their possession after their 1947 triumph. They were only being efficient in preparing a picture to be wired to the Atlanta papers after their anticipated victory. They succeeded, however, in only making the Goldblume stars testy, an emotion quickly shared with their teammates.

Whether this little episode had any bearing on the game's outcome is unknown. The Nashville players arrived at the gym feeling saucily confident, "giggling and loose as a goose." This second time around, the Blumes demonstrated their depth and reinforced their historic stature by defeating Atlanta in yet another very close game, 21–18. Led by Margaret Sexton, Billy Hudson's team slowed the game way down and held Banks to seven points in the final. Sexton was selected as the tourney's MVP, a most unusual reward for a defensive player. The Chatham Blanketeers beat NBC for third place. Hudson quit coaching after the 1948 championship. He considered this last club his best, quite a compliment considering the great success of the other Vultee/Goldblumes sextettes. AAU officials also pegged it as one of the outstanding teams ever.[14]

No team from Atlanta, rapidly emerging as the South's biggest metropolis, would ever approach the Blues' two-year 98–3 record during Alline Banks's tenure. The Atlanta team, consisting mostly of Tennesseans, disappeared as a factor in national competition after 1948. Anne Paradise went with Pat Carney to North Carolina to play for Chatham. Pat was dating that team's coach, and Paradise just felt like moving on. Alline Banks was getting tired of basketball and played in no more regular season games. She had married H. B. (Pete) Sprouse and was involved in her clerical work with an oil company. Thanks to H. O. Balls and some stretching of AAU rules though, her tournament competition was not finished.

NBC still had a good team, finishing fourth in the 1948 tournament. Balls was doubtless frustrated playing second fiddle to a local beer distributor's team and badly wanted a championship. His sports organization was suspect though, as NBC up to then only began seriously honing a team at tournament time. John Head was still commuting the thirty-five miles from Cross Plains and stocking the team with talented girls from his high school squad. NBC played only eight games before going to St. Joseph that year. The very young team needed a player with star quality, a go-to gal, someone who believed winning was her birthright. So next year Balls hired the ultimate ringer—Alline Banks Sprouse.

Sprouse's eligibility was, euphemistically, tenuous. She now lived in Atlanta and flew to the tournament to compete for a Nashville team. According to Sprouse, she resided in NBC's region and was, therefore, eligible. Did H. O. Balls pay the airfare for her long-distance commute? He probably did, again a certain violation of amateur rules. Regardless the legality of her participation, her body was not remotely ready for a week of hard basketball. Nevertheless, she staggered through the 1949 tournament to the finals, along the way scoring nineteen of her team's twenty-nine points in a semifinal win over Hanes Hosiery. However, NBC met a seasoned bunch of Goldblumes in the finals.

The Cook's team, now coached by Leo Long, was on its last competitive legs. Multi-All-Americans Mary Jane Marshall and Margaret Sexton Gleaves were, like Alline Sprouse, tiring of basketball. They remained tenacious though, and stomped NBC 35–17 to win (counting the Vultee years) their fifth championship in six years. Margaret won the battle against Alline on this night, holding her to three long-distance field goals. Goldblume team defense, one of their inevitable strengths, was incredible. In five of six tournament games, their opponents scored fewer than twenty points. They were also proud of their prevalence back home in the contemporary bedrock of women's basketball. A half century later, a steely-eyed Janie Marshall Ingram remembered passionately, if not entirely correctly, "We beat the crap out of NBC every time we played 'em."

Five Goldblumes (Marshall, Greer, Bruce, Cooper, and Gleaves) and two Nabucos (Sprouse and Gregory) made All-American. Tennessee dominance was greater than ever. Of the twelve starters in the final contest, only two, Pauline Lunn Bowden and Lurlyne Greer, were from somewhere other than a little Tennessee town. Even other tournament teams had Tennessee players. Pat Carney (Joelton) played for Chatham, and Jimmie Vaughn (Jackson) now played for Hanes Hosiery, her third championship-caliber club. (See Appendix A.)

The two coaches, Leo Long (Father Ryan) and John Head (who resigned his high school job in 1949), had earned their spurs in regional high schools. In his long AAU career, this was Long's only championship. In the time before NBC dominance led by John Head, Leo Long was considered the best basketball teacher in Nashville. Among those who played for several teams, there was almost universal endorsement of Long as the best coach. Alline Banks said, "He made me shoot with my left hand, polished my wheel shot, and taught me the value of floor play."[15]

Fittingly the decade ended with a game between two Nashville teams, and Alline Banks Sprouse was central to the outcome. After a second year of no regular season play, she again flew from Atlanta to St. Joe to play for NBC in 1950. Willing her way through the tournament, she concentrated on the offensive end of the court to the detriment of her former all-round game. The Goldblumes were seeded first and NBC second. Sportswriters agreed though that this was a tenuous ranking. The Cook's team was severely hampered by losing Janie Marshall. Late in the season, this competitive, very experienced player and 1949 MVP had severely hurt her knee in a game against Hanes Hosiery.

The semis matched the usual powers. Lurlyne Greer, with nineteen points, led the Blumes over AIB. NBC struggled against Hanes Hosiery, the crown princesses of AAU competition. Rallying behind Alline's late scoring, NBC squeaked out a 32–31 overtime victory, setting up another all–Nashville finale—the seventh consecutive year the city was represented in the finals.

NBC won its first national championship, 29–28; it would not be the team's last. Scoring over half her team's points in her swan song, Alline garnered her fifth championship and John Head his first. Most attendees thought that Lurlyne Greer, the consensus candidate to succeed Alline Sprouse as the best player extant, should have been tournament MVP; but, almost by reflex, the award was given to Sprouse. Half the All-American team came from Nashville teams—NBC (Sprouse, Doris Weems), Cook's Goldblume (Greer, Dot Bruce), and General Shoe (Agnes Loyd).

The Goldblumes began to scatter. Mary Jane Marshall turned to a new sport, softball; her knee kept her from playing basketball. Shortly thereafter she married her softball coach. Margaret Sexton Gleaves retired from sports to raise a family. It was unclear whether the Blumes would ever again be the team to beat, but unquestionably they had been the AAU women's basketball bullies of the 1940s. From 1941 to 1950, the team, whether as Bomberettes or Goldblumes, had won five championships and finished second twice. The decade had been theirs.[16]

The Hosiery Girls

Only three teams won AAU women's basketball championships in the 1950s, Hanes Hosiery of Winston-Salem, North Carolina, NBC, and a new and major player on the block, the Hutcherson Flying Queens of Wayland Baptist College in Plainview, Texas. The emergence of this major basketball power from a little-known college set up a vicious fifteen-year competition between them and NBC. But first there was the strong but transient reign of Hanes Hosiery.

Elva Bishop, principal recorder of the Hanes era, called the team "the last of the great industrial teams," meaning that the players had to work as well as play for their employer.[17] Actually, it may have been the only important women's team that could be so characterized. Eligibility requirements had always been flexible, and it was the rare team whose players were all obliged to the boss in any way other than winning basketball games. Players easily moved from club to club, and Hanes would so benefit during their reign. Hanes players did work at the plant, however, though in scattered departments so production would not suffer when they were off competing.

Hanes started its women's team in 1945 and immediately began climbing the AAU ladder. Their coach was key in this immediate success. Virgil Yow was recruited from the men's coaching job at High Point (North Carolina) College. A man way ahead of his time, he had supplemented his war-depleted team there with a good woman shooter in 1944.

By 1948, the "Hosiery Girls" had improved enough by play in the tough Southern Textile League of the Carolinas that they were invited to the AAU tournament. They lost in the quarterfinals. The next year they finished third, eliminated by NBC in the semifinals. The same two teams met in the 1950 semifinals, Hanes losing in overtime by only one point to the Nabucos. Along the way they captured several All-American honors, including Jackie Swaim Fagg and Jimmie Vaughn, late of NBC and the Atlanta Blues. The two recurring All-Americans that were the nucleus of the team during their championship years, however, were Evelyn (Eckie) Jordan and Eunies Futch.

Close friends Eckie (Li'l E) and Eunies (Big E) were basketball zealots and striking physical contrasts. They were Mutt and Jeff in satin shorts. Considered short even for her era, the stocky Eckie, 5' 2½", 142 pounds, was a classical point guard (a then uncoined term)—pushing the ball up the floor as fast as a couple of dribbles and sharp passing would allow, roving the court, and absolutely taking charge. The foot taller Eunies, 6' 2", 165 pounds, had a good outside shot and sometimes roved but was also a defensive specialist, usually covering the opponent's best inside player.

Two pals, Eunies "Big E" Futch and Eckie "Li'l E" Jordan. *Photograph courtesy of Evelyn "Eckie" Jordan.*

In 1951 the AAU tournament had a one-year stand in Dallas at the Fair Park Recreation Building. The site was convenient for the championship Dallas teams of 1928–1930 to have a reunion. Two Mexican teams crossed the Rio Grande for the games and graciously distributed sombreros as mementos of international friendship. The constitution of the big thirty-eight-team field showed that the Midwest, Southwest, and Southeast still dominated. There were no teams from west of Texas. The host state had seven teams; and Iowa, Tennessee (all Nashville), and Georgia had three each. From the East Coast, Massachusetts, Maryland, and Florida each supplied a team.

The AAU recognized the interest engendered by good defense and began to allow more aggressiveness by defenders. They experimented with actually allowing tying up the ball, an action previously reprimanded by a technical foul. After their elimination from the tournament, the Denver Viners and Atlanta Blues played an exhibition game using the risqué rule.

Alline Sprouse was supposedly going to ride into town again at the last minute and rescue NBC, but this time she could muster neither the will nor the way. Wayland College was an increasing presence and the Cinderella team of the tournament, upsetting both top-seeded NBC and AIB on the way to the finals. The Wayland appearance was the first time since 1939 that Texas, a state that had dominated early AAU competition, had a team in the championship contest.

In the semis, Hanes beat the last standing Nashville team, Cook's Goldblumes, 41–38. Eunies Futch held the Blumes star Lurlyne Greer to ten points and caused her to foul out with just over six minutes to go in the game. The absence of a Nashville team in the finals seemed queer. Considering the Vultee Bomberettes as the original incarnation of the Goldblumes, 1951 was the first time in seven years that team had not played for the championship. This was the Goldblumes' swan song. For unknown reasons, "Captain Johnny" Little disbanded the team after the 1951 season.

The Hosiery Girls defeated the Flying Queens in a yawner final, 50–34, winning the first of its championships. Jimmie Vaughn with fourteen and Jackie Fagg with thirteen points led the scoring. Coach Yow, though, asserted that Eckie Jordan, the peppery little Hanes floor leader, was the star of the tournament.[18]

The Hanes Hosiery 1951 AAU women's basketball champions: Eckie Jordan, Jackie Swaim, Jimmie Vaughn Williams, Irma Hedgecock, Sara Parker Stroud, Eunies Futch, Ruth Bingham, Coach Virgil Yow, Hazel Starret Phillips, Hazel Naylor, Joyce Mueller, Nancy Swigert, Cornelia Vaughn. *Photograph courtesy of Jackie Swaim Fagg.*

The 1952 season looked less promising for Hanes when they lost eight players. Some players quit to get married, and some married players quit at their husbands' behests. In the modern parlance though, they did not rebuild; they reloaded. Among the players attracted to the team and a job in the factory was Lurlyne Greer. When the Goldblumes disbanded, the talented Greer had no trouble finding a competitive team to join. She chose the best extant.

Hanes was undefeated through the 1952 season and dominated the season-ending tournament, now back in Wichita for a brief sojourn. They eliminated one of the persistent college presences, Iowa Wesleyan, 61–25, in the semis. Another Iowa team, AIC, was beaten in the finals, 49–23. AIC, featuring one of the first truly very tall players, Norma

An Iowa Wesleyan player feels the pressure of Eckie Jordan's defense. *Photograph courtesy of Evelyn "Eckie" Jordan.*

Schoute, had eliminated NBC in the semifinals. Schoute, a 6′ 4″ high school senior from Monona, Iowa, was the tournament's new sensation as she scored twenty-eight points. The stronger, more experienced Greer put a lid on her in the finals.

Nashville had good but not dominant teams in the tournament. Kathryn Washington, a high school senior from nearby Murfreesboro and their only All-American, led NBC. The Nabucos easily beat Iowa Wesleyan for third place. The Tennessee Highway Patrol Dreamettes featuring several former Goldblume players, including Pauline Bowden, were upset in the quarterfinals by AIC.

Hazel Phillips was the fourth straight Hanes player to win the free-throw championship in 1952. Yow required hours of free-throw practice, mandating an underhanded technique. His rationale was that women tired quicker than men and that the underhanded toss used less energy, especially in the closing minutes of a game when players were likely to be enervated. Four Hanes players, Futch, Greer, Jordan, and Sarah Parker, made All-American. Their two-season winning streak intact, Hanes Hosiery was unquestionably tops in AAU basketball.[19]

The 1953 tournament was a low point for Nashville. For the first time in ten years, there was only one Nashville team in the competition. However, that team was a history-making, powerful one. Led by Pauline Bowden and Katherine Washington, seven members of the NBC team had been on the United States contingent that had just returned from Santiago, Chile, where they had won the first women's World Championship. Though only seeded third, their talent and momentum made NBC a favorite to win the AAU championship. Whether from fatigue or overconfidence, they blew it. They lost to the low-seeded Sante Fe Streamliners of Topeka, 53–52. George Sherman, a longtime AAU observer, official, and coach, considered this the biggest upset in AAU women's basketball history. The Nabucos got little consolation from winning the rest of their games and finishing fifth in the tournament.

Aside from top-seeded Hanes winning out, the 1953 tourney was characterized by upsets. In addition to the NBC shocker, AIC and second-seeded Iowa Wesleyan lost early on. A Mexican team, the "popular" (as noted in a Nashville newspaper) Chihuahua Adelitas made it to the semifinals, the furthest any Mexican team ever advanced.[20]

For Hanes, the beat continued in 1953 as they added to one of the longest winning streaks in any sport. In the finals at Wichita, they beat Wayland 36–28 for the team's seventy-second consecutive win, becoming the third team to win three championships in a row. Tulsa Business College (1934–1936) and Vultee/Goldblume (1944–1946) had previously scored that hat trick.

Both the win and championship streaks ended in 1954. After 102 consecutive victories, Hanes, now coached by Hugh Hampton, lost in the AAU tournament semifinals to the Kansas City Dons, 44–41. They

Jackie Swaim receiving 1949 AAU Free Throw Championship trophy from Mrs. Irvin Van Blarcom. *Courtesy of Jackie Swaim Fagg.*

The 1952 AAU All-Star team (missing Louise Lowry). *Front row:* Katherine Washington, Sarah Parker, Lurlyne Greer, Eckie Jordan; *top row:* Janet Thompson, Dorothy Welp, Eunies Futch, Norma Schoute, Betty Clark. *Photograph courtesy of Diane Hall.*

derived some consolation by beating the champion Wayland Flying Queens in a post-tournament exhibition game 46–39. As part of the tryouts for the pending Pan-American games, that game was played using international, "men's," full-court rules.

Regrettably, Hanes Hosiery discontinued its women's team after the 1954 tournament. The regional textile league was crumbling. In a remarkably regressive move, the North Carolina legislature ended the

Beer Distributors, Business Schools, and Hosiery Girls

popular state tournament for girls, thus de-emphasizing the sport and limiting the supply of new players. Most Hanes players had come from the Carolinas, in line with the sponsor's initial plan to build the team from the area. In the words of their first regional star, Jackie Swaim Fagg, Coach Yow "made," that is, *molded,* the players on his first championship team.

That guiding philosophy was not sacrosanct, and as they became stronger Hanes used quite a few already-made players. The company recruited Eunies Futch when she was a fifteen-year-old high school junior in Jacksonville, Florida. She graduated from high school January 15, 1947, and played her first game for Hanes five days later. There were other notable transfers. Both Jimmie Vaughn and Lurlyne Greer, their best and most important player, were experienced AAU hoopsters before coming to Winston-Salem.

Virgil Yow coached most of the games in Hanes Hosiery's tremendous 102-game winning streak in the early 1950s. He was an early advocate of the five-player game and used an up-tempo pace, one of the first AAU coaches to encompass the entire ninety-four feet of court length into both the offensive and defensive games. He wanted his girls to "play like boys," that is, push the ball upcourt and play aggressive defense. They honed a remarkable fast break, even with only four players on the offensive end, and averaged almost sixty points per thirty-two-minute game. The Hanes teams were, therefore, necessarily well conditioned.

Such play was a predictable evolution enhanced by rules changes that earlier, talented players would have loved—liberalized dribbling, closer guarding (one could now tie up the ball), and being able to bring the ball in bounds under the basket. Yow deserves credit for taking advantage of this slowly changing philosophy of the women's game. The only coach to be inducted into the Helms Hall of Fame for contributions to both the men's and women's game, Virgil Yow led the United States team on its premier South American tour in 1951.

The primary motivation for most of the women playing AAU ball was simply the pleasure it gave them. The Hosiery Girls, especially, just seemed to enjoy playing basketball, radiating enthusiasm and conveying that emotion to loyal Tarheel fans. The team was always a social focus for Hanes employees and provided lots of excitement for regional devotees. Hanes Hosiery delivered a decade of brilliant basketball played by women who loved the game.[21]

Playing in the AAU

Whoever the AAU women's basketball champions might have been, they were little known or feted beyond their locale or by any significant number of fans other than a local cadre. The teams were low-budget operations playing far from the limelight. Nashville teams' experiences in the 1940s were representative.

Especially compared to the lives of current athletes, conditions were primitive. Unlike the well-heeled Atlanta Blues of the late 1940s and the Wayland Queens of 1950 onward, travel to the furthest competitions was usually in a caravan of two or three cars, often six riders with luggage per auto. Amenities were not a part of the program. After a several-hundred-mile car trip through several states to Iowa for instance, there was often no available shower for the players after the last of a two- or three-game weekend set against AIB and AIC. The players would then make the trip home as tolerable as possible by covering their unwashed bodies with their relatively clean and dry warmups and lots of deodorant. They alternated driving, amused themselves by singing songs, and slept on each other's shoulders when Morpheus beckoned. There was no time for dallying either. Monday morning and work obligations always came round. On teams of twelve to fifteen players, all the women were surely not bosom buddies. There can be no doubt, however, that camaraderie was strong enough to carry teams through scores of games under physically trying circumstances. In addition to loving basketball, the women had to at least like and respect one another.

Home games were usually played in a local high school gym or at a military induction center before a few hundred fans at most. Those fans did not have to break the family budget to attend games either. A late 1940s season ticket for the (Nashville) National Life Generals cost three dollars, including any necessary tournament contests! That ticket bought games against, among others, Hanes Hosiery, AIC, Mexico, NBC, Wayland College, Atlanta, and the Oak Ridge Rockets—quite a bargain.

The players were hot competitors, especially at tournament time, which they took real seriously. They were in it for the fun though, and basketball did not dominate their lives. They practiced two or three times a week at night in whatever gym was available. As Leo Long was the coach at Father Ryan High School, his AAU teams usually worked out at the school gym. Conditioning was not strict. The players generally behaved temperately, but there were no absolute lifestyle prohibitions from management. Many women smoked and considered a halftime puff a necessary pick-me-up. They would take a beer or cocktail with an after-practice meal, but there were no hard drinkers among them.[22]

For most AAU players, their security, life directions, and psyches did not depend on how they performed on a basketball court during their young lives. With varying degrees of commitment, they played for pleasure. To some of the women though, pleasure meant doing the absolute best one could at it. If basketball was a preoccupation, then "pleasure" could be real serious. Profiles of three superb players of this mid-twentieth-century era depict the gamut of attitudes they brought to the game. They ranged from players who did it strictly for the fun (Anne Paradise) to those who attained identity in an otherwise unre-markable life (Lurlyne Greer) to those who were obsessed with the game and the necessity to be successful at it (Alline Banks).

Anne (the Panther) Paradise

In addition to being very good athletes, the Atlanta Blues players were all attractive—southern belles in a city noted for such. Male fans and, especially, sportswriters appreciated this conspicuous team feature. Writers, whenever remotely possible, emphasized femininity to skep-tical fans during an era in which women's public participation in team sports cast doubt on the players' sexual orientations. The Atlanta Blues provided all the fodder they needed.

In a 1948 sports magazine article, Guy Tiller probably depleted his store of sexy descriptive adjectives in profiling the beautiful Blues. Calling them a team of "cracker-jacquelines" widely known for their "play and pulchritude," he somewhat dispassionately described each player's sports accomplishments, then ladled topping onto the journalistic sundae by emphasizing their looks. Green-eyed, freckle-faced "Red" Banks was attractive and, coincidentally, the best woman basketball player alive. Floor leader Doris Weems was "a dimple-faced blonde." Jimmie Vaughn in addition to being a free-throw champion and having a great outside shot was a "basketball beauty," most noted for being an AAU tourna-ment queen.

Then there was Anne Paradise. Paradise, a Lexington, Georgia, (yet another) country girl, was tall (5' 10"), fast, and graceful. In high school

The fetching Atlanta Blues. *Front row:* Blanche McPherson, Alline Banks, Dora McPherson, unknown; *top row:* Kathryn Williams, Pat Carney, Jimmie Vaughn, Doris Weems, Anne Paradise. Seven of these nine players came from Tennessee. *Photograph courtesy of Anne Paradise Hansford Langston.*

she was a star in track and field as well as basketball. A gifted jumper, she trained for the high jump by leaping over barbed-wire fences on her family farm. She briefly attended the University of Georgia where she coached girls' dorm hall basketball teams, played field hockey, and refused the pleas of the track coach that she join his team. Having left school because the university did not have an intercollegiate basketball team, she played on the first Atlanta team that went to the AAU tournament in 1943. Then followed a brief sojourn with NBC that included a trip to Mexico City for a tournament at which she became acquainted with Hazel Walker. Her two years (1946–1948) with the great Atlanta Blues team were the most important and successful in her basketball career.

Anne Paradise on her Harley-Davidson motorcycle, c. 1943. *Photograph courtesy of Anne Paradise Hansford Langston.*

Anne was striking, darkly beautiful, and free spirited—representative of the AAU players who, for a while at least, played ball and life for the fun of it. Because her father was supporting her, she needed no job and was, therefore, free to sit on her Harley-Davidson motorcycle instead of a desk chair. Attentive to the conservative morés taught in her youth, she refused offers to join the professional wrestling circuit or to go to Los Angeles and be photographed by a model agency in a bikini, the latest fashion scandal ("I'm not going to pose naked!").

Because of her smooth, long-striding running gait, an Atlanta sportswriter dubbed her "the panther." He also observed that "she looks just as good standing still, doing nothing." Her pleasant disposition and carefree reputation preceded her, and she was a natural focus for ribbing by opponents. When playing basketball, she wore her black locks in pigtails adorned with red ribbons. In the 1948 championship final between the Blues and the Goldblumes, the entire Cook's team arrived at the gym for the game with their hair styled in an Indian-like braid tied with a red ribbon—just like the Panther.

More important than her appearance, Paradise was a fine player. Multitalented, she was willing to be a role player to attain team success. With the Blues she was an All-American who deferred to Banks for most of the team's scoring. Just as was the case with Mary Jane Marshall of the Goldblumes, she got no statistical credit for the assists made to Alline Banks. She was the first Georgia woman selected All-American in basketball, being thrice so honored, and was inducted into the Georgia Sports Hall of Fame in 2003.

Paradise played one more year of AAU basketball with the Chatham Blanketeers after the Blues lost to the Goldblumes in 1948. Always believing that basketball was just a game, she then quit it and went home to marry her childhood sweetheart and raise a family. In contrast to her good friend Alline Banks, she put her play years behind her and is totally untroubled by lost games, ungarnered honors, or any other possibly negative aspects of her AAU experience. She remembers only the fun of it all.[23]

Lurlyne Greer

Lurlyne Greer was the best AAU women's player of the late forties and first half of the 1950s. She was born to play basketball. A big,

Anne Paradise in her signature game-time Indian braids. *Photograph courtesy of Anne Paradise Hansford Langston.*

strong, rawboned woman, she took to the game at an early age and succeeded at all levels of available competition except the professional for most of her first thirty years.

Greer was yet another basketball champion from the rural South. She was born in 1928 in Des Arc, Arkansas, a town with a 1930 population of 1,348 people and many rice fields. Her father was a farmer and her mother a White County schoolteacher. Early infatuated with the game, Greer happily recorded in numerous scrapbooks both anecdotes and pictures of the pleasure she got from playing the junior high school basketball in which her mother coached her. She was a good student, and her athletic skills provided notoriety in her high school graduating class of twenty or so. Girls' basketball was disorganized, and there was little discretionary money in Arkansas in the midst of World War II. There were no county or district tournaments during her junior year because of the diminished transportation associated with gas rationing. There was more gasoline and competition in 1943–1944, but Arkansas did not hold a state tournament until 1946.[24]

Various Little Rock teams began hustling Lurlyne during her senior year. At age seventeen she joined Little Rock Dr. Pepper, whose player-coach was Hazel Walker. Like all sports-knowledgeable Arkansans, she worshipped the famous Hazel, who was then precisely twice Lurlyne's age. After a tour of Mexico with that team, she went to the AAU tournament in 1946 but saw little action. Her obvious physical capability and exploits were well enough known though that teams from Iowa to Tennessee recruited her. Along with the equally young and strong Pauline Lunn of Des Moines, she chose to join the Cook's Goldblume team in 1946–1947, fleshing out one of the historical AAU juggernauts and replacing Alline Banks, who had fled to Atlanta.

Banks's Atlanta Blues beat the Blumes in overtime during Greer's first year with the team, and Lurlyne made All-American for the first time. The tables were convincingly turned the next two years as the Cook's team won in 1948 and 1949. Close observers felt that Greer had replaced Banks as the preeminent AAU player even though Alline-led NBC beat the Goldblumes for the championship in 1950.

Despite the fact that there was no financial or personal reward in the "flunky" work she did for her team sponsor, Southern Beer, Lurlyne loved Nashville. She enjoyed her friendships on both the Cook's

Lurlyne Greer, c. 1945. *Photograph courtesy of Diane Hall.*

basketball and softball teams. After the Goldblumes finished third in the 1951 tournament, Johnny Cook disbanded the team. Hanes Hosiery promptly found a slot for the now perpetual All-American. They were also lenient about her work in the "public relations department" (she wrote no copy), providing her employment during the season and letting her return to Arkansas to help on the farm in off-season.

The Hosiery Girls enjoyed two more championships led by the sturdy, 5' 11" Greer. Coach Yow said she made a good team "great." Not an overtly confident person such as Alline Banks or a great floor leader such as Hazel Walker, Lurlyne had to be encouraged to score more and not pass the ball so often to her new teammates. That unselfishness had previously enhanced the balanced attack of the Goldblumes and had been much appreciated by her Nashville teammates. Once unleashed, she could score though. In the 1951–1952 season, she made forty-one points in one game. She set an AAU tournament record that year in scoring thirty-five points against the Jackson (Mississippi) Magnolia Whips. Getting with Coach Yow's program, she became another Hanes player to win the tournament free-throw championship that year, hitting forty-seven out of fifty tosses. In 1952–1953, she averaged almost nineteen ppg, a very high tally for the time. She had both hook and jump shots and cashed in on rebound "put-backs." Her teammates called her "the Rock."

Though it started before she arrived, Greer had much to do with Hanes's amazing 102 games win streak that ended in 1954. She and the team were well recognized in regional papers, if not nationally. During that stretch she and two teammates were honored with the annual Louis Teague Award, given to the outstanding amateur men and women athletes in the two Carolinas. The team floor leader, Eckie Jordan, won in 1951; Lurlyne won in 1952; Eunies Futch won in 1953. Her time in North Carolina was complicated only by a short, unsuccessful marriage. Her betrothal to a marine sergeant in June 1953 ended less than two years later.

The Big and Little E's joined Lurlyne Greer Mealhouse on the first USA team competing in the Pan-American Games in 1955. Lurlyne captained the team. Her 18.3 ppg average was ten points higher than the second scorer and still ranks as the third-highest U.S. average in Pan-Am history.

When Hanes ended its women's program after the 1954 season, the

The 1955 USA Pan-Am team. Lurlyne (Greer) Mealhouse (#7) next to Coach Caddo Matthews, Eunies Futch (#3) in center, Mrs. Irvin Van Blarcom upper right, Eckie Jordan (#14) third from left, front row. *Photograph courtesy of Diane Hall.*

twenty-six-year-old was in her prime; but her best basketball was behind her. Not having established a two-month residency requirement, she was not allowed to play as a ringer for the St. Joseph Goetz Beer team in the 1955 tournament. The AAU finally seemed to be cracking down on late-season (i.e., tournament) migrations.[25]

Greer rejoined her original AAU coach, Hazel Walker, as a professional on the Arkansas Travelers for the 1956–1957 season. This was not a successful experience. According to Goose Garroute, longtime Traveler player and friend of Hazel, Greer just did not cut the mustard. Goose considered her "a good amateur player" but not up to the strain of travel and every night competition against men that was the fodder of the touring pros. She thought Greer neither fast nor tough enough for their game.

There must have been other factors. She had too much talent and experience to fail unless there were distractions or ennui. Perhaps her ardor for the game was dimming. Lurlyne had very successfully competed against the best AAU and international players. At any rate, Hazel "let her go" after that season, and she played no more organized basketball.[26]

Greer migrated to Philadelphia and learned the cemetery business. She did not like the city life and returned to Arkansas. There in the early 1960s, she married Frank W. Rogers. The two developed a cemetery in Heber Springs, Arkansas, a retirement and vacation area north of Little Rock. In her latter years she rarely strayed from there, enjoying her work, hunting and fishing with her husband, and occasionally hosting old AAU teammates. A habitual smoker like many ballplayers of her generation, Lurlyne Rogers died of a pulmonary malignancy on February 16, 2001.

Greer's off-court personality was quite different from the aggressiveness with which she played basketball. She was open, kind, and friendly. Many former teammates described her as "sweet." Though frequently designated as "boyish" by former AAU players, she was a handsome woman whose personal warmth shone through a big smile.

During her lifetime, the career of this publicly taciturn, country cager did not gain the plaudits it warranted. Its ten-year span was less than that of other stars such as Hazel Walker and Alline Banks. Though she was selected into the first Helm's Hall class of women basketball honorees in 1967, she is not in the Arkansas Sports Hall of Fame or, not surprisingly, the Naismith Hall. She was posthumously selected for the Women's Basketball Hall of Fame (WBHOF) in 2004. Lurlyne Greer was All-American eight times, a proven international star, and the best player on two of the dominant AAU teams of all time, Cook's Goldblume and Hanes Hosiery. The relative lack of accolades recedes, though, beside the fact that basketball gave her some notoriety and loads of pleasure. She was mighty good at it and for it.[27]

Alline Banks

Before the institution of late-twentieth-century sports bureaucracy, eligibility rules at all levels of organized sport ranged between absent and illusory. The invocation of residence and eligibility requirements depended on the wishes of the person doing the invoking, team need, and player preference.

Mary Alline Banks grew up in Coffee County, Tennessee. She learned toughness and masculine moves from playing basketball against her brothers on their outside court, a familial athletic nurturing precisely like that of Hazel Walker and numerous other AAU players. All three Banks kids played basketball in the town of Buchanan in neighboring Rutherford County. The school principal there readily admitted to recruiting Alline and felt it was well worth any abuse that might be heaped on him for doing so. As a forward, she played the three-division game just before it was replaced across Tennessee by the two-division court. Called a "point-a-minute" player, she averaged thirty-six points per thirty-two-minute game as a senior in 1938–1939, scoring fifty-six points in one game—really big numbers for that or any time.

High schools were the farm clubs for AAU women's teams. Scores of the best players somehow skirted school attendance rules to take a week or so off from school in March following the completion of their high school basketball careers to begin AAU tournament competition. As a seventeen-year-old senior, Alline Banks joined the NBC team when it went to the national tournament in Wichita. Though only playing part of a game on a team early eliminated, she earned honorary All-American honors. Alline always noted this award at the beginning of a career that would be filled with high accomplishment and honors as one of her greatest thrills.

Banks's real coming-out party was the following year at the first St. Joseph Tournament. At 150 pounds, the 5' 10", fair-skinned, freckled redhead was big enough and quite tall for her era. Often called "Red" by casual acquaintances and sportswriters ("My friends never called me that!"),[28] her good looks made her a prime candidate for tournament beauty queen.

She, though, was only interested in playing ball. She led NBC to an upset win over the defending champion and highly favored Galveston

Alline Banks as a Vultee AAU star. *Photograph courtesy of Jane Marshall Ingram.*

Anicos in the semifinals before they lost to the Little Rock Flyers in the 1940 tournament finals. Named Most Valuable Player of the tournament, Banks won her first of eleven consecutive All-American and nine MVP awards.[29]

Alline enjoyed running the court and was usually the rover, although she definitely enjoyed the offensive end more. Often put at the low post, she could move well in either direction and was adept at getting open. She especially enjoyed getting an opponent on her hip in the low post and firing in a flat, quick, deadly hook shot. Though rarely relying on the outside shot, she had an excellent one. Especially considering her height advantage, one observer felt she would have cashed in beyond the three-point line, had there been one. She felt she should never miss a free throw. Like all good shooters, she always thought her shots would go in. A half-century after her heyday, she felt the same as when she was dominating the AAU game. "I had all the shots."[30]

Her mates did not universally adore Banks. Teams rarely kept or preserved statistics. Even records of such obvious stats as individual scoring averages are hard to find. Alline in her prime usually averaged between fifteen and twenty ppg. They certainly were not counting assists, a critical aspect of basketball. There was no doubt though that Alline preferred being the assisted rather than the assistor. She wanted the ball, and coaches wanted her to have it. Some capable forwards begrudged a coach turning to Alline at tournament time after they had demonstrated their own scoring skills during the season.

There were no divisive enmities on her teams; and, in retrospect, jealousy may have inspired some of the negative feelings about her. The only characteristic rivaling her physical ability was her sense of confidence. She basked in the limelight and bore herself as the star, which she was. George Sherman felt her star quality was obvious and was intimidating to opponents. He compared her mystique to that of Joe Dimaggio's in baseball. She definitely had "an air" about her. There was no doubting Alline's dedication to basketball. She did not smoke, drink, or carouse on the road. Banks enjoyed horseback riding and tennis; but, unlike many of her mates, she played no organized off-season sport. Basketball was what she loved and did.[31]

The prevailing feature of Banks's career was success, wherever she played. In 1940 and 1941, the teenager led mediocre (compared to future powerhouses) NBC teams to the finals, losing both years to the Hazel Walker–led Little Rock Flyers. As Walker's career eased onto the down slope, Banks's took off; she was the MVP of both those tournaments. A trend had been set. By 1945, she was called the "world's best known women's basketball player."[32]

Banks played AAU basketball with four teams from 1939 to 1950.

Alline Banks with one of her many (1945) AAU MVP trophies. *Photograph courtesy of Alline Banks Sprouse.*

She was with NBC from 1939 to 1943, Vultee Aircraft from 1943 to 1945, Cook's Goldblume in the 1945–1946 season, Atlanta Sports Arena from 1946 to 1948, and NBC again in 1949 and 1950. Banks's teams won five national championships—two with Vultee (1944 and 1945), one with Cook's Goldblume (1946), one with Atlanta Sports Arena (1947), and one in 1950 with her first team, NBC. She was on runner-up teams four times (1940, 1941, 1948, 1949) and the third-place team in 1942. There was considerable variance in quality of these winning teams. The mid-decade Bomberettes and Goldblumes were conspicuously strong. The unifying characteristic of them all, however, was the presence of Alline Banks.

Banks's last two years of competition with NBC dramatized her innate athletic capability as well as the flexibility of AAU rules. In these years, H. O. Balls somehow made her eligible to play for NBC in the AAU tournament while she was living in Atlanta. Whatever the legality of her participation and in spite of being in no condition to play basketball either year, her skill and nerve propelled NBC to a second-place finish and a championship. Gasping for breath and clutching her last MVP trophy, she then retired from basketball at age twenty-nine. Only one other player would ever be so outstanding in women's AAU basketball.

Banks's excellence in her sphere was appropriately recognized during her athletic career. She was the Helms Foundation Athlete of the Year in 1947 and a nominee for the Sullivan Award in 1948. Bob Mathias won the award that year; Alline finished sixth out of six nominees. In addition to her All-American and MVP awards, she was selected to the AAU, Helms, Georgia (1972), and Tennessee (1974) Halls of Fame. She was in the charter class of women basketball players selected to the Helms Hall and the second woman, after golfer Louise Suggs, selected to the Georgia Hall. In the *Sports Illustrated,* millenium-ending survey of the fifty greatest twentieth-century sports figures from Tennessee, Alline Banks Sprouse was ranked twentieth.

Yet sports fans are rarely historians and have notoriously short memories. There are only two AAU women players in the Naismith Basketball Hall of Fame in Springfield, Massachusetts, and Alline Banks Sprouse is not one of them. According to many, a more flagrant omission occurred in 1999 with the induction of the initial class of honorees into the spanking new WBHOF in Knoxville, Tennessee. Selectors emphasized contemporaneous, international diversity over U.S. prevalent historic excellence. Of the twenty-five original inductees, none honored as a player had competed earlier than the mid-1950s. Only two were AAU players. Then followed a year of indignant protest from knowledgeable coaches, now senior fans who had seen Alline play, and former AAU players. Her exclusion only reinforced a simmering distrust of the current basketball establishment by AAU players, who feel their era has been forgotten. Sprouse was added to the WBHOF in its second class in 2000.

In her ninth decade, Alline Banks Sprouse still relives her basketball career. As an old woman, her pride mirrors the image she conveyed as an intimidating winner who just happened to be the best woman basketball player in the world for a decade. That basketball career remains at the center of her existence. She was the best and, assuming regained youth, feels she would be today. Her attitude remains as strong as her talent was. Pleasure in basketball for Alline was not something frivolously attained. It meant doing it better than anyone else and, always, winning.[33]

The Best Women's Basketball in the World

By the end of the Hanes Hosiery era, the few observers there were of it thought that United States, that is, AAU, women's basketball was the best in the world. That impression had not been tested in significant international competition. Despite the cultural barriers of the cold war, that challenging opportunity was opening up. If there were people in remote corners of the world who still were unfamiliar with this game invented in the United States, they were about to be exposed to it.

The AAU women's basketball program had persisted through the Great Depression and World War II. Rules were continually being modified to make the game faster and more like the men's game. Attendance of teams and fans at national tournaments held in midsized cities was consistently good. In its own milieu it seemed as strong as ever.

Yet that milieu was not expanding to the general public. The opportunity for girls to play high school basketball was spotty. Like the best AAU teams, girls' high school teams were mainly in the Midwest, Southeast, and Southwest. Publication of AAU teams' triumphs was rarely more than local in scope. Who outside these pockets of regional interest knew or cared who the women's national champions were? The AAU teams pleasurably and without the illumination of publicity were keeping lit the historic torch of women's basketball in the United States and, to some extent, the world. Recognizing this and wondering why no one seemed to be paying attention then or remembering now over a half century later, the septuagenarian and 1940s AAU All-American Jane Marshall Ingram questioned why people did not concede that "we blazed the trail" for all the good things that happened for women's basketball later in the twentieth century. The question was not hyperbolic.[34]

That happy pursuit of basketball superbness continued for a couple more decades after the Hanes era until women's basketball took a dramatic turn following the passage of Title IX. There would be expanding international competition, two excellent teams (some of the most dominant ever), and a player better than any seen before or (some say) since.

CHAPTER FOUR

Expansion and Consolidation

*"I only want to give my best, Lord,
And in thy strength alone be strong."*

—From "A Player's Prayer"
by Patsy Neal, Wayland
Flying Queen

For the duration of its influential period until its demise in the 1970s, AAU women's basketball would expand and contract. It expanded internationally. As long as it was the only significant outlet for elite players, it influenced the creation of U.S. national teams. The FIBA, the USA Olympic committee, and the State Department all enlisted the AAU's help in the rapidly expanding international competition.

This occurred for two reasons. First, the sport was becoming as popular internationally for women as it already was for men. Secondly, communist bloc countries increasingly used their national teams as propaganda tools, seeking to show the superiority of their societies through the accomplishment of their athletes. This included women's basketball. The United States slowly began to respond to this impetus. By providing most of the USA teams, the AAU thus abetted international contact and understanding, two scarce items during the cold war.

Paradoxically, AAU women's basketball began to contract in a couple of ways. The breadth of competition decreased due to decreasing popularity of industrial leagues. For whatever reasons, women workers were less interested; and employers saw no yield in paying for programs that neither improved employee *espirit* nor evoked public exposure for their companies. The breadth of competition at national tournaments gradually waned.

Its depth of quality did not suffer, as another consolidation occurred. Two tremendous teams dominated the game for two decades. Wayland College came first, followed by Nashville Business College. Despite a shallow level of good quality teams just below them, these two powers unquestionably ruled the AAU roost. Sue Gunter, recently retired Louisiana State women's basketball coach and former NBC player c. 1958–1962, characterized the teams as the respective "Cadillac and Lincoln Continental" of the era.[1] Because of the proliferation of good international teams, even these great teams would not be rulers of the world, something they might reasonably have considered a historic birthright.

Basketball across Borders

As the most influential governing body of amateur athletics in the United States, the AAU encouraged international basketball competition. This was a philosophical bent not necessarily backed by subsidization from the organization. Funding of competition outside the country was often an uncertain thing, usually left up to teams with such ambitions and enough money to pay their own fare.

Perhaps the first Western Hemisphere, cross-border women's basketball competition for U.S. women was with the Edmonton (Canada) Grads. Graduates of Commercial High, the first successful Canadian high school program in Edmonton, Alberta, formed that semipro squad which remained strong from 1915–1940. Coached by Percy Page, the Commercial Graduates' Club teams had little personnel turnover and were very disciplined. They attained their first international fame by crossing the Atlantic and defeating the London Shamrocks. Beginning in 1923, winners in a challenge competition between American and Canadian teams won the Underwood Trophy. The Grads had an advantage, as at least half the games were played using the full-court, five-player game, rules the Canadians normally used and which the Americans were slow to adopt. Despite this disadvantage, the OPC Cardinals whipped the Grads in three straight games in 1933. For unknown reasons, this competition ended in the late 1930s.[2]

For U.S. women, playing basketball against foreigners, especially on their home turf, was often a dicey proposition. Well before international rules were even partially standardized, a team, whatever its capability, could find itself in a hopeless situation. The Oklahoma City Cardinals learned this lesson the hard way. They represented the U.S. in a so-called World Championship competition in London in 1934. There were only three teams in the mini-tournament. After Finland was eliminated, the Cardinals played a French team in the finals.

Despite having obvious advantages in size and skill, the Yankee interlopers had no chance in the European venue. Using five-player rules on a dirt, outdoor court, the Oklahoma players faced an unexpected opponent in the one referee. As described in the AAU's magazine, "Amateur Athlete," the "short, fat Frenchman" spoke not a word of English and dressed incongruously in a "Swiss yodeler's outfit." Regardless the language barrier, he would not talk to the Americans about his strange rules interpretations. The Americans were not allowed to pivot or dribble. Not until late in the game did the Cardinals recognize that he was taking the ball from them for letting it touch parts of their body other than their hands. Some concluded he was not even a referee and had wandered in off the street and assumed the role. *Zut alors!* The French team could understand him and accommodated enough to beat the befuddled Americans, 34–23. In a xenophobic snit, a Polish coach had warned Cardinals coach Sam Babb that the French might hedge the rules a bit, their supposedly having cheated his national team out of the European championship. Now the shocked U.S. coach could only cry at the awards ceremony that "my girls were a lot better."[3]

Early in the AAU era, a warm, sometimes hot, and prevailing competition between North American neighbors took place across the United States' southern border. The AAU began inviting Mexican teams to its tournament in the 1930s. Because of contiguity, Mexican and Texas teams frequently played regular season games. Arrangements were made by coaches, not governments. Cross-border games with Mexican teams continued even during World War II. Among the teams the Vultee Bomberettes beat in their undefeated 1943 regular season on their home court of Nashville Father Ryan High School were the Mexican champions, the Politas of the Labor Department. Mexican teams continued to travel to middle Tennessee for games into the 1950s.

During their heyday in the late thirties and early forties the Little Rock Travelers frequently did just that—to Mexico. Hazel Walker's olive skin and dark hair made her especially popular in Mexico, where she was inundated with flowers and gifts. The trips highlighted different cultural attitudes toward the game, or how a "homer" can influence events. Sometimes pragmatism just trumps rules. Though certainly not limited to Central America, rigging a contest could be accomplished south of the Rio Grande. Margaret Dunaway, widow of the Travelers' coach, Bill, described one way of doing that.

When the Little Rock team played a best-two-out-of-three tournament in Mexico City, Coach Dunaway was assigned a translator. With that linguist's aid, he agreed to the first game conditions; and the Travelers won in a waltz. Dunaway's second pregame meeting with referees and opponents was without translator, who was mysteriously absent. After Dunaway agreed to a bunch of rules he really did not understand because of the language barrier, he watched his team get beat by many strange foul calls and rule interpretations. With translator, the third game went according to talent, another easy Little Rock victory. After discussing all this with the translator, Dunaway understood that the Mexican team had to win a game in order to realize three nights' worth of gate receipts.

Nashville teams traveled down Mexico way after the war to play basketball. On different occasions both the NBC and Goldblume teams crammed into a couple of cars and drove to Mexico City, playing games in the capital and surrounding towns. The conditions and the competition were rough. Teams were still appropriately called cagers. The Mexicans prudently maintained wire cages around arena floors to protect the players from the fans. Said fans did not take too kindly to losing, and postgame riots were considered an occupational hazard. The NBC and the Little Rock Dr. Pepper teams were the only *Estados Unidos* squads in an international tournament in Mexico City in 1945. Two NBC players at that competition ambivalently remembered the cultural contacts. Pollye Hudson described the Mexican players as "little but mean." Anne Paradise was not bothered by any hostility and

Group picture of friendly competitors, Convair Bomberettes and Mexican Politas in Nashville, 1943. *Photograph courtesy of Jane Marshall Ingram.*

recalled the fans' constantly tugging at their clothing to get a souvenir from the visiting cross-border celebrities.

Janie Marshall (Ingram) recalled that on a Mexican trip later in the forties with the Goldblumes there were few stores or gas stations between the border and Mexico City. With a screwdriver, the hot, rumpled women ate peanut butter purchased in Texas. Conditions were apparently a tad less threatening this trip. There were Hollywood stars in the gym (Bette Davis and Gary Merrill), and players were awarded silver bracelets in addition to a huge silver trophy for winning a tournament. The players were fascinated that games could not be played on Sundays because they would conflict with the bullfights. Despite the

BASKETBALL

MARTIN SQUAWS
— vs —
MEXICO CITY CHIHUAHUAS

Left to Right — All American Katherine Washington, Mary Jo Worley and All Regional Anna Hill

MARTIN COLLEGE GYM
PULASKI, TENNESSEE

WEDNESDAY, JANUARY 13, 1954
8:15 O'CLOCK
ADMISSION: 40c AND 25c

Ad for basketball game in Pulaski, Tennessee. *Photograph courtesy of Kermit Smith.*

debilitating features of travel, the Blumes enjoyed mixing with their opponents and returned undefeated from that sally into Mexico.

This evermore cordial competition between international neighbors continued for decades. It was enhanced, beginning in 1949, by the Mexican tours of the Wayland College teams. Mexican teams toured the strong southern AAU states throughout the fifties and sixties. There was never any cultural or racial animosity among the players. According to Jane Marshall, the competitors got along fine; and the Mexicans were "just another team."[4]

U.S. men's teams demonstrated basketball at the 1904, 1924, and 1928 Olympic Games. When it became an official sport at the 1932 Los Angeles Olympics, Dr. James Naismith tossed up the ball for the opening tip. Strong consideration was given to the inclusion of women's basketball in the 1940 Olympics planned for Tokyo. The AAU All-Star team was to be the U.S. representative. As Japan pursued military empire in Asia, numerous nations began to boycott the pending games; and the Japanese backed out of their host role. With World War II came the cancellation of the Olympic Games. Among many others, Alline Banks anticipated the adventure of playing for the United States in international competition and always regretted the lost chance. At that time the United States women would likely have encountered little significant opposition.[5]

The USA and AAU did enter another important theater of international women's competition in the early 1950s—the World Championships. In the absence of the Olympics, that would have to do and would be a good gauge of U.S. women's basketball standing around the globe. The United States decided to send a women's team to the first World Championship tournament in 1953.

Two years earlier another U.S. team had learned all about basketball the South American way. The Chilean Basketball Federation had asked the AAU to send a team to tour much of the continent—Ecuador, Peru, Paraguay, Argentina, Brazil, and Chile. Anticipating the growth of interhemisphere competition, the AAU accepted the invitation.

Coached by Virgil Yow of Hanes Hosiery, the ten-woman team included two players from tiny Cross Plains, Tennessee, Agnes Baldwin and Fern Nash. Both had played under John Head at Cross Plains High School. The team learned about the full-court game and the smaller ball then used in international play. In her letters home, Agnes noted that some of the better opponents played "just like boys too" and that away from the court things moved more slowly in South America. In a grateful letter to this highly motivated woman that autumn, Coach Yow regretted losing six games, thinking the team should have won all but one.[6]

That extensive intercontinental tour paved the way for success in 1953. The first World Championship was held that March in Santiago, Chile. There were only ten teams in the tournament, all but France and Switzerland from the Western Hemisphere. A strong USSR team had been expected, but their trip was canceled following the death of Premier Joseph Stalin on March 5.

Coach John Head led a nine-woman squad consisting of seven NBC players and two players from Iowa. Janet Thompson was on the Iowa Wesleyan team, and Betty Clark played for AIC. There were three Cross Plains, Tennessee, women—Agnes Baldwin, Betty Murphy, and Fern Nash. In discussing why so many NBC girls were on the team, the Iowan Thompson opined it might have become a matter of convenience as much as talent. She said several women were selected who simply could not afford the time off from work or school. So John Head fell back on his NBC players, not a bad option considering how good they were and that they were used to playing as a team.

Janet Thompson chose to take a semester off from Iowa Wesleyan, but financing the experience was a near thing. Her parents could not help. Her coach, Olan Ruble, paid for her train tickets and motel in Miami, a legal impossibility under today's college athletic rules. Her brother provided one hundred dollars for incidental expenses. The Chilean government financed their flights from Miami.

Travel to and within South America was still a multistage, multi-mode adventure in 1953. The U.S. team's stages included stops in Panama to enjoy sightseeing and in Cuba to pick up that nation's team. Planned trips to Ecuador and Nicaragua were canceled because of riots. Plane trouble caused a two-day delay before they finally arrived in Lima. After competing there in outdoor arenas, whatever the weather, the team bused to Santiago. That leg was characterized by numerous stops for peasant boarding, flat tires, and the carburetor's struggle through 10,000 feet of altitude.

After the travel, competition was a relative breeze. The U.S. team won all its exhibition games before the tournament and went 5–1 in the competition, losing to Brazil in a preliminary round. The final against host Chile demonstrated the value of the experience gained from previously playing on tour before hostile Latin crowds. Fervid, home rooters threw rocks; and the U.S. substitutes sometimes dove under the bench for protection. The game had to be temporarily stopped when demonstrations by the thirty thousand fans erupted after the Chilean star fouled out in the third quarter. At the beginning of the fourth, the crowd sang a rousing version of the Chilean national anthem. Led by Pauline Lunn Bowden, the tallest member on the team, and Katherine Washington, the youngest at twenty, the United States prevailed, 49–36, a triumph not only for the nation but for the AAU and a bunch of country girls from Tennessee and Iowa as well.

After the game, the team enjoyed refuge at the United States Embassy and did some partying, including dancing with the handsome marine guards. A commemorative picture of the team surrounding the huge winners' trophy was made there. That remains the last image of the trophy. Because of its size, the Embassy staff was to dismantle it and send it piecemeal back to the States. They never did return this totem of the first World Championship in women's basketball.

This had not been an easy victory. The resourceful players had to overcome travel fatigue, gastrointestinal disturbances, pinching fingers of admiring men, the absence of positive fan support, and the hostility of Chilean fans. The championship also showed how far ahead the United States was in women's basketball. That this superiority came from AAU talent was well demonstrated by the first-round AAU tournament loss later that month of the NBC team, who had constituted the majority of the victorious USA team. They were perhaps travel fatigued and surely took their obscure Topeka, Kansas, opponent for granted. They paid an ignominious price. Back in the United States, they were just another part of the crowd at the top of the AAU heap.[7]

They were nevertheless world champions. As the United States extricated itself from the Korean War, as U.S. citizenry settled into the relatively placid 1950s, and as Hanes Hosiery discontinued its basketball program, the AAU seemed secure and supreme in the small world of women's basketball. That sport was expanding around the globe, but consolidation of power in AAU women's basketball was imminent.

USA, winners of the first women's World Championship in basketball, with their huge trophy. *Front row:* Agnes Loyd, Coach John Head, Mildred Sanders, Fern Gregory; *top row:* Tennie McGhee (national AAU rules chairman), Agnes Baldwin, Janet Thompson, Betty Clark, Pauline Bowden, Betty Ann Murphy, Katherine Washington, Mrs. Irvin Van Blarcom (AAU women's basketball chairman). *Photograph courtesy of Agnes Baldwin Webb.*

The Flying Queens

The Hanes Hosiery players were understandably proud of their 102-game victory string and expected the mark to endure indefinitely. They quickly learned that one of the certain maxims of sport is that records not only are meant to be but usually get broken. The close (39–38) victory of the Wayland Queens over the Kansas City Dons in the 1953 AAU final was the first championship by a four-year college. Led by Coach Caddo Matthews, whose teams never lost an AAU game, the Queens were undefeated in their first championship year. Wayland had been a force for several years, but this victory was the true opening of a real big AAU act. The Flying Queens began several years of dominance and inaugurated a rivalry with NBC that would put most other competitors in their rearview mirrors.

As was the case with the players, who usually hailed from little rural towns, the few colleges that participated in AAU competition since the 1930s were obscure and small. In the absence of organized intercollegiate competition for women, those little schools were going far afield to provide high-level competition for their athletic coeds. One of these enlightened schools was located in west Texas.

Wayland Baptist College began classes in Plainview in 1910. It was a very small school. Its student enrollment only exceeded five hundred in 1948 and was usually far less than one thousand during its years of basketball eminence. After sporadic interest in club and interscholastic basketball competition, the college formed a women's team in 1946, to be coached by the men's coach, one Harley Redin.

Evolution of the team's name was unique. Known initially as the Wayland Lassies, they became the Harvest Queens in 1948 because the local Harvest Queen Mill had donated the team's uniforms. The final amplification of its name and the Queens' introduction onto the national stage both occurred in 1949–1950. Led by Coach Sam Allen, the team beefed up its schedule, traveling east to take on AAU powers in Nashville, Atlanta, and Winston-Salem. Despite losing all seven games on that tour, the team was strong enough to be invited to the AAU tournament, where they lost to their soon-to-be perennial rival, NBC.

Prior to the 1950 tournament, the Queens had played a game in Mexico City, an experience that launched a tony mystique that abetted the athletic excellence of the women's basketball program at the obscure Baptist school. The college president had persuaded Mr. Claude Hutcherson, a Wayland grad and prominent local businessman, to use some of the planes from his air service business to fly the team to Mexico. On that trip Mr. Hutcherson supposedly became enamored of the team and its potential. This was an era of very few women's college basketball programs. It was also an era bereft of intercollegiate regulation. With Wayland's unblushing approval, Mr. Hutcherson became the team sponsor and sank hundreds of thousands of dollars into that hobby. His signature investment was the provision of transportation for the players in four white Beechcraft Bonanzas (four passengers per plane), a classic two-prop cruiser with a V-shaped rear stabilizer. Thus the team acquired a long, distinctive moniker—the Wayland Baptist College Hutcherson Flying Queens.

This flying transport provided a physical as well as psychological advantage for the Wayland players, minimizing travel fatigue and time away from school. A home-and-home schedule against a distant opponent was much more difficult for the team without the airplanes. In order to play in Plainview, over one thousand miles from Nashville, NBC required a five-day commitment, two days of enervating auto travel each way and one day for the game. When the Flying Queens traveled, they had to commit only two days and a lot less time in cramped quarters.

In addition to the best transportation of any AAU team, the Queens were correct in comportment and current in accouterments. Stylishly coifed by a hairdresser hired for the team, they had several uniforms with various combinations of blue and gold, the school's colors, and smart traveling outfits of skirts and matching blazers or sweaters with the Wayland logo on the pockets. Claude Hutcherson's wife, Wilda, was especially influential in assuring the women were tastefully garbed. The college and the Hutchersons engendered a family atmosphere surrounding the team. Mrs. Hutcherson saw them as surrogate daughters, frequently hosting dinner parties for them or just having the young ladies out for soft drinks and snacks. Margie Hunt McDonald considered the experience of being a Queen as "almost a fantasy experience," a feeling that took her the better part of two years to shed.

Financing was obscure but plentiful. Harley Redin said the college paid his salary. Local booster clubs and Hutcherson paid for much of the first-class operation. Some portion of that unaudited pot purchased eight-hundred-dollar scholarships for thirteen players in the 1950s. Wayland College was the most beneficent collegiate women's program in the country at that time.

The Wayland basketball program attracted the best young players who could adhere to the school's standards. They claimed to award

1958 Wayland Baptist Flying Queens in front of one of the "team buses." *Photograph courtesy of Wayland Baptist University Office of Communications.*

scholarships on the basis of three "Bs," brains, beauty, and ball handling. Most of the players came from the basketball-rich Texas panhandle, the southern extent of which Plainview bordered. Some had been recruited. Others came to the school because of its burgeoning basketball reputation. If the coaches had not seen them perform, the players undertook a pilgrimage to Plainview where they underwent tryouts. Forty to fifty young women did so each year.

In Forrest, Mississippi, Carla Lowry learned about the Wayland program from a *Parade Magazine* article on the Queens while they were

Claude and Wilda Hutcherson. *Photograph courtesy of Wayland Baptist University Office of Communications.*

in the midst of a monstrous winning streak. Lowry's visit to Plainview was successful; she won a scholarship. After graduating from high school in 1956, Patsy Neal of Elberton, Georgia, saw a newspaper ad about the Wayland program. Desperately wanting to extend her basketball career, her family drove thirteen hundred miles for a tryout. To her chagrin, her parents sold one of her pet 4-H cows to finance the trip. Harley Redin liked what he saw. Neal earned a scholarship, won the

AAU free-throw championship her freshman year, and became a multiple All-American.

Not all of the players were just out of high school. Lu Nell Selle played ball at Wayland after a stint with the great Hanes teams. Wayland offered NBC's Agnes Baldwin, an All-American who played on the 1953 World Championship team, a scholarship when she was twenty-four years old. Katherine Washington of Murfreesboro, Tennessee, graduated from high school in 1952. She immediately went to the AAU national tournament with NBC. During a two-year career at Martin Junior College in Pulaski, Tennessee, she was a member of the United States national team and an All-American. One of the greatest AAU players, Washington was rejected by Wayland after a tryout, taught school for a year, went back to NBC for a couple of years, then after a second audition was finally given a Wayland scholarship. "Wash" played three years for the Queens, where she was again an All-American. She graduated at age twenty-six.

Wayland coaches had the best of teaching situations. They were presented with talented women who loved basketball and hungered to play it. Players were willing to live in a small west Texas town bereft of trees but full of loyal, friendly fans. The restrictive rules at the Baptist school prohibited dancing and other such overt secular delights, prohibitions not so uncommon or unthinkable as now. The women had no great problem with rules either on or off the court. They applied their intrinsic discipline within their academic and athletic milieus to get good educations, travel extensively, and play ball. Most were the epitome of what modern sports publicists only fantasize about; they were student-athletes.

Stories abounded about straight-laced Wayland players letting down their hair when competing internationally, far from their campus and coaches. Such tales only reassured that the young women were, thankfully, human; but the episodes of falling off the moral wagon constructed for them were rare. The players well understood the rigid standard to which they were supposed to adhere and feared being kicked out of school if they strayed. The team's abiding reputation remains that of focused, extremely mature people who worked hard at succeeding in basketball, school, and life.

The Queens conveyed an intimidating aura with their successful precision. Some of their opponents detected a swagger in their bearing. John Head's wife, Verna, doubtless seeing the Queens as the eternal enemy, described stereotypical Texas arrogance when she called them "bugeyed Petes." Their pregame warmup weave was a rapid-fire exhibition of dribbling and passing suggestive of a Harlem Globetrotter drill. To their detriment, wary opponents sometimes paid more attention to that basketball ballet than they did to their own game preparation.[8]

Harley Redin, a former World War II marine bomber pilot, returned as Wayland women's coach in the 1954–1955 season. He is given most credit for the team's dominance in the 1950s. He also served as one of the Bonanza pilots on "road trips." Redin took over a program then unique in women's collegiate athletics, following successful coaching regimes of Sam Allen, Henry Garland, and Caddo Matthews, who bequeathed an AAU championship and a forty-three game win streak. He was well ready to take advantage of the situation.

Wayland began its decade of dominance in 1954. Iowa Wesleyan College and NBC unsuccessfully nipped at their well-drilled and stylish heels the whole time, playing them close in the regular seasons and in tournaments; but the Queens firmly established themselves as the team of the fifties.

Hanes Hosiery was toppled from their throne in the 1954 AAU semifinals by the Kansas City Dons, a huge upset. Barbara Sipes, a strong 6' 1" center who would frequently represent the United States in international play, had made her AAU debut the previous year in the upset of the NBC team just back from the World Championships. Despite the Topeka native's twenty-one points, Wayland won the 1954 championship, 39–38.

Another important player made an inauspicious tournament entry in 1954. Nera White, a shy, lanky high school senior, played for NBC, scoring thirteen points in one game. The polished Waylands blasted both her and NBC in the tournament quarterfinals. Thereafter such victories would not be so easy.[9]

Colleges were becoming more interested in women's basketball. In the hotbed of that sport, midwestern schools competing in the 1955 tournament were Arkansas Tech, Clarendon (Texas) Junior College, Eastern Oklahoma A & M, Iowa Wesleyan, and Wayland. No national newspaper splash occurred, but AAU fans observed with wide eyes the

peaceful tournament participation of another team from the region—
Philander Smith of Little Rock, Arkansas, the first team from a black
college to come to the competition.

Other than her home county newspaper, hardly anyone noticed
that Nera White made All-American for the first time in 1955. As she
entered stage left, the most recent "best" AAU player exited on the
other side. Tennie McGhee as AAU women's basketball chairman
refused to let Lurlyne Greer Mealhouse play for St. Joseph Goetz
because the star had not satisfied a two-month residency requirement.
Finally relegated to an ancillary role, Alline Banks Sprouse, the most
accomplished and famous AAU player to that time, aided in passing out
trophies that year.

Sprouse passed out the big trophy to the Wayland Queens, who were
not being terribly tested during their decade of dominance. Led by Ruth
Cannon, Lometa Odom, and freshman Kaye Garms coming off the
bench, the mid-century dynasty beat Omaha Commercial Extension,
30–21. The consistently strong Omaha business school team had earlier
upset third-seeded NBC in the quarter-finals. St. Joseph Goetz Beer finished third, the highest finish ever for a team from the Missouri host city.

The All-American team had representatives from many clubs,
though the champ Queens had the most, three. Many of these players
would go with Coach Caddo Matthews to represent the United States
in the Pan-American Games that summer.[10] (See Appendix A.)

In 1956 Wayland became the fourth team to win three in a row,
retiring another AAU Traveling Trophy. While striding through the
brackets, they burst Philander Smith's brief bubble by walloping them,
80–19. They also began a tournament supremacy over their fellow collegians, Iowa Wesleyan, in the semifinals. Led by their big, smooth, four-
time All-American center, Lometa Odom, the Queens beat a rapidly
solidifying though unseeded NBC sextet 39–33 in the finals. On the way
there, NBC had upset both the second (Omaha CE) and third (Midland
Jewelry) tournament seeds. The Nabucos were back as an AAU force,
and the NBC-Wayland late-tourney pairing began cropping up more
and more. Fewer and fewer other teams would have a chance.[11]

That match-up was stymied in 1957 when Iowa Wesleyan, now
led by Sandy Fiete and the experienced Barbara Sipes, beat NBC in the
semifinals. The Tigerettes became the first Iowa team to be in the finals

since 1943. Their euphoria was short-lived, as Wayland continued to beat them, this time in a close one, 36–33. This was one of Redin's most talented teams, with multiple All-Americans Rita Alexander, Alice (Cookie) Barron, and Kaye Garms. Along the tournament trail, the Queens surpassed Hanes ostensibly unbeatable streak of 102 consecutive wins and became the first team to win four consecutive AAU championships. The winning streak was a mixed blessing, burdening Redin and his team with lots of pressure. Would anyone ever beat them again? Well, yes.[12]

Joan Crawford and Nera White, a NBC tandem that would go very far, came back from the 1957 World Championships in excellent shape and hungry for basketball success.

Wayland beat NBC twice during the regular season, but the Queens were losing the intimidation factor against the Nashville squad. In the AAU semifinals NBC used a new offensive set against Wayland, moving White down low to create a double-post with Crawford. It worked. Led by Nera's scoring and Joan's rebounding, NBC upset Wayland, 46–42, ending the Queens' amazing winning streak at 131 games. The euphoric NBC coach John Head showed little perspective but well described how he and his team felt when he called it "the greatest victory that's ever been." It was Wayland's first loss since the finals of the 1953 tournament. NBC's 46–40 defeat of Iowa Wesleyan, again led by Barbara Sipes, in the finals before twenty-five hundred fans seemed anticlimactic.

If they did not have grounds to do so before, the late 1950s Wayland players began to truly dislike NBC after their win streak was broken. John Head commended them on being good sports but confided to reporters back home, "it like to have killed them." Nashville got somewhat excited and welcomed the new champs back home with a fifty-car motorcade of open convertibles carrying some tall, happy women. In addition to the championship and All-American honors (see Appendix A), six of the NBC team were selected for the U.S. squad that went to the USSR to play various teams in that vast confederation.[13]

NBC was not yet as dominant as it would be, and Wayland was not yet through. Rather, they seemed to have revenge on their minds. After beating NBC four times during the regular season, Wayland cruised through the 1959 tournament hitting high percentages of shots and win-

Joan Crawford and Nera White, NBC's terrific twosome. *Photograph courtesy of Joan Crawford.*

ning by big margins. Both White and Crawford had good tournaments; but Wayland shut Nera down in the finals, holding her to eight points. With seventeen points, the Georgian Patsy Neal led the Queens to a final margin of 43–37. The fifties ended appropriately with the Wayland Flying Queens, the team of the decade, as AAU champions.[14]

Harley Redin

Wayland Baptist College had a successful program before Harley Redin became its coach. Way before there were glitzy basketball programs such as those of the Universities of Connecticut and Tennessee, there was Wayland Baptist College basketball. By the turn of the millennium, Wayland Baptist (now University) was the only collegiate women's program to have won more than one thousand games, clarifying the magnitude of that long record. Caddo Matthews, a practicing Baptist minister as well as the Queens' coach, was undefeated in AAU competition and led the Queens to their first championship in 1953. That tremendous record has almost been forgotten in the shadow of his successors. Harley Redin took over for Matthews in 1954–1955. He had been a boys' high school coach and was the Wayland men's coach when he succeeded Matthews. Redin and his players continued the streak started by Matthews, resulting in the Queens' unsurpassed 131 successive wins.

Wayland was the best AAU team of the 1950s and NBC's tough rival throughout that team's dominant 1960s. Redin's teams were highly disciplined and featured the fast break, a weave offense in the halfcourt, and man-to-man defense. He was an early and forceful advocate of the five-player game, the shot clock, and liberalization of dribbling. His record with the Wayland women was 431–66, an amazing 87.6 percent winning record. Before his retirement in 1973, his Wayland teams had won seven AAU championships and were second as many times, usually to NBC. Redin saw the college game quickly filling the vacuum left by the AAU demise and accommodated in 1969 by helping start the National Women's Invitational Tournament (NWIT) in Amarillo, Texas, a tournament that the Queens dominated for several years. His international record included coaching two USA Pan-Am teams (1959, 1971) and one USA team at the World Championships (1964). He led teams on tours of Mexico and Europe and competed against the Soviets on their United States tours.

Harley Redin loved coaching women, finding them more receptive to teaching than men. He exulted in the unique history of the Flying Queens, with their usually ample money, the flashy transportation in Claude Hutcherson's Beech Bonanzas, the opportunity to cull the best high school players vetted for character as well as basketball ability, representing the United States in evolving international competition, and the long-running duel with John Head and NBC. Redin was selected to

One of many AAU championship teams from Wayland, the 1959 Flying Queens. *Front row:* Margaret Odom, Jan Wiginton, Nelda Smith, Patsy Neal, Mona Poff, Joyce Kite; *back row:* Wilda Hutcherson, Claude Hutcherson, Katherine Washington, Betty Halford, Carla Lowry, June Stewart, Carolyn Miller, Marsha Scoggin, Coach Harley Redin. *Photograph courtesy of Wayland Baptist University Office of Communications.*

the Helms Hall of Fame and was in the first class inducted into the WBHOF in 1999. He was awarded the Jostens–Berenson Service Award by the Women's Basketball Coaches Association in 1992. In *Sports Illustrated*'s special century-ending issue, Redin was forty-second on a list of the fifty most important twentieth-century athletic figures from Texas. Although nominated thrice, as of 2004 he was not in the Naismith Hall of Fame.[15]

Coach Harley Redin. *Photograph courtesy of Wayland Baptist University Office of Communications.*

Here Come the Russians (and Others)

Preeminence of USA women teams around the world in the 1950s became uncertain. U.S. teams would prevail in most of the important tournaments, but by smaller margins. The rest of the world was catching up.

Prior to the inclusion of women's basketball on the Olympic program in 1984, Western Hemisphere teams could compete internationally in the Pan-American Games as well as the World Championships. Held on odd years before the Olympics, the Pan-Am tournaments were very competitive; and athletes were honored to be on their national teams. There had been episodic attempts at holding such a competition since the 1920s. Buenos Aires had been selected as the host city for the 1942 Pan-Am Games, and the 1941 AAU All-American team was to represent the United States. Organizers of those games must not have been reading the newspapers. World War II nixed their plans. With continuing interest by countries of the Americas, the inaugural Pan-Am Games finally opened in February 1951, in that same Argentine city. Over twenty-five hundred athletes from twenty-two countries participated in the competition.

Women's basketball was not on the 1951 Pan-Am program but was in 1955 in Mexico City. Team selection by the AAU was systematic but typically late—only a couple of weeks before the games. After an early March AAU tournament, four teams, Hanes Hosiery, Wayland College, the Kansas City Dons, and the Amarillo Dowell's Dolls, played a round-robin qualifying tournament, won by Hanes. Selected from the players on those teams, the USA team consisted of six Flying Queens, three Hanes Hosiery Girls, one Doll, one Don, and an additional player from the Midland Jewelry team—a true cross section of AAU talent. Caddo Matthews of Wayland was the coach. Several games were close, but the United States compiled an 8–0 record against the five-team field. Lurlyne Greer Mealhouse was the scoring leader, compiling an 18.3 ppg average.[16]

John Head again coached the USA team at the second World Championship tournament in Rio de Janeiro in October 1957. The field was bigger (12) and women's basketball more advanced worldwide than had been the case four years before. Looming in Rio was the first major competition with the USSR, a basketball power that had emerged since the last World Championships. They had won four consecutive European titles. There was considerable doubt the USA women could maintain their place atop world's women's basketball.

The team again consisted of the best AAU players—four from NBC, three from Midland Jewelry, two from Wayland, and one each from Platt College, Iowa Wesleyan, and Clarendon Junior College. Rita Alexander, Barbara Ann Sipes, and Katherine Washington (in her second Worlds) provided some international experience. Playing together for the first time were a notable duo of Nera White and Joan Crawford, who would soon be teammates for NBC.

Again the USA team was compiled just before the trip to South America and had only one week of practice together before the competition began. Nera White remembered a bunch of country girls being in very strange and high cotton. Housed in a luxury hotel on one of Rio's gorgeous beaches, their eyes were big and their jaws slack. The ambience was definitely a distraction to the competition.

Lucille (Ludy) Davidson was a 5' 6" guard on the squad. In her mid-thirties, she was also a teacher in the Kansas City area. In contrast to the current year-round practice and subsidization given USA national teams, her school district awarded her three weeks off work without pay to represent the nation. A diary she compiled for the Rio Games well represented the conditions she and other dedicated players experienced and, mostly, enjoyed.

She described the curiosity and effervescence of the Brazilians, the inevitable struggles with diarrhea despite the use of bottled water, the strength of the Czech and USSR players, the heavy and small international basketball, the beauty of an opening ceremony in which Dr. Naismith was honored, and the chaos of playing before thirty to forty thousand screaming, unbridled fans. Her own experience was complicated by catching a dental bridge in her uvula, resulting in near asphyxiation and subsequent infection. Breathing, much less basketball, was difficult.

The U.S. team lost a close game to Czechoslovakia in preliminary competition but advanced to the final round. There they earned a 6–0 record, winning three easy games, close ones against Hungary and Czechoslovakia, and a final doozey against the USSR. The acknowledged world's best player, Nera White, was kneed in the mouth in the second quarter of the USSR game, was ineffective thereafter, and fouled out in the third quarter. The Soviets led most of the way, but a late rush by the U.S. quintet led to a 51–48 victory. The losers were surprised and crushed. Ludy Davidson noted much Brazilian enthusiasm for the United States victory whereas earlier in the competition the locals had seemed to be against the defending champs. These pleasant, fair, and skilled women had been the best possible representatives of their nation.

So the U.S. women's basketball team once more ruled the world—the last time they would for many years, as a Soviet juggernaut would soon dominate internationally. Not that all this seemed so important back home. Following the long flight to New York, there were no AAU or U.S. Government officials to meet the victors. They were held hostage in customs because of excess baggage weight, including the sixty-two-pound trophy they had worked so hard for. After financial obligations in customs were finally corrected, the team dispersed to their homes, comforted by their wonderful team accomplishment despite its obscurity in the United States.[17]

The next major international competition of the decade for AAU players was the 1959 Pan-Am Games. It could have been subtitled the Wayland Flying Queen Show. It was a good one. Seven of the twelve-woman squad were Queens. The team was only together ten days before going to the games. Because they were held in Chicago, travel problems were not a worry. Nera White was selected as a team member but did not compete, giving the ever-enthusiastic and available Ludy Davidson an opportunity to win another international medal. The team went 8–0, as the United States remained undefeated in Pan-Am play. Leading scorers were Rita Horky (11.9) and Joan Crawford (11.4). Though Brazil was getting stronger, the USA team remained the best in the West, winning this tournament's games by an average of twenty-two points.

As team manager, Laurine (Mickie) Mickelsen was impressed with how well these mature young women represented the United States, winning Western Hemisphere friends as well as games. She also had to change some feelings she had had about men coaching women. As women struggled to achieve major status in elite athletics, Mickelsen had felt that they alone "would have to do it" and that the presence of a male coach only introduced another element of controversy. In Chicago in

1959 though, she came to respect both Harley Redin's coaching ability and his "mannerly" treatment of the players.[18]

Systematic cultural diplomacy between the USA and foreign nations, particularly the USSR, began in 1954. An interchange of artists and athletes performing demonstrations and/or competing would remain a staple of U.S. diplomacy whether under the aegis of the State Department or the United States Information Agency (USIA) until 1993. The AAU was an early contributor to international teams participating in this program, and the first participation of women basketball players in the exchange program between the nations took place in the spring of 1958.

An ominous inkling of the diminishing relative power of USA women's basketball was gotten from that first tour of the USSR. In April 1958, the U.S. team, coached by John Head, went 4–2, losing the first two games to the Russian National Team while adjusting to their AAU All-Star teammates' games and the small, hard international basketball. Prior to the 1959–1960 season, Harley Redin coached the Americans when the USSR team returned the visit. The initial game of that series in November 1959 was held in Madison Square Garden, the first women's game to be played in that great venue. The bigger, better-conditioned visitors dominated the subsequent cross-country competition, winning all six games against various U.S. teams. It was difficult to quantify the yield in cross-cultural understanding attained by these basketball contests between USA and USSR women's teams. Quantification of competitive results was obvious.[19]

CHAPTER FIVE

NBC, "The Greatest"

"Losing is the bottom."

—Nera White

Nashville Business College's championships of 1958 and 1960 were only a preview of an unparalleled era of AAU dominance by the Nabucos. (Nashville sportswriters no longer favored that nickname, but the team never adopted another.) Wayland and the strong Iowa teams were still around, would provide some competition, and even prevent a sweep of the decade by NBC. Unquestionably though, NBC owned the 1960s in AAU basketball.

Much of the team's success stemmed from stability of a talented lineup. By 1960, Nera White had been AAU All-American five times. The other player that would anchor the team through its dominant era was Joan Crawford, a quiet woman from Van Buren, Arkansas. After playing a couple of years at Clarendon Junior College in Texas, she had joined NBC in 1957. Wayland had recruited her and anticipated her becoming a Queen. At 5' 11", "Jodie" was tall for her era and strong. She played a true center or "post." A gifted rebounder, her featured soft hook shot was a reliable offensive weapon. To these bulwarks

Coach John Head would add numerous women who would compliment them and make All-American themselves.

John Head had no trouble recruiting and, unlike Harley Redin at Wayland and Olan Ruble at Iowa Wesleyan, did not have to worry about players graduating. If not matriculating at the business school, they could work for one of Mr. Balls's enterprises. Head looked for players with quickness, grace, strength, and big hands. Though benefiting from the rich high school basketball feeder system in middle Tennessee, Head also recruited throughout the upper South. In 1960, nine of NBC's eighteen-woman squad (no scholarship limitations here!) were from contiguous states; four were from neighboring Arkansas. Because NBC was at the forefront of women's basketball, it was very attractive to the best young players. The team was conspicuously good and, with major stars such as White and Crawford and a proven coach in John Head, gave every indication they would stay that way. Best to join a winner . . .

International competition was heating up, and NBC teams were regularly playing in Europe and Central and South America. On a postcard featuring a formal picture of the 1963 team posed in front of the Parthenon replica in Nashville was the bold phrase "TRAVEL IS ONE OF THE BEST FORMS OF EDUCATION," certainly a valid enticement to most of the rural, untraveled players the NBC recruited. In addition to playing against the Russians on their U.S. tour that year, the NBC players competed in Mexico and in the Pan-American games in Sao Paulo, Brazil. The team did get around. Finally, many young women wanted to further their educations. Some were satisfied with the clerical training at the business college, but many pursued baccalaureate or more advanced degrees at regional universities.

In order to make seasonal play more meaningful to teams and to stimulate fan interest, two AAU coaches, Gene Agee Jr. and George Sherman, created a conference, the National Girls' Basketball League (NGBL). Gene Agee coached the consistently good but never championship caliber Omaha Commercial Extension Comets. George Sherman, a resident of St. Joseph, had covered AAU tournaments as a reporter and revered the history of AAU women's basketball. When the league was started during the 1959–1960 season, he coached the St. Joseph Platt Business College team. In addition to these coaches' teams, the other ini-

Joan Crawford leaps for a layup. Note the relatively uncluttered court associated with the "rover" rule. *Photograph courtesy of Joan Crawford.*

tial league members were NBC, Wayland, Iowa Wesleyan, and Northeastern Oklahoma A & M.

Claiming they could not be competitive because of student turnover, the Oklahoma squad dropped out after one year. (Neither Iowa Wesleyan nor Wayland seemed to have this problem.) League results tended to mirror those of the AAU competition; that is, NBC, Wayland, or both were usually at the top. There were trophies, all-star

NBC, 1963 AAU basketball champions posed in front of Nashville's Parthenon replica: Coach John Head, Mrs. John Head, Beth Adkins, Shannon Osborne, Sally Nerren, Judy Coble, Nera White, Joan Crawford, Doris Rogers, Doris Blackwelder, Doris Barding, Linda Singleton, Mr. H. O. Balls. The text on the postcard on which this picture was used proclaimed, "THE PEERLESS SIX—the most famous Girls' Basketball Team in the world." *Photograph courtesy of Joan Crawford.*

teams, and listings of conference standings in the newspapers. League popularity and importance, however, depended entirely on that of women's basketball in general. In the 1960s that was an uncertain thing.[1]

NBC and Wayland dominated seasonal play and the 1960 tournament. More colleges were bringing teams to the tourney. They were still small schools from out-of-the-way places. Wayland whipped the perennial bridesmaid Iowa Wesleyan in the semifinals, 61–36. After expeditiously dispatching the Platt College Secretaries 59–34 in the semis, NBC signaled that the Flying Queens' reign was about over by easily beating them in the finals, 48–29. It was not that close; NBC led 25–4 at halftime. Nera White scored twenty-seven points, 56 percent of her team's total. White, Crawford, and two Mississippi women, Sue Gunter and Jill Upton, made All-American for Nashville.[2] (See Appendix A.)

At the 1961 tournament, Wayland was recognized as the regular season champion of the two-year-old NGBL. Wayland had gone 8–0 in league play against NBC (6–2), Platt College, Iowa Wesleyan, and Omaha Commercial Extension. A familiar trio of teams, Iowa Wesleyan, NBC, and Wayland, plus Platt College, a team from the host city, made the AAU semifinals that year. The dominant duet, NBC and Wayland, played in the finals. The Queens won 39–29, avenging the previous year's loss with gusto. They held Nera White to one point in the finals. This was the Queens' sixth victory in eight years. They did not recognize it and would never have admitted it at the time, but this was their triumphal swan song of the strong AAU era.

Wayland's Laura Switzer, who featured a gorgeous hook shot, was the 1961 tournament MVP. Both NBC and Wayland placed three players on the All-American team. (See Appendix A.) Seven Queens were the nucleus and Harley Redin the coach of a United States team chosen to tour the Soviet Union that spring. They surely hoped to revenge a 0–6 record posted against a touring USSR team in 1959. Both John Head and Nera White declined to take the trip.[3]

The year 1962 was the beginning of a supremacy by one team that was unparalleled in AAU basketball. The Tulsa Stenos, Little Rock Flyers, Nashville Vultee/Goldblumes, Winston-Salem Hanes Hosiery, and Wayland teams had each enjoyed several years of national preeminence. NBC would put those teams' marvelous records in the shade.

Iowa, Tennessee, and Texas teams again filled the AAU semifinal slots at St. Joseph that spring. NBC stomped a team from Sioux City, Iowa, 79–30, while Wayland again beat the always-close-but-no-cigar Iowa Wesleyan Tigerettes, 48–35. The final was not competitive, NBC scored 63 points, Wayland, 35. NBC's narrowest victory margin of the tournament was fourteen points. Their All-Americans were Rita Horky, a woman who had previously played for Iowa Wesleyan and Topeka, Nera White (MVP), and Joan Crawford. (See Appendix A.) There was another post-tournament tour for the NBC team, this time to Mexico, an old AAU stomping ground, where the champions swept three games from that country's national team.

In other business at the tourney, officials announced that three new teams had been added to the NGBL—Great Southern (Houston), Real Refrigeration (Milwaukee), and the Boosters (Topeka). The creation of North and South divisions of the conference was another effort to stimulate fan interest in the regular-season schedule.

A tour of the United States by the USSR team in November 1962 dramatized the Soviets' status as the world's number-one national women's team. The players were full-time athletes who outweighed their American opponents by an average of twenty pounds. In three games each against NBC and Wayland and two against Iowa Wesleyan, the Soviets were unbeaten. Eastern Europeans were well launched into several decades of international dominance in women's basketball.[4]

NBC entered the 1963 tournament with five of their six starters from the previous year and a 22–2 record, having split four games with Wayland during the season. Twenty-four teams went to St. Joseph, down from the thirty-two that had competed in past AAU championships. This lesser number than in most years past was a factor in NBC's 1960s dominance. There was simply less competition. Most teams were still from the Southeast and Midwest. There were more from Kansas and Nebraska but noticeably fewer from Texas and Oklahoma, states that had provided the strongest teams in the early years of competition.

The Nashville juggernaut again waltzed into the finals. One of the teams they trounced actually consisted of the scrubs on the deep Wayland squad, entered as T F & R of Silverton, Texas, a town just up the road from Plainview. The players were Wayland freshmen hoping to win scholarships and some talented high school players who had finished their seasons. The Wayland varsity broke a pretty good sweat against Iowa Wesleyan in the semis before yet again dispatching them. The final before four thousand well-entertained fans was close. After Wayland rallied to tie at 41 all, NBC scored on a set play to Nera White and prevailed, 45–41. Representative of the increasing presence of college teams, Ouachita College of Arkadelphia, Arkansas, won both the consolation game and, in the person of Peggy Holt, the tournament queen award.

John Head attributed much of his 1963 team's success to a mysterious food supplement with which he dosed his players at halftimes. (Nera White thought its main ingredient was caffeine.) Quite possibly it was because they usually had the best six players on the court. NBC had four

All-Americans. Joining Crawford, White, and Horky was Doris ("Gunner") Rogers, a player who had joined the team in 1962 and who would be a mainstay in its years of consecutive dominance. Joan Crawford averaged 18.7 ppg during the tourney and was the MVP. Wayland had three All-Americans, Iowa Wesleyan, two. A player qualified for the AAU Hall of Fame by making All-American five times. Sandy Fiete (Iowa Wesleyan, St. Joseph), Rita Horky (Iowa Wesleyan, Topeka, NBC), and Barbara Sipes (Topeka, Kansas City, Iowa Wesleyan) garnered that honor in 1963.[5]

NBC won its third consecutive championship in 1964. The total of six in the team's history tied it with Wayland. Though there were teams from afar—Milwaukee, Oakland, California, Washington, D.C.—the prevalent powers were the same. For the fourth straight year, Wayland beat Iowa Wesleyan in the semifinals. In 1958 Wesleyan had been the last team other than NBC and Wayland to play in the finals. The competitive stuck record took another turn in 1964 as NBC again prevailed over the Queens, 58–46. Joan Crawford was the tourney MVP for the second straight year. Deanna Grindle of Russel's Sporting Goods hit an amazing ninety-nine of one hundred free throws in two rounds of that competition. Harley Redin led an all-star team on a post-tournament tour to Lima, Peru. Naturally, the NBC and Wayland players dominated the squad.

Laurine Mickelsen, the new National Girls Basketball chairman, announced a signal rules change at the tournament. The unlimited dribble was to be tried on an experimental basis for two years. Though Senda Berenson and James Naismith might not have approved, the players did. Those founders had done their work in the nineteenth century. AAU women were competing in the twentieth.

The teams were playing faster, more polished basketball. Both John Head and Harley Redin used very sophisticated and effective zone defenses. International competition with its full-court, five–player game had sped up the game. In addition to scoring more, good teams were shooting in the mid- to high 40 percent range from the field, almost ten percentage points higher than a decade before. Twenty years earlier, Coach Percy Page of the famous Edmonton Grads, one of the world's best semipro teams, had pridefully noted his squad's amazing 1938 shooting average of 37.7 percent.[6]

A starting lineup of the 1958 Iowa Wesleyan Tigerettes, one of the school's two AAU runners-up: Sandy Fiete, Judy Hodson, Glenda Nicholson, Coach Olan Ruble, Rita Horky, Shirley Hoeppner, Carol Fay. *Photograph courtesy of Iowa Wesleyan College Archives.*

Though the AAU tournament script was repetitive in 1965, the stage on which it played changed considerably. For the first time in its history, the competition was held in the far West, not the heartland. After being in St. Joseph for twenty-two of the last twenty-four years, the tournament went to Gallup, New Mexico. The Missourians' ardor for the tournament had waned, and Gallup wanted it. An enthusiastic priest/coach, Father Dunstan Schmidlin, and the local Chamber of

Commerce led the effort to sell the AAU on this most unlikely site for a national tournament. The AAU accepted the best bid and thought it might help to get more western exposure, especially hoping to attract more California teams.

Gallup was an obscure town on the western side of the continental divide, almost in Arizona. Founded in the late nineteenth century, it was on the famous U.S. Route 66 and the southern route of the transcontinental railroad. In 1960 the trading town had a population of fewer than fifteen thousand people consisting of a polyglot of Anglos, Indians, and Mexicans. Called the Indian Capital of the World, numerous tribes, including the Acoma, Hopi, Navaho, and Zuni, had lived in the area for centuries. Though unknown elsewhere as a basketball center, there was a growing interest in the sport, especially among local Indians.

Gallup's geographical remoteness exemplified the general and persistent national disinterest in the women's tournament. Of all the obscure places the AAU held its tournament, Gallup was by far the most obscure. A local Catholic school gym where preliminary games for the national championship were played was far from New York's Madison Square Garden, Philadelphia's Palestra, UCLA's Pauley Pavilion, or any other nationally recognized basketball venue of the time where men's tournaments were being contested. Because of the hospitable work of locals and the AAU players' abiding enjoyment of the game, this was not athletic hell. From a national perspective though, it was a kind of purgatory. Whether AAU officials recognized or admitted it, their women's basketball program was, like the sun, sinking into the west.

Tournament flavor, itself, had changed significantly. There was a constantly changing roster of teams and diminishing depth of strength in the tournament. Among twenty-four competing teams, the field was diluted by five New Mexico teams, including the host Gallup Catholic Indian Center Falcons coached by Father Schmidlin. There was a noticeable diminution of industrial sponsors, who no longer saw the need to invest money in nonprofessional basketball. The era of long-term sponsorship by business colleges, manufacturers, bottlers, brewers, and insurance companies was about over.[7]

None of the new teams, including the first from a major college, the University of New Mexico, had the history or talent of NBC and Wayland College. The quarterfinalists included traditional AAU powers

NBC, Wayland, and Iowa Wesleyan. Others were the Omaha Aces, Omaha Comets, Look Magazine (Des Moines, Iowa), Raytown (Missouri) Piperettes, and the Orange (California) Lionettes.

Only Raytown among the newcomers would provide any consistent competition. Mr. Leroy Cox, the owner of a pipeline company in the Kansas City, Missouri, suburb, sponsored the Piperettes. Mr. Cox had subsidized his daughter Alberta's athletic career in both basketball and horse showing. Alberta had played for the Midland Jewelry Company of Kansas City, Missouri, and Platt College of St. Joseph. After formation of the Piperettes, she played for and coached that team. Leroy Cox generously funded college educations for several players, many who became coaches in the subsequent flowering of college basketball. Alberta Cox played for the U.S. national team and was a team coach after 1965.[8]

After beating Raytown in the 1965 semis, Wayland once more confronted Nashville basketball (er, Business) College. Although more interesting than some recent finals, NBC's great talent and experience carried the day, 47–42. In shooting 49.7 percent for the tournament, NBC won by an average score of 67.7–39.2. There was less and less mystery to the AAU women's tournament. Doris Rogers, whose sister was now on the NBC team, was the tournament's leading scorer with seventy-five points. NBC and Wayland again dominated the All-American team.[9] (See Appendix A.)

The 1966 tournament was even less competitive—perhaps even boring or anticlimactic to those who did not have a prayer going into the games. The finals were reminiscent of most baseball World Series in the 1950s, when the New York Yankees seemed always to beat out the Brooklyn (or Los Angeles) Dodgers. In the AAU tournament, NBC played the role of the always-winning Yankees; the Wayland Queens were the always-second-place Dodgers. In beating Wayland 59–33, NBC became the first AAU team to win five consecutive championships.

The thirty-year-old Nera White probably reached her basketball apogee in 1966. John Head thought it was her best year, and Harley Redin anointed her the greatest woman basketball player in history. "She's the only woman who can do everything—rebound, defense, handle the ball, and score."[10]

Though more colleges sent teams in 1967, none was as strong as the established programs such as Wayland and Iowa Wesleyan. The competition was increasingly unbalanced. In a preliminary round, NBC walloped an Albuquerque team, 101–23. For the first time since 1958, NBC had a new opponent in the 1967 finals, as Raytown upset Wayland in the semis. The finals outcome was familiar though—NBC, 49, Raytown, 37.

The Helms Basketball Hall of Fame inducted its first class of women at the 1967 tournament. Of the sixteen, half had played most of their ball for Nashville teams, including two active players, Joan Crawford and Nera White, and several retired ones—Margaret Sexton Gleaves, Mary Winslow Hoffay, Rita Horky, Mary Jane Marshall Ingram, Lurlyne Greer Rogers, and Alline Banks Sprouse. Little Rock women were also well represented—Leota Barham, Lucille Thurman Berry, Loretta Blann Gregory, and Hazel Walker. Other inductees were Alberta Cox (Raytown, Missouri), Alberta Williams Hood and Correne Jaax Smith (Wichita, Kansas), and Evelyn Jordan (Winston-Salem, North Carolina).

Though nostalgic recollection for the "old days" is notoriously subjective, many AAU players of past decades thought the current field weaker as well as smaller. Through possibly clouded retrospective lenses, several of the ladies opined that the depth and quality of competition simply was not up to that of their era. Some unhesitatingly said their teams could have handled even the NBC juggernaut with no trouble. Well, we'll never know.[11]

The 1968 tournament received even less publicity than usual. During the week prior, a beleaguered Lyndon Johnson had announced he would not stand for reelection to the United States presidency. The country reeled with grief and riot when Martin Luther King Jr. was assassinated on April 4 as the tournament got underway. Sport of any kind, especially women's basketball, was on few minds and in few newspapers.

The NBC team motored the fifteen hundred miles to Gallup with a 20–0 season record and had no difficulty with the competition. A Nashville sportswriter called the tournament a "Tennessee Waltz." More teams from obscure, small colleges were in the twenty-four-team field. In addition to Wayland and Iowa Wesleyan, there were teams from Ouachita (Arkansas) Baptist College, Midwestern College (Denison, Iowa), Wayne State (Nebraska), Temple (Texas) Junior College, and Mississippi State College for Women.

Raytown squeaked into the finals with a 48–46 win over Ouachita. The final was a reprise of the previous year, as NBC polished off Raytown 56–43 in their closest game of the tournament. Nera White led NBC with twenty-five points. Barbara Sipes led the Piperettes with nineteen. The finalists dominated the All-American team. For the first time in sixteen years, no Wayland player was on the honorary squad's first team.[12] (See Appendix A.)

The Helms Foundation basketball honorees for the year included supporters, coaches, and players of AAU ball. The supporters were H. O. Balls, who had sent his NBC team to the national tournament more than any other sponsor, and his niece, Tennie McGhee, who had been the AAU basketball chair from 1958 to 1963 as well as dean at the Nashville Business College.

As director, McGhee had followed Mrs. Irvin Van Blarcom, one of the mainstays of AAU women's basketball from its inception. Always stylishly adorned with gloves, high heels, hat, and fur, the doyenne Van Blarcom had been the basketball chair from 1929 to 1954. She had written the basketball articles for *Amateur Athlete,* supervised tournaments, and chaperoned numerous U.S. international teams. Though some latter-day players considered her somewhat prim, most approved of her demeanor and her work. Hanes Hosiery's Jackie Fagg considered her "a gracious and perfect lady."

Other honorees were Olan Ruble, longtime successful Iowa Wesleyan coach, Lee DuBois, an AAU game official, and Lyle Foster, former AAU basketball chairman. Inducted players were Babe Zaharias (Dallas Golden Cyclones), Lometa Odom (Wayland), Sandy Fiete (Iowa Wesleyan, St. Joseph), Barbara Sipes (Iowa Wesleyan, Raytown), and Katherine Washington (NBC, Martin Junior College, Wayland, Pasadena, Texas).[13]

There was increasing consultation between AAU officials and the Division of Girls' and Women's Sport (DGWS), seeking uniform rules that would bring women's rules closer to men's and allow U.S. teams to prepare better for international competition. In addition to the overdue change to unlimited dribbling, the inevitable transformation to the five-player game loomed. Even with fast, skilled players like those on the best AAU teams, the six-player rover game just was not the same as competition between all players on five-woman teams running the court, the game all the rest of the world was playing.

The octogenarian H. O. Balls did not believe in the full-court game for women. Despite the performance evidence that his brilliant NBC

NBC, 1968 AAU women's basketball champions. *Photograph courtesy of Joan Crawford.*

athletes had not been harmed by the most vigorous international competition, he did not think the women's game should emulate the men's. Senda Berenson and traditional physical educators for women certainly would have concurred. Young basketball players bursting with talent and aerobic capability, however, doubtless saw Balls as a historical basketball artifact. The game and women's obvious ability to play it had simply come too far for such a conclusion.

NBC was finally showing some sign of getting a tad long in the tooth. The team had lost three out of four to Wayland during the 1968–1969 season. Joan Crawford did not even play during the regular season and came out of retirement for the tournament. Nera White was now thirty-two years old. Still, there was promising youth on the team, including its first black player. Sally Smith had led her Waverly, Tennessee, team to the high school state championship in 1968, scoring almost 3,800 points in her career and averaging 46.1 ppg her senior year. As a rookie, she was beginning to establish herself as a potent AAU player.

As business sponsorship waned, there were even more colleges in the tournament. The big schools with big athletic budgets still eschewed women's basketball. At the 1969 tournament in Gallup, NBC players must have wondered where they were. Wayland was there, but where were all the traditional rivals that had provided historic competition— Little Rock, Hanes Hosiery, AIC, AIB, Tulsa Business College . . . ? NBC was an experienced, talented, semipro team that was now literally out of its league.

The results showed. When NBC met Wayland in the semifinals, they substantiated the adage that the regular season is just good for getting into shape for the playoffs. NBC beat the collegians, 56–42. In the finals they stomped John F. Kennedy College of Wahoo, Nebraska, 69–37. The Kennedys had won a final berth by beating Midwestern College.[14]

The tournament had been a laugher for the vastly experienced NBC team. Their average margin of victory was almost twenty-five points. They dominated the All-American selections. For the first time in history, *all six* of a team's starters were selected for the twelve-woman squad. (See Appendix A.) Sally Smith was voted AAU Rookie of the Year. Nera White was yet again MVP and was on the All-American team for the fifteenth consecutive year.

When the AAU took up the five-player game, Balls did as he had threatened and withdrew NBC from competition. He was probably correct in his assertion that with Head, their reputation, and their recruiting ability, they could have kept winning; but the old sponsor stood by his guns in rejecting the men's game for his women. Perhaps he was also cognizant of his own mortality and the gradual replacement of private business schools by state-sponsored technical schools.

NBC's reign and AAU's dominance in U.S. women's basketball ended after 1969. Since the format was to change and the AAU was losing its control over elite women's basketball, the NBC record of eight consecutive championships would

Mr. Herman O. Balls. *Photograph courtesy of Mrs. John L. Head.*

never be surpassed. Whatever the caliber of their competition, NBC had beaten 'em all. The team was phenomenal and only improved with age. They enjoyed nearly a decade of a stable core of superior players, one of whom may have been the best. Their star in the basketball firmament grew ever brighter until it flamed out. With year-round training and some size supplementation, could they have competed against today's best? You betcha! Elva Bishop was correct. At the end of the AAU era, NBC had been "The Greatest Ever."[15]

Nera

Nera Dyson White was the best AAU women's basketball player in history. The only uncertainty is whether she was the best of all time—any era, any league, any nation. Her leadership of the NBC team to unprecedented dominance and her individual statistical feats are well documented. A more private person than stars such as Alline Banks and Hazel Walker, not that much is known about her as an individual. Her motivation to pursue such a long athletic career without remuneration or real national fame is, therefore, less understood.

Nera White was the oldest of seven children. Born in November 1935, she was raised on a farm near Lafayette, a town of less than two thousand on the eastern Highland Rim in middle Tennessee, just south of Kentucky. Her father, Horace, had lost a leg in a baseball accident at age fourteen. An infection sustained while sliding into second base became gangrenous, requiring a very high amputation. Nevertheless he continued to play ball, coached baseball to youngsters, farmed, and taught school. All the Whites pitched in on the farm, and Nera was a co-mother to many of the younger siblings. Nera was conspicuously taller than her siblings, because, according to her, she "got the first milk."

She was a good but unheralded athlete in high school. She averaged twenty-five ppg as a high school senior but was only on the *Nashville Banner*'s All Middle Tennessee (not All-State) second team. John Head was constantly mining for rough athletic diamonds in small towns. In addition to scouting White in basketball, he also watched her compete successfully in men's baseball. Head recognized her remarkable potential and persuaded her to continue her basketball career with NBC. Before graduating in 1954, she played for NBC in the AAU tournament in St.

Joseph, hitting for double figures in one game. Though one observer thought her the best player at St. Joseph the next year, her first selection as All-American was mostly unnoticed in 1955. Among women's basketball devotees, that obscurity would quickly disappear.

While working in H. O. Balls's mailing department and playing basketball, the intelligent Nera went to George Peabody College for Teachers in Nashville, a prestigious school that teammates Sue Gunter, Jill Upton, and Doris Rogers also attended. She completed all the requirements for a bachelor's degree in education except student teaching, an activity she could not muster the courage to do. As she entered onto bigger stages than her comfortable, rural hometown—Nashville, AAU and international competition, college, the business world—Nera became more rather than less shy, a characteristic for which she had long been known. Despite a lifetime of public display as an athlete, White could never relate to audiences who were not fans in a gym. She was warm and pleasant among small groups of friends such as her teammates but could never speak in public or manage a classroom—thus no college degree.

Much of her insecurity and timidity had to do with her appearance. In addition to being tall, her face usually showed a dour, flat affect. There were constant whispers about her masculine appearance, and sometimes razzing at games was not so quiet. Softball fans often yelled "Mr. White" at her. Though respected as a player, cruelty about her appearance and masculinity continued throughout her career. Some players, whether jealous or amazed, questioned her anatomy. Worse, according to George Sherman an opposing coach once demanded before an AAU championship game that a physician examine Nera to see if she were really a female—a request immediately denied. In response to all this she remained an uncommunicative person—rarely trying to overcome with personal engagement an initial impression based on appearance and hearsay.[16]

So Nera settled into a nonprofessional life of working in one of Mr. Balls's enterprises and, mainly, playing basketball.[17] All NBC players were good, a few outstanding. Joan Crawford was a thirteen-time All-American and tournament MVP twice. Doris Rogers was All-American seven times. White and Crawford are the only two AAU players currently in the Naismith Basketball Hall of Fame. However, Nera was the

Photo of Nera White, used for her 1992 induction into the Naismith Basketball Hall of Fame. *Photograph courtesy of Nera White.*

star. As described by Dixie Woodall, a former teammate, everyone else was a "spear carrier" for Nera. With her skills and leadership by example, the team won ten championships during her career. Totally unselfish and not at all concerned with personal statistics, she did whatever necessary to assure her team's success. The limelight was not her goal.

Though she did not take every opportunity to represent the nation, White was an obvious first selection for United States international teams. In addition to various squads that toured Latin America and

Europe, she led the U.S. team in the 1957 World Championship in Rio de Janeiro. In the finals, the USA team narrowly beat the USSR 51–48, the second team John Head coached to win the championship and one of the last major triumphs over that increasingly professional team for almost three decades. At age twenty-one, White was named the outstanding player in the world after that tournament.

White rapidly cooled on the international experience for financial and athletic reasons. She had to farm or work for Mr. Balls in the summer to make ends meet. The manner in which USA teams were put together irritated her. Always done at the last minute and sometimes influenced by politics, the teams were fortunate to do as well as they did against polished national teams. The first time the victorious 1957 World Championship team practiced together was on an outdoor, concrete court in Brazil, very close to competition time. No wonder they lost a preliminary game to Czechoslovakia! Nera did not enjoy such makeshift teams.

White enjoyed competition in off-seasons from basketball. Some believed she was a better softball than basketball player. Playing centerfield and shortstop, she was twice selected to the "All-World" team. Her skills included a strong arm, the ability to hit with power and for average, and amazing speed. Supplemented by men at the pitcher and catcher positions and to considerable ballyhoo, her team once played a state champion men's team. Much to the chagrin of the fellows, White won the game, 1–0, with an inside-the-park homerun. She was supposedly the first woman who could circle the softball bases in ten seconds. A la Jackie Robinson, she was always a threat to steal home from third base.[18]

At 6' 1" White was big but not a giant for her era. She had to work during the season to keep her weight above a satisfactorily strong 150 pounds. At first glance her body did not look intimidating. She was slender, with narrow hips, sloping shoulders, a long neck, and one of John Head's critical criteria—big, strong hands. Her expression was usually unemotional, whether in competition or not. In the midst of that expression were a couple of cold, clear, light-blue eyes that conveyed will, intelligence, and Scots-Irish, dormant rancor that rivals were ill-advised to awaken. Ever lurking beneath her inscrutable demeanor was a reserve of skill and competitiveness that could be mustered in critical moments— the driving characteristic of a dominant athlete, the ever-elusive, ill-defined will to win. To quote the subject, "Losing is the bottom."[19]

Only when this machine revved up did one realize she was a special athlete. White could out-leap and out-muscle all her peers; but graceful, seemingly effortless speed was probably her most remarkable physical attribute. Carla Lowry, a Wayland opponent in the early 1960s, marveled at White's ability to instantly attain maximum speed yet be able to pivot or stop on a dime. George Sherman, who covered and coached AAU ball for thirty years, considered her one of the fastest people he ever saw. He thought that, if given the opportunity, she could win Olympic medals in individual as well as team sports. She actually became interested in such an athletic opportunity at the urgings of a friendly Nashville track coach. A rumor that she might be trained by Ed Temple of Tennessee State, developer of the famous track-and-field Tigerbelles and an Olympic coach, came to naught.

Her physical talent translated into some remarkable, some perhaps mythical, some groundbreaking skills. Though never documented in competition, Nera watchers, including teammate and retired Louisiana State University coach Sue Gunter, asserted the leaper could dunk a basketball. She was a very good outside shooter, allowing her to lure a slower defender to the open spaces of the outer court. She credited Leo Long with teaching her a jump shot, making her one of the first women practitioners of that currently standard offensive weapon. Should she choose to go inside from the perimeter, she had a quick, long "first step" and a "reverse dribble," in a time when those terms were unminted.

Despite all these weapons, Nera felt her role was not to be the scorer. There was so much offensive punch on the NBC team that her first responsibility was to assist. If she were (rarely) ill or hurting or if the opponents were defensively double-teaming her, she would find the open teammate with a variety of passes. Seldom did she get under the basket to form a double-post with Joan Crawford. The offense usually began with her out front.

During her career, the allowable dribble evolved from two to three to unlimited. None of the restrictions was particularly hindering to her. She had no problem gliding from midcourt to the basket in three long, fast dribbles. Just like Julius Erving and well before his time, numerous opponents, teammates, and fans asserted she could take off from the foul line and scoop the ball into the hole.

Nera White soars toward the goal. *Photograph courtesy of Jill Upton*

The competitive White was an early and very effective woman practitioner of the dawning concept that, unlike what Dr. Naismith originally suggested, basketball was not a noncontact sport. Depending on the game's flow, she could be silky smooth or very rough. Oh yes, she could play defense and rebound.[20]

Despite her personal reserve, all those preeminent accomplishments led to lots of "Nera" stories among AAU basketball fans. She *was* competitive and intimidating. As a sophomore near the end of the Wayland bench, Margie Hunt (McDonald) quaked at a sudden command by the great Coach Redin to go in and guard Nera. It was no contest; Nera scored at will. The resourceful soph though had one last bullet to fire. Margie proceeded to "take a charge" for the team—that is, flop to the floor after contact from the offensive player, a notorious challenge for officials to differentiate from blocking, a foul on the defensive player. After the ref whistled a violation against Nera, Margie was happy for her team and grateful to see the famous Nera reaching down to pull her off the floor. That proximity to greatness and all its facets was clarified as White muttered to Hunt, "You do that again, you little shit, and I'll kill you!" She didn't. Nera was subsequently unencumbered by any defensive effrontery from the young Flying Queen.[21]

Carolyn Moffatt coached a successful, financially hand-to-mouth basketball program at Ouachita Baptist College in Arkadelphia, Arkansas, in the late 1960s. As referees, she sometimes hired male students—all trained and reasonably impartial. During a heated contest with the visiting NBC team, one of these young men told Coach Moffatt that he would be leaving quickly after the game and would not be available for conversation. After his last foul call against Nera White, she had advised that she would meet the official outside after the game. Was she serious? Probably . . .

Moffatt also observed how Nera could turn it on or off, depending on the team's need. Her Ouachita team in one of its early AAU tournament appearances was seeded quite low and drew NBC in the first round. The game was out of hand in the second half when the frustrated player guarding Nera decided to challenge her. Whenever the great one would dribble across the midcourt line, the resigned opponent would question that Nera could score from some spot a challenging distance from the hoop. When Nera repeatedly answered with a goal, the game became the Nera show, much to the delight of fans and her opponents, who realized they could never stop her.

At another contest an unsophisticated fan said to Moffatt that this Nera White wasn't so hot, as she had not scored in the second half of the game. The patient coach pointed out that NBC was in no trouble and that White was just playing around and concentrating on assists, especially lobs to a leaping Joan Crawford for gimmes. She used whichever of her skills was needed at the moment.[22]

Bob Spencer was coaching the John F. Kennedy team of Wahoo, Nebraska, in a tournament game against NBC in the late sixties. At halftime his exasperated players asked what they should do about Nera, who was tearing 'em up. He resignedly suggested they just get out of her way and let her score. He didn't want any of them getting hurt.[23]

Off the court, however, Nera was a very different person. Her obvious personal reserve made her unapproachable and discouraged casual interchange. Yet those who knew her well universally agreed on her loyalty, kindness, and generosity. To her friends she was true. There were just as many stories dramatizing these aspects of her character.

Even as she recognized her own "maladjustments," Nera reached out to those around her needing help. Joan Crawford had a serious speech impediment, though Nera and her teammates well understood their star forward. Early in their mutual NBC careers, Nera noticed Joan's frustration at ordering meals in restaurants. Thenceforth Nera made sure to sit next to Joan while on the road in order to communicate with waitresses whose ears were not tuned in.

Ann Matlock was one of the many Raytown Piperettes who enjoyed success in AAU and international ball. During the 1969 AAU tournament, her mother became so ill that Ann was called back home to Oklahoma. When her mother rallied, Matlock took the long trip back to Gallup to finish the competition. Nera White, the opponent whom she usually guarded, was waiting at the station at two A.M. when Ann's bus pulled in. Nera just had to show her concern for Ann's mother and her worried daughter.[24]

Nera adopted a teammate's child at his birth and just as NBC was quitting basketball. She raised him to successful adulthood in Nashville. Jeff White remembers nothing awkward about being the child of his single, nonbiologic mother. As do all Nera White's friends, he testified that she was and is warm and generous—"would do anything for anybody."[25]

White's basketball career ended with the cessation of NBC's program in 1969. This event was more accurately defined than its editors could have imagined when the front page of an issue of *Amateur Athlete* announced the event as "the end of an era in women's basketball." Life after basketball for Nera was often unpleasant and very uncertain. She supported her little family by working for an hourly wage in one of Balls's printing operations. When the man who had been her protector and sponsor died in 1977, Nera shortly thereafter lost her job. As allegedly promised, she had not been mentioned in Balls's will. His nephews and heirs had little interest in the NBC team's incredible history (all team trophies have been lost or thrown away) nor any loyalty to the player most responsible for that history. After they let Nera go, she was economically high-and-dry in her early forties and with a young son. White could not find another printing job. She attributed some of that rejection to her appearance, which had become harsher and more masculine with age.

In 1982, Nera returned to her family place, where she has since been a solitary farmer, raising beef cattle, silage, and tobacco. Some years have been good, others not so good. She has mostly subsisted on the farm and has bemoaned the loss of earning opportunity during her years invested in basketball. She is as comfortable in Macon County with her fellow farmers as she was with her teammates. The respect with which those homefolks hold her was shown when State 50N was named the Nera White Highway. To reporters, however, Nera remains reclusive and usually inaccessible.

Nera White and Lusia Harris, a 1970s Association for Intercollegiate Athletics for Women (AIAW) All-American from (Mississippi) Delta State, became the first two women players inducted into the Naismith Basketball Hall of Fame in 1992. Letters supporting White's nomination had come to the Hall for over a decade before women other than coaches (e.g., Margaret Wade) and supporters (e.g., Senda Berenson) were finally honored. She almost did not go to Springfield for the induction. In her Naismith Hall file is a letter saying she could not attend because of "irrevocable previous commitments" and suggesting that all subsequent communication go through Doris Rogers.[26]

White finally acquiesced and participated, supposedly commenting on her selection that "it's about time!" In addition to the illogical and unjust delay, White had wanted the honor before her parents died so they could also enjoy it. She even gave an in-depth interview, one of a couple such permitted during the 1990s. In these she publicly unburdened many of her disappointments and animosities, especially against male chauvinism and the discriminatory value modern society put on female beauty. As she told Larry Taft in 1992, "I'm sure I've had discrimination based on appearance. Most of the time they didn't even know me. Had never even talked to me. Never got to know me. That's just the way life is."

She also conveyed a hardy independence honed by heartbreak and tempered by the love of family, friends, and sport—at which she was a nonpareil. Long after achieving a measure of financial security and raising her son, White described that necessary independence. "The main thing is I'm not dependent on anybody now. There's nothing they depend on me for. Or me them. There are no illusions here. In Nashville, I did depend on somebody."[27]

There were other honors. She surpassed her teammate Joan Crawford and another middle Tennessean, Alline Banks, in being selected AAU All-American fifteen times. Ten of those years she was Most

Valuable Player of the honored team. Like Banks and Hazel Walker, she was a Sullivan Award nominee, finishing fifth in the 1965 balloting. Another cager, Bill Bradley, won the award that year. The usual "halls" other than the Naismith—Helms, Tennessee State, AAU—added her to the roster as soon as she was eligible. Along with Coach John Head and teammate Joan Crawford, she was in the first class selected to the WBHOF in 1999. That year *Sports Illustrated* ranked White seventh on a list of fifty greatest Tennessee sports figures of the twentieth century.[28]

Even some latter-day stars, all better known to the public, began to recognize her. When she was coach in the late 1990s of the Detroit Shock in the Women's National Basketball Association, Nancy Lieberman was continually regaled with stories about the seemingly mythical Nera. She called White, attempting to lure her to Detroit for an award ceremony of some sort. Not surprisingly, the solitary Nera refused. In a couple of telephone conversations, Lieberman thanked White for her contributions and asked her if she really had "game." They discussed a recent highlight "move" of Michael Jordan's in which in midair at the last split second he transferred the ball to his unguarded left hand and scored against the Los Angeles Lakers. White snorted that that was a part of her repertoire in the 1950s.[29]

Was Nera the greatest women's basketball player in history? Postgame analysis is cheap, plentiful, and as subjective as it gets. She did not play with or against scientific, well-funded college teams or, excepting some of the Eastern European teams, international programs replete with big players toughened by weight training and year-round basketball. Current players, on the other hand, did not play against an earlier, distaff version of Earvin ("Magic") Johnson, the modern player to whom she is most comparable. White was a big, strong player, toughened by year-round farm work as a youth and year-round athletics until she retired. She had absolutely all the skills, was able to play forecourt or backcourt, loved the game, produced for her team when needed, and durably towered over the world's best players for fifteen years.

Sue Gunter was an NBC teammate of Nera's from 1958 to 1962. Gunter became one of the most enduring and productive woman's college coaches in history. She also had considerable international experience and was to coach the women's team at the 1980 Olympics, which the United States boycotted. Coach Gunter unhesitatingly says that

Nera White was the "greatest player I've ever seen." In addition to her panoply of skills, Gunter was most impressed with her unselfishness and basketball intelligence—a characteristic her friends recognize in other aspects of her life.

In Nera White's last season, 1968–1969, Sally Smith was an eighteen-year-old rookie who was in awe of her own NBC teammates and extremely appreciative for the opportunity to play with them. She was deferential to the great players who supported her as the first black NBC player. Because she continued in basketball for almost twenty-five years, she could put White's ability in perspective. As an assistant coach at Kansas State, she recruited both Sheryl Swoopes and Cheryl Miller, players whom modern fans inevitably refer to when debating the "greatest." Miller's proud father asked Smith if his daughter were not the best woman basketball player she had ever seen. The candid and confident recruiter (who among other athletic attributes claimed a forty-inch vertical leap) quickly rejoined that she knew two who were better—herself, Sally Smith (Anthony), and, especially, Nera White. Just like Gunter, Sally Smith after close observation for decades said as of 2002 that White was unequivocally the best.

To put Nera White's talent into better perspective for modern fans, opinions from a couple of old Wayland opponents who have participated in and paid attention to the evolution of women's basketball are helpful. Perhaps their views were retrospectively hazy, but "they were there" against Nera. After watching the brilliant Diana Taurasi of the University of Connecticut play ball in 2002, Carla Lowry commented that if this player were twice as good as she currently is, she'd be almost as good as Nera. When being interviewed by *USA Today* for an article about Harley Redin, Margie Hunt McDonald compared Nera to the University of Tennessee's Chamique Holdsclaw, another candidate for the most talented collegiate player ever and the only woman basketball athlete to win the Sullivan Award. Margie averred that this "Coldslaw" person couldn't lace Nera White's shoes! Oh, yea . . .[30]

So Nera White was unquestionably one of the best women basketball players of all time. She should also be recognized as one of the best all-round female athletes, included with such elites as Babe Didrikson, Marion Jones, and Jackie Joyner-Kersee. Those familiar with White's skills and accomplishments have no trouble with this categorization, and they would likely argue that she was better than any of the rest. Because of the relative obscurity of her sport and her reclusiveness, the general public remains unaware of either her accomplishments or, absent the ubiquitous contemporary press agent, what a good and valuable person she is. Likely that's just the way the secure and secretive Nera wants it.

John Head

John Lyman Head coached Nashville Business College, a team that reigned over AAU women's basketball longer and more certainly than any other. Like most of his players, Head's background was rural. He played basketball through his freshman year at Union College in Jackson, Tennessee, but turned to coaching and officiating because of his small stature. His first championship team was a sorority he coached in an intramural tournament. Beginning in the late 1930s, he won big with boys' and (mainly) girls' teams in country towns north of Nashville—Cedar Hill, White House, Cross Plains. H. O. Balls recruited him to coach NBC in 1947. Head commuted between Nashville and Cross Plains for a couple of years before devoting all his energy to the business college in 1949.

In coaching that team to eleven national AAU championships before Balls folded it in 1969, he posted a 689–95 record. That 87.8 percent winning record was 0.2 percent higher than Harley Redin's and is better than those of the most famous coaches readily recognized by the public, including Mike Krzyzewski, Adolph Rupp, Pat Summitt, and Dean Smith. As his prime 1960s team coasted through the AAU competition, its record for the last four years was 113–4. He constantly stressed fundamentals, especially defense and rebounding. With fewer set plays and more emphasis on situational reaction, his offense was less complicated than Redin's at Wayland.

Coach John L. Head. *Photograph courtesy of Mrs. John L. Head.*

Head was a quiet, patient teacher more than a loud top-sergeant type. His player development was obviously impressive. Nera White was a strong athlete, not a basketball player, when she came under Head's tutelage. His eye for talent from wee burgs was keen; and, once they were recruited, he related well to the players. Twenty of them earned sixty-one AAU All-American awards.

His teams' records against foreign competition were 40–15. More important than numbers though was the fact that Head and his NBC teams, in part or whole, were there at the very beginning of international women's basketball competition. Head's patriotism in representing the United States was effusive and overt. He coached the first two United States World Championship teams (1953, 1957) and the victorious 1963 Pan-American Games team. He led successful USA team tours of Europe in 1958 and 1965 and was an assistant to Alberta Cox on the USA team that was preparing for the 1972 Olympics—an opportunity that was delayed until 1976, bitterly disappointing team players, coaches, and staffs. Head's international tally might have been even mightier except that on several occasions he and some of the best NBC players demurred from touring with the U.S. team because of job responsibilities. They had to make a living.

The long duel between Head's NBC and Harley Redin's Wayland teams was close and intense. Their players were loyal to their own coaches and usually did not enjoy playing on all-star teams coached by the other one. Each coach and team knew the other was their main hurdle to AAU dominance. In the fourteen years they coached against each other (1955–1969), Head's and Redin's teams met sixty-three times with the Queens winning thirty-two. In twelve AAU tournament finals between the two, the Nashville women were clear winners, 9–3.

John Head died of a heart condition in 1980. Nera White said, "He was like another father to me." Like Redin, Head was in the first class inducted into the WBHOF in 1999 and is also in the Helms and Tennessee State Halls of Fame. The Naismith Hall apparently has not even considered his membership in that basketball shrine.[31]

The USA as an International Also-ran

Nera White's aversion to last-minute international teams to represent the United States was based on the sure recognition that such quick amalgams did not create cohesive teams such as the international squads that played together all the time. That was only one aspect of the USA method that was bound to lead to defeat, something Americans were not used to on the world stage. For a brief time in the early sixties USA teams continued to have the success they had initially enjoyed in international competition. That illusory experience quickly evaporated as the decade progressed.

One of Joan Crawford's most memorable years was 1963. After the quiet business college center was selected MVP at the AAU tournament where her team was on a decade-long roll, she was outstanding at the Pan-Am Games in Sao Paulo, Brazil, one month after the end of the AAU season. After less than two weeks practice, John Head led a USA team that featured six of his own players and three Wayland Queens. The field consisted of only four teams—the United States, Brazil, Chile, and Canada. The competition showed the increasing international vulnerability of United States teams. Led by Crawford's 16.3 ppg average, the United States won the tournament with a 6–1 record. However, in a preliminary round its Pan-Am winning streak was ended at twenty-one games by second-place host-Brazil in front of thirty thousand delighted fans.[32]

Despite increasing cooperation between sports governance bodies such as the DWGS and the United States Olympic Committee (USOC), rules were not changing fast enough. Not enough attention was being paid to USA women's teams in order to maintain their competitiveness against highly selective international teams. While governments of their opponents were subsidizing year-round training and travel of their national teams, U.S. teams were still put together at the last moment before international tournaments. Understandably, no effort was made to tap any talent pool beyond the AAU; there really was no such source. The albatross of six-woman rules remained round the USA shoulders. After taking another U.S. team to the USSR in 1961 and going 4–4 against their regional teams, Redin was even more anxious about the future of American women's basketball unless it switched to the five-player rules.[33]

Those chickens came home to roost in the April 1964 World Championships in Lima, Peru. After winning the first two Worlds, the U. S. had not competed in the 1959 Moscow tournament, won by the USSR. Though most anticipated a USA-USSR showdown nicely in

The U.S. team plays against a USSR team before a packed house in Moscow in 1961. According to Jill Upton, Cosmonaut Yuri Gagarin attended this game, only weeks after he became the first human space orbiter. *Photograph courtesy of Jill Upton.*

tune with the ever-hot cold war, that was not to be. Within a month of the AAU tournament, Harley Redin led to South America a U.S. team with five Wayland and three NBC (none of which was Joan Crawford or Nera White) players on it. This first truly "world" championship with thirteen entrants was dominated by Iron Curtain teams. The United States finished fourth, going 5–4 overall, losing twice to Bulgaria, once to Czechoslovakia, and ignominiously (71–37) to the Soviets, who won the tournament with a 6–0 record. It would not have been hard to convince U.S. participants at that debacle that it would be over two decades before our women were again supreme in international play.[34]

The USA women's team sank to its nadir in 1967. The AAU still led in forming and training national teams, but AAU teams were fewer and weaker. NBC bestrode a U.S. basketball world that had less depth and quality than in the past. Alberta Cox had long been an important contributor to U.S. women's basketball, especially in the Kansas City,

Missouri, area. A multiple All-American and veteran of international play, she now had the responsibility of coaching the United States team. She was the first woman to coach a United States basketball team on foreign soil.

A major step toward rectifying the team's problems took place in the unlikely site of Blue Eye, Missouri, that spring of 1967. There the AAU and the USOC (somewhat lukewarmly) sponsored the first national development camp for the USA team. This site in a remote resort area of southwest Missouri near the Arkansas border was chosen because sponsoring officials wanted the players' minds only on basketball. The Leroy Coxes had vacation property there and knew that extracurricular entertainment opportunities were simply unavailable in Blue Eye.

Because there was planned wholesale turnover in the national team, going from seasoned to promising young players, the team was known as Young USA ("you-suh"). In addition to older players such as Rita Horky, Barbara Sipes, and Dixie Woodall, there were several in their early twenties. With five players, the AAU runner-up Raytown Piperettes had the most representatives. There was again an ominous

Alberta Cox. *Photograph courtesy of Laurine Mickelsen.*

absence of NBC players, five of whom had made All-American at the AAU tournament.

A quick trip to South America before going to Europe illustrated just how hazardous international play still was. The People to People program sponsored the team's visit to Arequipa, Peru, to celebrate that city's one hundredth anniversary. The competition may have been helpful, but the local politics were unexpectedly dangerous. Because of some stirring by (Fidel) Castroist rebels across the border in Bolivia, the telephone lines and airport at Arequipa were shut down as the team prepared to leave. As the team cooled their heels, the U.S. Consulate could not help. Team members were considered safe, as many were lodging with known communists. When the airport briefly opened up, the team, with the financial aid of Alberta Cox's parents, hied out of there to Lima and Panama City, Panama. Though it was unclear whether the USA team was prepared for the World Championship, they at least were wise to the ways of revolution.

Despite the concentrated training at Blue Eye and the short, hectic tour to South America, the team was inadequate by mid-April to the competition at the fifth World Championships in Prague, Czechoslovakia. They laid a big egg with a record of 1–6, finishing eleventh and last in the field. Their mix of experienced and new players was no match for well-oiled international fives. The average (losing) differential between the USA and its opponents was sixteen points.

It was not surprising that the Soviet Union went undefeated and won the tournament. Very surprising was the second-place finish of South Korea. That team's upset of host Czechoslovakia for the runner-up slot was considered perhaps the biggest upset in the World Championship's (admittedly short) history.

Mickie Mickelsen was traveling with the team as an AAU official. She shared in their misery. On a European stopover heading back home, she recognized a celebrity, Loretta Young, in the first-class airplane cabin. Mickelsen introduced herself to the movie star, told her of the U.S. team's despair, and wondered if she would perhaps console the players. Miss Young demurred, pointing out that should she walk down the plane aisle, her fans might create some undesirable chaos, an experience with which she was undoubtedly familiar. Afterward, however, she remained true to her reputation as a considerate person, sending Miss Mickelsen a lovely, handwritten letter to share with the team:

Dear Miss Mickelson (*sic*)–

Please tell the other ladies I know all too well, the terrible feelings
that accompany defeat, especially when one has tried his best—Its
(sic) happened to me many time (sic) in my life and as corny as it
may sound, believe me it is only a steping (sic) stone to a greater
success, some time, some where in the future—Disappointments
(if we're wise) bring humility and humility they say is the basis for
real success. God love you all for trying—there is no need for any
thing else–

> Sincerely
> Loretta Young

Essentially the same USA team, absent Rita Horky, did better in
the Pan-Am Games that summer in Winnipeg, Canada, but still lost its
nation's hemispheric dominance. The oncoming Brazilians finally prevailed and ended the U.S. Pan-Am gold streak. The red-white-and-
blues tied Brazil's record (6–2) but had to settle for silver because of
their two losses to the Brazilians. Leading scorers for the USA were
Barbara Ann Sipes (13.5) and Carole Phillips Aspedon (11.5).

Conspicuously there were no NBC players on the Pan-Am team.
Though she would have obviously been everyone's first pick, whether
competing on the playground or in an international venue, Nera White
did not enjoy making these trips. There was the additional pressure
from the boss. H. O. Balls wanted his employees, including Nera and
Joan Crawford, working if they were not competing for the NBC team.

It was now quite clear that the United States had fallen behind the
rest of the world in women's basketball and could no longer count on
just showing up to play the game they had invented and assume that
victory would be theirs. Squads were selected at the last minute and
mainly consisted of AAU tournament all-stars who had no opportunity
to meld as a team. Many changes would have to be made for United
States women's basketball to regain its international luster.

No one was more aware of this than Alberta Cox, who continually pushed for national training camps. There was relatively little U.S.
interest in the international politics of this competition. Cox, Harley
Redin, and others had long harped on the adoption of full-court, five-
player rules. International travel was always enervating. Additionally,
players could not quickly adjust to a very different basketball scenario

characterized by rougher play, bigger players, wider free-throw lanes, and different in-bounds rules. Cox felt that because her players entered international frays without adequate experience and under such conditions that they had to overcome a tipoff deficit of ten points.

It was also clear that the United States should not hope to compete well if it did not, because of financial considerations, send its best players. Whatever the morality of amateurism versus professionalism, it was unreasonable to expect part-time players with jobs to compete with state-subsidized teams whose only responsibilities included blocking out and guarding the baseline. The USA team of the late 1960s might have done a tad better if it had included NBC's Joan Crawford, Doris Rogers, and, especially, Nera White.[35]

The Road to Recovery

Women basketball players still made few headlines. No one was paying much attention to the sport. It simply was not on the national radar or television screens. Women's basketball was not on the program in any of the three Olympics of the 1960s. Though U.S. collegiate players did compete in the 1967 World University Games, there were no organized sports programs in most colleges. The only game in town for elite players remained the AAU; and, as the decade progressed, the general quality of that had waned.

Substantive and attitudinal changes were afoot, however, in the 1960s. The American Medical Association (AMA) reversed course, changing from its traditional caution against excessive physical activity for women to now encouraging athletics as healthy for both genders. President Kennedy encouraged exercise for all and created a Commission on the Status of Women to assess the prevailing state of women and to influence the directions in which they should subsequently move. That group concluded that traditional impediments to women's participation in many formerly excluded societal activities should and would be obliterated. Women's basketball was about to emerge into the public limelight through these changing social perspectives and with federal legislation of the next decade.

The Division of Girl's and Women's Sports tacked. They moved away from the sanctification of intrascholastic (intramural) competition and the preservation of the "women as different" philosophy toward developing opportunities for the best women athletes in interscholastic (extramural) competition. In forming the Commission on Intercollegiate Athletics for Women (CIAW), they thus recognized the desirability and necessity of varsity athletics. Another turnabout was DGWS's increased cooperation with the USOC, an organization that had long championed the development of elite athletes. Even before Alberta Cox's Blue Hole training camps, the DGWS and USOC had jointly sponsored National Sports Institutes to develop coaching and officiating skills in numerous sports, said skills to be thence spread onto school playgrounds as well as Olympic stadiums.

The DGWS and AAU were also cooperating. Recognizing the stolidity of the multiple court-division games and the flow and speed of the "rover" game long used by the AAU, the DGWS adopted it on an experimental basis. This was much to the chagrin of traditionalist women physical educators, who inevitably decried any emulation of the men's game.

By decade's end though, such mutterings were drowned out by the clamor to do just that—make the women's game as fast as the men's. The continuous dribble was comprehensively adopted in 1966. Then followed the most heinous heresy or exciting advance, depending on one's viewpoint—the approval of full-court, five-player competition on an experimental basis in 1969 (to be formally adopted in 1971). These two rules plus the addition of the thirty-second clock revolutionized women's basketball. Encouraged leaders of the women's basketball now only needed societal and legislative (i.e., financial) support to bring their movement to public awareness.[36]

CHAPTER SIX

Looking Back and Ahead

"I am still learning about you gals and guess I never will know everything that there is to know about the fairer sex."

—C. Virgil Yow, letter to Agnes Baldwin, October 11, 1951

This history of women's basketball covers 111 years, extending from 1893 when Senda Berenson tossed up that first competitive ball through the 2003–2004 collegiate season. AAU women's basketball spanned the years 1926–1979, almost half that duration. Nearly all that time the AAU game was the best in the United States and nurtured the evolution of women's basketball for much of the world. Results having been recorded and main movers introduced, it is appropriate to put the AAU era into context, address what has happened to women's basketball since then, and summarize how the AAU women's program contributed to the game's current status.

The Amateur Athletic Union

No one has comprehensively addressed the history and huge influence of the AAU on sports in the United States subsequent to Robert

Korsgaard's mid-twentieth-century dissertation on the organization. Since then, universities, governments, and professionals have encroached on the union's former turf and reduced it to an associate status with stronger organizations such as the United States Olympic Committee and the NCAA.

Entering the third millennium CE, its primary emphasis was sponsoring competition for younger athletes through the Junior Olympics. The AAU began sponsoring meets for pre-college athletes in 1949. That effort was sporadic until the 1960s, when leaders such as Laurine Mickelsen recognized that this then-secondary AAU effort would shortly become its *raison d'être*. Starting in 1967 with its first big national meet in Washington, D.C., the AAU's Junior Olympics have provided off-season competition for thousands of pre-collegians in multiple sports. The program is now huge. In 2001, over thirteen thousand athletes competed in twenty-four sports.

The downside of this successful reorientation has been the perverse influence of some nonacademic coaches and college recruiters who have used the program as a tryout venue for potential scholarship athletes. Formerly rivals of the AAU for athletic talent, college coaches now use the junior program to scout and recruit players for their teams. Though this relationship often provides opportunity for previously undiscovered athletes, the meat-market aspect in certain sports, especially basketball, has encouraged violations of the AAU's amateur code.

Since its fall from national preeminence in amateur athletics (possibly a modern oxymoron), the AAU has exhibited considerable organizational chaos. During the last decade its national headquarters has moved from Kansas City to Indianapolis to Orlando—not a good sign. As former AAU activist and longtime basketball chairman Laurine Mickelsen bemoaned, the "old AAU [is] gone, finished."

None of that devolution negates the importance of AAU sponsorship of women's basketball for a long time when no one else was willing to do so. For half a century the union conscientiously sponsored the only major national competition for women basketball players, struggling all the while to finance the program and maintain their concept of amateurism, sport unsullied by filthy lucre for people who looked upon the activity as an avocation.

In their effort to preserve athletics in a theoretically pristine state, they mandated some foolish rules and judgments that clashed with reality. No women got rich playing AAU basketball. Still there was some obvious fudging. Though the union surely recognized that some players may have had cushy jobs marginally related to the sponsor's business or were in other cases getting some overt perquisites (e.g., the Atlanta Blues' provision of a house for some of its players), they insisted on a patina of total amateurism. Occasionally this patina was a piece of tape. The Cook's Goldblume players had to so cover the word "Beer" on their warmup jackets at tournament time. Like a lot of ostensibly altruistic organizations, the AAU was prone to hypocrisy in things large and small.

Women basketball players repeatedly ran afoul of the organizational idealism. After the great Babe Didrikson left basketball to pursue a living in various kinds of professional sports, she returned to be with her former team, the Dallas ECC Golden Cyclones, at the 1933 national tournament. The AAU absolutely refused to let her perform an "exhibition stunt" (nature unknown) at one of the halftimes, apparently concluding that even the sight of someone making money from sport would pollute the environment. After college in the mid-1940s, Ludy Davidson worked as a physical education teacher. The AAU considered her a "professional" in that occupation, nixing for several years an opportunity to play AAU basketball. During that same time, Agnes Baldwin lived in Nashville's YWCA while playing ball for NBC and struggling to make ends meet. Although she was allowed to coach "Y" teams, in order to maintain her amateur status she was forbidden pay for the work.

Perhaps the most ridiculous, though illustrative, example of the AAU's self-destructive obsession with their rigid concepts of amateurism was the case of Patsy Neal. While pursuing a graduate degree, the Wayland All-American, U.S. international representative, 2003 WBHOF inductee, and current executive director of that Hall continued playing basketball and helped finance a Denver team in AAU competition. She also had the temerity to write a book on basketball, *Basketball Techniques for Women*. For this marvelously motivated, academic effort to teach the sport, Neal lost her amateur status. Thus disregarding the best motives of its members and their need to make a living, the AAU continued to cut off its competitive nose to spite its philosophic face.[1]

Game Governance

AAU women's competition did not end in 1969. With NBC's withdrawal and the quick rise of the college game in the 1970s, however, it precipitously dwindled over the next decade and became less than a shadow of its former self. There was ever-decreasing industrial sponsorship of teams, and women workers were not clamoring for them. Its death knell was certainly the passage of Title IX and all the changes that legislation wrought. New opportunities for girls and women to participate in sport beyond the AAU would soon open up.

Except for one year in Council Bluffs, Iowa, the home of Midwestern College, Gallup continued to host the national tournament through 1976. In 1977 the tournament was held at Cypress College in California. The last two AAU women's tourneys were played in Allentown, Pennsylvania. Wayland Baptist succeeded a while yet, winning four more championships—1970, 1971, 1974, and 1975. John F. Kennedy College won championships in 1972 and 1973 before the school went belly up in 1975. Other winners in the 1970s were National General West in 1976 and Anna's Bananas, 1977 through 1979. The latter two teams were from California. The AAU had succeeded in its long-held goal to attract California teams even as it recognized the obvious necessity to discontinue its women's competition.

As colleges geared up, the stars of the few remaining good AAU teams were current and former college players. Anna's Bananas and Allentown featured some of the first widely recognized modern women players, including Carol Blazejowski (Montclair State), Tara Heiss (University of Maryland), and Ann Meyers (UCLA). Meyers was on the 1976 USA Olympic team and Blazejowski the 1980 team that did not go to the Moscow Games. All three have subsequently been inducted into the WBHOF, and Meyers is in the hallowed Naismith Hall.[2]

As the AAU basketball competition sank, a mad fifteen-year fight for governance and philosophy of women's basketball ensued. There were several contestants in the bureaucratic struggle. Physical educators represented by the DGWS, a division of the American Association for Health, Physical Education, and Recreation (AAHPER), seized the initiative in the 1960s. As in the past, they hoped to avoid the commercialization and cheating that seemingly had always characterized men's collegiate sports.

The Commission on Intercollegiate Athletics for Women formed by the DGWS got underway in 1967.

That original governing body expanded in 1971–1972 into the Association for Intercollegiate Athletics for Women. For a decade the AIAW was a pacesetter in establishing national tournaments and visibility of collegiate women's sports. It then had to battle for the control it had originally established against the eight-hundred-pound gorilla of college sports, the NCAA. The opponents in that struggle were well defined by gender. Over three-quarters of AIAW convention delegates in the 1970s were women, while over 90 percent of NCAA delegates were men.

The CIAW and the AIAW had idealistic and now seemingly quaint ideas about how college women should pursue interscholastic athletics. They believed in the "education model." They felt that women athletes should maintain the same eligibility standards as those pursuing other campus activities. This philosophy led to rules that are anathema in today's college sports environment such as limited recruiting, immediate eligibility for a transferring athlete and, most shocking, no athletic scholarships per se. The AIAW had to almost immediately cave on the last rule when faced with a class action suit by potential scholarship athletes in 1973.

Another problem was the paradoxical influence of Title IX. As the AIAW worked to enlarge sport for women, the NCAA fiercely fought the federal mandates. Yet feminists in and out of the AIAW increasingly defined attainment of the status enjoyed by men as the final goal of sports expansion for women. The NCAA did not want to be left out of the money inherent in coverage of the increasing international competition for women, especially the Olympics. As the NCAA began to realize they would not beat Title IX in court and that there were real commercial possibilities in televising women's sports, even basketball, they turned on a dime and proceeded to squeeze the AIAW out of power. Regardless the opportunity for more revenue, the NCAA had a broader goal of maintaining control of as much of college athletics as possible.

Despite increasing its membership by multiples, the AIAW had neither the money nor the philosophic staying power to prevail over the NCAA. The NCAA began sponsoring women's sports championships in 1980. Both organizations held national basketball championship tournaments in 1982. The NCAA purposefully held its on the same dates as the AIAW's. Rutgers defeated Texas in the AIAW finals in the Philadelphia Palestra that year, while Louisiana Tech beat Cheyney State in the NCAA championship at Norfolk, Virginia. As larger institutions began to flee the AIAW and television contracts were lost to the NCAA, the bigger, older, stronger, and richer organization thereafter took over major college women's basketball.

It is difficult today to find women's college basketball fans who begrudge the demise of the idealistic, pioneering AIAW. As their game grows in fan popularity and revenue, the worst features of men's intercollegiate basketball (recruitment and academic cheating, early "hardship" departure from college, etc.) may come to characterize the women's game. Though the fiscal and marketing aspects of the game have bloomed, the philosophical outcome of the now-resolved governance hassle remains unclear.[3]

The Colleges

College basketball success in the AAU women's tournament began with the Oklahoma Presbyterian Cardinals, who won championships in 1932 and 1933. The team from Durant was one of many junior colleges that participated in the tournament. Among other JCs that successfully competed over the years were Martin (Tennessee), Seminole (Oklahoma), and Temple (Texas).

The first team from a four-year college given a realistic chance to compete for the championship came from Iowa, the only state that continually encouraged and provided girls' high school ball through good times and bad. Iowa Wesleyan College (IWC) is a Methodist institution in Mt. Pleasant (population around seven thousand) that claims to be the "oldest college west of the Mississippi River." Like Wayland it is small. Only a boost from the baby-boomer population bubble brought the school's student population over one thousand for a couple of years in the mid-1960s. During its other years of high-level women's basketball competitiveness, there were fewer than eight hundred students in school.

Beginning AAU competition in 1943, Iowa Wesleyan was first invited to the national tournament in 1945. The Tigerettes were always a force, just never a champion. They competed in twenty-one AAU tourneys and were in the top four nine times from 1956 to 1964. Thirteen players were All-American, many competing for U.S. national teams. Iowa State's most noted players were Sandy Fiete, Rita Horky, Barbara Sipes, and Janet Thompson. Despite these big, groundbreaking accomplishments, Iowa Wesleyan was to play second fiddle to Wayland in AAU competition. (See Appendices A and B.)

The Wayland Flying Queens won lots of AAU titles—ten of them, though four were after NBC had left the fray and the field was small and weak. The Queens were the dominant team of the fifties and a constant burr in NBC's saddle during their run of championships. Wayland's prevalence over IWC was clear cut. In addition to winning all those titles, Wayland seemed to continually beat the Iowa team in the semifinals prior to meeting NBC in the AAU finals. It was done with a system of persistent recruitment and consistent on-court work. Wayland produced thirty-nine AAU All-Americans, though none had long AAU and international playing careers such as those of IWC matriculators Horky and Sipes.

Neither Harley Redin nor Olan Ruble, the IWC coach, had to struggle with roster limitations imposed on modern collegiate teams. Wayland had so many players that during the 1960s they fielded a second team, the T F & R Queen Bees. An IWC team picture in a 1959 *Amateur Athlete* showed forty-three players. Twenty-six players on that squad periodically "dressed out" for games.

From 1970 onward, all college teams associated only with the dwindling AAU women's basketball program were desperately looking for an official athletic home. For a decade these teams could play several college tournaments as well as the AAU tournament. Carol Eckman is usually given credit for starting the first exclusively collegiate women's invitational tournament at West Chester State (Pennsylvania) in 1969. However, in that same year several midwestern schools began the National Women's Invitational Tournament (NWIT) in Amarillo, Texas. The NWIT date was conveniently the week before the AAU tournament, then still held not so far west of there in Gallup. Formerly exclusively associated with the AAU, coaches at the tournament founding schools had flexibly recognized that their teams' future orientations would be collegiate rather than AAU. Among the schools were Wayland, Midwestern, Ouachita, John F. Kennedy, and William Penn

Coach Olan Ruble and his 1959 Iowa Wesleyan Tigerettes. *Front row:* Coach Ruble,
C. Fay, D. Hoppe, C. Phillips, D. Ramsbottom, R. Horky, R. Wilslef, J. Hodson,
D. Bodansky, L. Nelson, P. Sword; *second row:* J. Bates, C. Linder, J. Hoove, J. Shay,
E. Eighme, J. Cameron, L. Marker, D. Fitzsimmons, M. Seiver; *third row:* D. Graf,
J. Koch, F. Ford, S. Vaughn, M. Dalrymple, P. Smith, J. Sandquist, P. Berrie.
Photograph courtesy of Iowa Wesleyan College Archives.

College of Oskaloosa, Iowa. Wayland won that tourney for eight consecutive years until large schools such as UCLA, Old Dominion, and
Texas began to show up. Unlike the 1969 West Chester tournament,
the NWIT has continued to the present, in both preseason and post-
season forms, though it is no longer held in Amarillo.

Taking over for the CIAW, the AIAW started its national tournament in 1972. Always concerned with emulation of the seemingly year-

round men's competition, the organization left it up to the individual schools whether they should participate in both the NWIT and AIAW championships. The AIAW continued to stress scholarship for its athletes, for instance not allowing John F. Kennedy College to participate in its 1974 tournament because the school was not accredited.

When the AIAW tournament was started, there was considerable concern regarding whether schools just beginning play at the national level could compete with such AAU teams as Wayland that had long given scholarships. Not to worry—the best finishes for Wayland were a third, a fourth, and two fifth-place finishes in the national tournament. Harley Redin always regretted retiring in 1973 because he did not anticipate just how quickly the college game would expand. He felt he could have kept Wayland at championship level during those early years.

However, the Flying Queens no longer enjoyed a corner on the market for the best players, and high school girls were playing basketball in increasing numbers all over the country. Wayland's women's basketball team eventually settled into being respectably competitive under the aegis of an athletic governance body other than the NCAA, the National Association of Intercollegiate Athletics (NAIA). Their historic place was well established by signal success. Because of their strong and lengthy head start on the rest, the Queens have a unique place in collegiate women's basketball history. In addition to their ten AAU championships, they have recorded since 1948 far more wins than any other college, over thirteen hundred as of 2002.

Just as was the case with AAU basketball, the initially successful teams in the increasingly organized world of women's college ball were not traditional athletic or academic powers. The first three AIAW tournaments were won by Immaculata College (Pennsylvania), the next three by Delta State (Mississippi). Other "powers" were West Chester, Mississippi State College for Women, and Queens (New York City). The bigger schools such as Louisiana State (LSU) and University of California-Los Angeles (UCLA) finally geared up their programs and became more prominent. The final four teams in the 1980 AIAW tournament were all big state universities—Old Dominion, University of Tennessee, University of South Carolina, and Louisiana Tech. The age of small college dominance of women's basketball, whether in the AAU or AIAW, was over.

As women's college basketball bloomed in the 1970s and, especially, in the 1980s after NCAA takeover, the obscure teams that had done so well in AAU competition reverted to even greater obscurity. Several schools—John F. Kennedy, Midwestern, Parsons (Fairfield, Iowa)—failed financially. (When Midwestern College went out of business, the women's basketball team transferred *en masse* to Parsons.) The sponsoring schools had always had some of the same characteristics that the best AAU players had—little money, the absence of a national reputation, and rural origins. The obverse of these seemingly unattractive features is that the schools supported basketball for the best of reasons—to provide opportunities for exercise, honing of otherwise lost skills, travel, and prestige, sometimes as much foreign as domestic. The schools profited regionally from the *elan* always associated with successful athletic programs. They enjoyed a coterie of fans, and their reputations enhanced student recruitment. Yet these were not money making or nationally prominent programs. They existed to help women continue the enjoyment of elite athletics beyond high school, something the biggest, most prestigious colleges and universities had not seriously considered until they were forced to or recognized potential financial reward.[4]

The Coaches

The most successful AAU coaches had a couple of similar characteristics. In contrast to AAU players, many of whom were peripatetic, they usually stayed with one team throughout their careers, sometimes for more than two decades. Also, most were men.

Frances Williams was a pacesetter for women coaches in the 1930s. The multiple All-American (Appendix A) coached the Galveston Anicos from 1938 to 1940, leading them to a championship in 1939. Even by the early 1960s, perusal of AAU tournament programs showed that only one-fifth to one-quarter of the coaches were women. There were more by the end of that decade, the most successful being Alberta Cox (Raytown Piperettes, Topeka Boosters), Shirley Martin (Milwaukee Real Refrigeration), and Carolyn Moffatt (Ouachita College). Alberta Cox believed the early women coaches were resented somewhat. AAU basketball to her seemed a "good ol' boys' game."[5]

Any attempt to designate the best AAU coach of all time would

result in a typical subjective sports argument about titans who dominated various sports in various eras—Ted Williams v. Barry Bonds,
Helen Wills v. Chris Evert, Red Auerbach v. Phil Jackson, etc. In this
case, the endless and irresolvable discussion would be Harley Redin v.
John Head.

Sam Babb and Virgil Yow, though not productive as long as these
two, were notably stellar coaches. In his book on Missouri basketball,
George Sherman, who surveyed most of the strong AAU era, listed sev-
eral other of the better coaches. Among those were Ruben Bechtel—
AIB, Leo Schultz—AIC, Les Majors—Denver Viner Chevrolet, Johnny
Moon and John McCarley—Atlanta, and Chuck Ransom and Don
Johnson—Kansas City. Others were more obviously successful.

Much was made of Hanes Hosiery's three-year AAU championship
streak being only the second after Tulsa's in the 1930s. Not true; Billy
Hudson had actually done it with Nashville teams in the forties.
Hudson's AAU tournament coaching experience went back to 1931
when he took a team from the National Life Insurance Company to
the Dallas competition. His "WSM Girls" (named for the Nashville
insurance company's radio station) were pasted there by the Dallas
Cyclones 58–11. That was not a precedent for his subsequent record.

Hudson's winning Vultee Convairs/Bomberettes of 1944–1945
migrated with their coach to the Cook's Goldblumes championship
squad of 1946. That Goldblume team, one of the strongest in AAU history, also won in 1948, giving Hudson-coached teams not only three
straight championships but four in five years. His only championship
loss during that run was an overtime one in 1947 to the Alline-Banks-
led Atlanta Blues.

Some Nashville players never considered Hudson to be as good a
teacher as a couple of other local coaches, Leo Long and John Head.
His record suggests he was doing something other than just throwing
the ball out onto the court. Though coaching records in semipro
leagues are occasionally imprecise, Hudson's winning percentage was
apparently in a class of its own. Heading into the 1947 AAU finals, his
overall coaching tally in industrial leagues and AAU competition was
reported to be 304–12; and his Goldblumes at that time had won 100
of their last 101. Hudson's teams won somewhere between 95 and 98
percent of their games! Billy Hudson died of a heart attack in 1977.

Judging from his obituaries, few Nashvillians recalled him or his teams' tremendous accomplishments.[6]

The energetic Olan Ruble was long the mainstay of the Iowa Wesleyan College Athletic Department. At various times he coached football, men's basketball, baseball, and track. It was as coach of the basketball Tigerettes though that he established national and international reputations. In creating a women's basketball program at IWC in 1943, Olan Ruble did something that was long overdue. Iowa Wesleyan became the first four-year school to have such a program in a state long enamored of girls' basketball. Prior to then, the best Iowa high school girls had only the business school or industrial league teams to turn to after graduation. They now had academic and athletic opportunities at once, and Ruble had easy recruitment pickings.

Ruble retired from coaching college ball in 1965 with a career IWC women's basketball record of 626–127 (82.9 percent). He was pleased to see women's basketball included in the 1976 Games just as he retired after twenty-five years of service on the U.S. Women's Basketball Olympic Committee. Ruble served as an assistant coach on several USA international teams. The all-round teacher of athletics was selected for the Iowa Football Coaches Hall of Fame (1977) and was the first women's basketball coach selected for the Helms Basketball Hall of Fame (1965). Dying in 1982 at age seventy-six, Olan Ruble well deserved the honorific title of Coach.[7]

Bob Spencer was a gentleman who with enthusiasm and success coached in several eras of women's basketball—AAU, AIAW, and NCAA. He came to the newly created John F. Kennedy College in Wahoo, Nebraska, in 1965 as a dean cum coach and started what he claimed to be the first comprehensive intercollegiate athletic program for women, with competition in basketball, softball, and track and field. The school's basketball team was immediately successful, becoming strong enough in AAU competition to be the last team NBC defeated for a title in 1969. Among Spencer's players at JFK was Colleen Bowser, one of the first two black women to play on the U.S. national team. JFK remained strong after Spencer's five years there until the school folded in 1975.

Spencer's subsequent career was nomadic and successful. After JFK, he coached at Parsons College (his alma mater and a school that also failed), William Penn College, and Fresno State University. Spencer and several other midwestern AAU/college coaches started the National Women's Invitational Tournament in 1969. For his lifelong service to women's basketball, the Women's Basketball Coaches Association in 2001 gave him the prestigious Jostens-Berenson Award.[8]

These coaches and their teams refined and perpetuated elite women's basketball for forty years. Their professional heirs filled the numerous jobs that became available in the 1970s. Teaching, especially before the feminist movement of the sixties and seventies, had always been a prime occupation for women. Many educated AAU players turned to that profession, usually at the secondary level, after their playing days. Some taught other subjects; but the job for which they were most qualified and that they usually wanted was coaching girls' basketball. Many former players enjoyed a career as "the coach" of the local team.

As women's college basketball waxed after the waning of the AAU and the advent of Title IX, there were scores of new coaching jobs at schools beginning intercollegiate programs. Many former AAU players filled that new job vacuum. Most were in their thirties or early forties, stuffed with basketball experience and knowledge, and blessed with the energy to teach something they loved.

This was a time of flux in women's college ball, as schools and athletic directors wondered how many resources to put into their programs, most of which had no immediate fan base and did not offer any obvious financial return to their departments. There was considerable variance in commitments to these new programs. As Bob Spencer noted, his teams at William Penn or Parsons, both with student bodies of fewer than three thousand, easily competed with UCLA with its student body of over twenty thousand.

A partial listing of AAU players and the schools where they coached illustrates the immediate effect these women had on college basketball. Many of them were the first coaches of brand-new teams. Because of the uncertainties by athletic department chairmen about whether women's basketball was worth the investment, taking a job as women's basketball coach was not a guarantee of long-term security. Many of these pacesetting women, therefore, did not stay long at the helm:

Rita Horky (Iowa Wesleyan, NBC)—Midwestern,
Northern Illinois
Carla Lowry (Wayland, Pasadena, TX)—Sam Houston State
Ann Matlock (Raytown)—Colorado State
Sheila Moorman (Raytown)—James Madison
Margie Hunt McDonald (Wayland)—University of Wyoming
Ellen Mosher (Midwestern)—UCLA, University of Minnesota
Patsy Neal (Wayland)—Montreat-Anderson College
Karen Williams Nicodemus (JFK)—Cochise Community
College
Pam Parsons (Raytown)—University of South Carolina
Pat Ramsey (Ouachita, Raytown)—Seminole College, Lamar
Cherri Rapp (Wayland)—North Texas State, Texas A & M
Sally Smith (NBC)—Tennessee State, Palm Beach Community
College
Linda Tucker (Wayland)—Rice
Jill Upton (NBC)—Mississippi State College for Women
Linda White (JFK)—Phoenix Community College
Cathy Wilson (Wayland)—Wayland
Dixie Woodall (NBC, Raytown)—Seminole (Oklahoma)
Jr. College, Oral Roberts
Mary Zimmerman (JFK)—University of South Dakota

Because they enjoyed professional longevity, several former AAU players had careers that spanned the AIAW and ongoing NCAA eras. Lynn Suter Hickey, another woman from a small town (Welch, Oklahoma), was an AAU All-American at Ouachita and played one year for Raytown. She was head coach at Kansas State from 1979 to 1984, going to five straight NCAA tournaments. Her next ten years in coaching were at Texas A & M. In 1994 she quit the bench after an overall coaching record of 279–167 for a desk, rising steadily in the A & M athletic department administration. In 2002 she became the athletics director at University of Texas, San Antonio. In 2003 there were twenty-four women filling such NCAA Division One positions.[9]

Juliene Brazinski Simpson barely made the cutoff of the AAU era, graduating from John F. Kennedy College in 1974. At twenty-four years of age she started coaching at Amarillo Junior College. Subsequent coaching jobs were at Arizona State, Whitworth College, Bucknell, and Marshall. She is now head coach at East Stroudsburg (Pennsylvania) University.[10]

Marsha Sharp was another who experienced AAU basketball as its influence waned. A 1974 Wayland graduate, she began coaching even before graduating. She has been a highly successful coach at the major level since becoming head coach of the Texas Tech women in 1982–1983. After the 2003–2004 season, her record there was 533–167 (76.1 percent). With Sharp as coach, the Red Raiders have won eight conference championships, gone to the NCAA tournament seventeen times, and won the national championship in 1993. That year she was National Coach of the Year and coached Sheryl Swoopes, the National Player of the Year and one of the best collegiate players of all time.

Sharp's influence at Tech and for basketball has gone far beyond the hardwood. Her players always score well academically and have posted a 99 percent graduation rate. She donated $100,000 to Tech for an academic center for student-athletes. A continual coaching contributor to the Olympic movement in the "off" season, Marsha Sharp's career is far from over. A 2003 inductee into the WBHOF, she ranks in the highest echelon of great women's coaches.[11]

Marian Washington also played during the last halcyon years of AAU competition and participated in even more women's basketball milestones. As coach of the West Chester State (Pennslyvania) Ramettes, Carol Eckman promoted the first national women's collegiate tournament at her school in 1969. West Chester won that tourney; and Marian Washington, a black woman from nearby Philadelphia, was a team star.

Washington's AAU experience was with the Raytown Piperettes. She made the U.S. national team from the Piperettes in 1971, one of the first two black players on the national squad. The versatile, tremendous all-round athlete also participated in international track and team handball.

Washington began coaching the Kansas University Jayhawks in 1974. She has been her conference Coach-of-the-Year twice, has coached internationally, and coached Lynette Woodard, one of the major players in women's basketball history. During her fruitful tenure at Kansas, she served a stint as athletic director and started the women's track program. At the end of the 2002–2003 season, the winning percentage of this fifteenth winningest coach in NCAA history was 61.5 percent. She retired from coaching midway through the 2003–2004 season. In 1991 Washington was awarded the Carol Eckman Award, an honor bestowed on a coach who epitomizes Eckman's values of sportsmanship, ethics, and courage—a fitting award for one of Eckman's premier players and one of the most respected women in U.S. basketball history. Coach Washington was elected to the WBHOF in 2004.[12]

Sue Gunter, another Carol Eckman Award winner (1994), has had the longest and one of the most productive coaching careers at the highest levels of any former AAU player. The Walnut Grove, Mississippi, native took full advantage of Nashville's educational opportunities during her 1958–1962 playing career with NBC, graduating with bachelor's and master's degrees from George Peabody College in 1962. After launching her coaching career at Middle Tennessee State College (1963–1964), her subsequent twelve years at Stephen F. Austin produced a 266–87 record and four top-ten AIAW rankings. She became head coach at Louisiana State University in 1983. Playing in the tough Southeastern Conference, she was twice SEC Coach-of-the-Year and won numerous national awards. Along the way she has been head coach of the U.S. National Team (1976, 1978, 1980) and was the U.S. Olympic coach in 1980 when the nation boycotted the Moscow Games. Gunter has posted some historic numbers. After the 2003–2004 season, she was the third winningest NCAA women's basketball coach (708 games), had coached the third most NCAA games (1,003), had coached the second most NCAA seasons (34), and was fourth on the list of coaches posting twenty-win seasons (22). All told, Sue Gunter coached over 1,000 collegiate wins. After LSU reached the NCAA Final Four at the end of the 2003–2004 season, Coach Gunter retired. John Head would have approved.[13]

These accomplished women still reminded, for those who ever knew or could recall, that AAU women's basketball produced outstanding coaches as well as players. The AAU flame, though flickering, was still burning, especially in the person of Marsha Sharp, on the modern women's basketball scene.

International Competition

Major international competition in women's basketball can be dated from the 1953 World Championships in Chile. The United States, led by AAU players, won that tournament and was dominant for most of the next two decades. As USA and AAU basketball weakened in the 1960s, world teams got much stronger, especially in Eastern Europe and South America.

Almost a decade of women's basketball development following Title IX and adoption of the five-player rule would pass before the United States returned to eminence. National basketball governing bodies had to recognize the necessities of early formation of teams and prolonged training before entering major international meets. The Pan-Am Games have remained competitive, but the U.S. teams are now once more at the top of that heap, winning a gold medal in 1975 and rarely finishing below second since then. Two eighth-place finishes in the World Championships would be realized before the USA team won again in 1979. In the six subsequent Worlds, Team USA has had one third-, one second-, and four first-place finishes. After winning the silver at the 1976 Oympiad, the first at which women's basketball was contested, Team USA has won every other Oympic competition it has entered.

Whatever the competitive outcome, the benefits accruing to AAU women basketball players when they represented their nation internationally were certain. The epistolary, gee-whiz observations of Agnes Baldwin during that first South American tour in 1951 were representative of the pleasure and reward gained by AAU players. Most of these women were from small, rural communities and, except for basketball, might not have seen much of the world beyond their county seats or state capitals. International travel with national teams brought education, sophistication, and the opportunity to rub elbows with luminaries such as Eva Peron.

After she won her Wayland scholarship in the early 1950s, Patsy Neal saw the world starting from Plainview, Texas. In addition to many trips to Mexico, she played for the United States in the 1964 World Games and against the USSR, both when the Soviets came west and the USA team toured Europe. She experienced the excitement of opening ceremonies as she carried the team flag and the stimulation of getting to know players from other countries. Conversely, she had to learn to play on dusty outdoor courts in the wind and how to somehow overcome the apparently inevitable agonies of gastrointestinal distress. She and her teammates also learned about host nation cultural preferences, such as the Soviets not approving of players appearing in shorts for any occasion other than competition.

Portrait of Eva Perón autographed to Agnes Baldwin. *Photograph courtesy of Agnes Baldwin Webb.*

There was no guarantee of safety during such international competitions. From the difficult travel and hostile crowds the 1953 World Champions faced to the South American revolution encountered by the 1967 national team, occasional danger added a frightening flavor to the experience. The players tended to, at least in retrospect, dismiss all that. Margie McDonald remembered a rock being thrown through the team bus window at the 1964 Worlds in Peru. The message on paper wrapped around the missile, "Yanks go home," was soon supplanted by huzzahs from Peruvian fans appreciative of both the Americans' athletic skills and their diplomacy.[14]

They had plenty of opportunity for such broadening experiences. As well documented by the rosters of U.S. participants in international competition, all the USA coaches and players came from the AAU ranks before the blossoming of the U.S. college and professional basketball. Of the twelve U.S. coaches leading a team in the World Championships through 1998, five were from the AAU. The two colleges who had contributed the most players to those teams were the Universities of Tennessee and Texas, with seven each. The AAU teams with the most players in that competition were NBC, Raytown, and Wayland, each with thirteen players. Similarly in the twelve Pan-Am Games through 1999, five of twelve U.S. coaches were AAU coaches. Stanford and Tennessee had each contributed five players to those games. From the AAU, Raytown had contributed eight players, the Wayland Flying Queens twenty-six.[15]

Halls of Fame

Any cataloging of honors bestowed on those excelling in athletics as player, coach, manager, or supporter usually includes whether the achievers have been selected for enshrinement in whatever halls of fame that represent the Valhallas of their sports. A look at the history of those pinnacles of sports recognition shows their popular and economic uncertainty. In the 1990s as a huge new building for the Naismith Hall was being contemplated, both that institution and the Baseball Hall of Fame faced inadequate funding and deficits. The subjectivity of the process used to select honorees occasionally also rankles. Perhaps because AAU women's basketball during its preeminence was so little noticed by the general public, there has been meager recognition by halls of fame of these athletes who perpetrated those decades of round-ball excellence.

Such was not the case with the Helms Hall of Fame, a regrettably evanescent institution. A baker, Mr. Paul Helms, started the Helms Hall in Los Angeles in 1936, the same year the Baseball Hall of Fame began in Cooperstown, New York. The initial materials for this all sports museum were the sports memorabilia of Mr. Bill Schroeder, a southern California athlete, banker, and sports enthusiast. The collection eventually contained materials as esoteric and valuable as a Jesse Owens's track shoe, a Jack Dempsey set of boxing gloves, a Ty Cobb bat, and baseball uniforms of Babe Ruth, Lou Gehrig, and Joe DiMaggio.

The Helms family owned and managed the hall until 1970, when various institutional and individual owners began a tortuous fifteen-year struggle to keep it afloat. It failed financially in the mid-1980s, in large part because of competition from halls established for individual sports. For example, the Naismith Hall of Fame opened in Springfield, Massachusetts, in 1968. The Helms Hall's priceless artifacts, books, film, and so forth were donated to the Amateur Athletic Foundation of Los Angeles (AAFLA). That institution's goal was and is the education of southern California youth about sport. During relocations between various sponsoring institutions while the Hall gradually died, the massive collection of artifacts disappeared. Its components have probably been disposed of in the ever-efficient memorabilia black market.

The Helms Hall had a category of world-class athletes that included AAU basketball players Babe Didrikson and Hazel Walker. In 1966 they established their own Women's Basketball Hall of Fame. Because the AAU Women's Basketball Committee was given the opportunity to make the selection nominations, deserving AAU players, coaches, supporters, and officials enjoyed several years of well-justified public recognition. Like smoke though, those accolades as well as the associated artifacts went away. Many interviewed AAU players bemoaned the Helms Hall's failure, the disappearance of their donated uniforms, and the apparent loss of their historical basketball perpetuity.[16]

This resentment is compounded by the noticeable disregard of AAU worthies by other halls, principally by the Naismith Hall, the one that counts. In 2003, of the 127 players in the hall, ten were women. Of those, six were AIAW players, one was an international player, and one an NCAA player. Of the two AAU players, Nera White in 1992 was one of the first two women players inducted into the hall. (The Naismith Hall recognized late that women had been playing basketball.) Joan Crawford is the other (1997). There can be no disputing the appropriateness of White's selection. Crawford was a fine player too, surely one of the most important in AAU history, and deserved Naismith Hall recognition. But was she as important as Alline Banks, Lurlyne Greer, or, especially to the history of basketball, Hazel Walker? Likely not! Only the historically challenged perspectives of selection juries can explain these oversights. Many of the noted unselected have had good cases made for them. Nera White's name had been before the Naismith Hall for a decade before she was finally selected, probably because of social pressure to get some women in.

Of the sixty-nine coaches in the Naismith Hall in 2003, five were women. Unbelievably, there were no AAU coaches. Harley Redin has not been selected after three nominations. John Head, winner of almost seven hundred games, eleven AAU titles, and the first two World Championships, has never been nominated.

There are forty-six electees in the Naismith "contributor" category. Senda Berenson Abbott rightly leads the list for reasons beyond her name being at the first of the alphabet. There are no AAU contributor honorees. Perhaps knowledgeable basketball people have not nominated them. Still, it is doubtful that a contemporary jury would be aware of seminal AAU contributors such as Claude Hutcherson, who bankrolled and gaudily transported the great Wayland teams; Glenn Martin, the aircraft inventor and magnate, who similarly subsidized the Iowa Wesleyan program; W. L. Moody III, who sponsored the Galveston Anicos and contributed so much else to amateur athletics in his city; H. O. Balls, who sponsored a team in the AAU tournament for almost forty years; Mrs. Irvin Van Blarcom, who as chairman of the AAU Women's Basketball Committee organized and publicized competition and accompanied (chaperoned) U.S. international teams for twenty-five years; Mr. Leroy Cox, who financed the teams of his daughter, Alberta, and paid college expenses for scores of women on those teams; or Alberta Cox, herself, who prodded the AAU and USOC to systematize and subsidize the selection and training of United States women's basketball teams.[17]

The opening of the Women's Basketball Hall of Fame in Knoxville, Tennessee, in 1999 was hailed by all associated with the sport as a big boost to its advocates, past and present. Here in a museum of their own was a chance to teach the history of women's basketball and to inspire the improvement of the future game.

The early results of that hall have been a mixed bag. No interviewed inductee, board member, or casual fan had anything but enthusiasm for the project. For those studying women's basketball though, the hall's philosophy has been frustrating. The decision to concentrate on maximizing attendance to the exclusion of any archival function has prevented use of the institution as a significant source of knowledge.

Additionally, the criteria for induction into the hall have been controversial. Most interviewed former AAU players were aghast at the number of selected foreign honorees and University of Tennessee women in the Hall's short history while, in their opinions, important AAU players were overlooked. Several independently described the first big class of twenty-five as "a joke." Causing the most frustrated anger was the exclusion of Alline Banks Sprouse, a player almost universally conceded to be the best in the United States for a decade. Two Soviets and one Korean were in that first class.

Subsequently the WBHOF seems to have rediscovered the AAU. Sprouse was included in the second class; and eighteen (one supporter, two coaches, fifteen players) of the seventy-nine inductees through 2004 had AAU connections. The 2004 class included Lurlyne Greer Rogers and Marian Washington. The major accomplishments of Sue Gunter, Billie Moore, Marsha Sharp, and Marian Washington occurred during their post-AAU coaching careers. *In toto* then, almost 23 percent of the WBHOF inductees had their roots in the AAU. Even disregarding those honored for their collegiate coaching careers, almost one-fifth were chosen on the basis of their AAU records.[18]

So that early grousing by the AAU vets may have been just part of the recurring and understandable refrain that they have been unrecognized historically. Those overseeing the WBHOF apparently have made their choices based on considerations both fiscal and philosophical. The board obviously has wanted an international flavor, to honor coaches at all levels of play, and, like all halls, to stimulate tourism. With time and the attainment of such niggling necessities as floor space and endowment, the Women's Hall may offer archival and research services, just as does the Naismith Hall. However questionable to various critics management and selection decisions have been, the Women's Basketball Hall of Fame exclusively honors only those contributing significantly to *women's* basketball—an overdue state of affairs and one worth nurturing.

The Game

It is difficult to compare athletic accomplishments of different generations, whether by players or teams. Improved medical care, bigger players, a steadily growing economy, better training methods, more broadcast coverage, and technique refinements have certainly yielded continued performance improvements. No matter the glory they achieved in their time, only die-hard loyalists could believe that Vince Lombardi's Green Bay Packers could defeat today's Super Bowl teams or that the best NBC team could match up with current WNBA champions. The only fair comparison is between competitors of the same era. Using that parameter, AAU women's basketball was an interesting game played by very good players whose teams were the world's best for almost two generations.

The quality of AAU play probably ascended until the mid-1960s. It was initially compromised by a lack of depth associated with the lack of high school competition. This was especially true in the 1930s as school systems reacted to the depression and a backlash against the athletic freedom enjoyed by women in the previous, more pleasure-oriented decade. The shallowness of AAU women's competition during the 1930s even allowed numerous of the stronger high school teams in the regions of host cities to compete in season-ending tournaments.[19]

The game itself was long locked into a stultifying set of Senda Berenson's rules. Although the 1926 tournament was played using men's rules, the AAU quickly reverted to a two-division game, including such time-consuming rules as a center jump after each made goal. Institution of the innovative "rover" in 1936 opened the game to full-court running by players necessarily skilled in both offense and defense. Fast breaks were possible, and outside gunners became as important as the big, usually slow inside players formerly relied on for most scoring.

The AAU women's game always featured good passing. Because there were a maximum of eight players on a court half after the rover rule, there was more space for this often-neglected basketball skill. Even when players were limited to one dribble, the action was crisp, with the ball zipping around as in a schoolyard game of keep-away. This ball movement was abetted by the three-second rule and a prohibition until the late 1940s against grabbing or tying up the ball. These rules along with limited dribbling actually satisfied one of Dr. Naismith's main characteristics of his new game—no running with the ball, as in football or rugby. As dribbling rules were liberalized, there was similarly more space for the ball handler. The few extant films of AAU play, usually in the 1960s, show fast players using passing lanes, dribbling between defenders to shoot or pass off, and superb long-range shooting—an interesting game without the congested crunching inherent with ten players in the half-court.

After liberalization of the rover rule, the uncertainty concerning just who would cross over when the ball changed hands led to lots of midcourt line tactics. If a team were loaded with runners and shooters, the opposition was always guessing who would go to the offensive end. A player on one side of the court might fake crossing while a teammate on the other sideline was streaking away from her deluded defender to receive a long pass for an easy shot.

As educators and coaches slowly recognized that female players did not have to be confined to half a court, girls' and women's leagues considered the rover rule in the late 1960s. Because U.S. teams were at an increasing disadvantage in international games, momentum toward the five-player game was overwhelming by then; so the rover game was never taught to the general public. Many interviewed former players, while recognizing the necessity for the inevitable evolution to five-player sides, still regretted the loss of the graceful, distinctive AAU women's game with its less crowded court and emphases on passing and shooting.

One modern change in women's basketball that the AAU vets are universally contemptuous of is the smaller ball used by today's amateur players. After the NCAA took over the game in 1982, they changed the official ball diameter for college women from the traditional size for both sexes (29.5"–30" in circumference) to at least an inch smaller

(28.5"–29"). Thus the current collegiate women's basketball has a diameter of nine inches, one-half the diameter of a regulation goal (18"). This flagrant violation of the feminist orthodoxy that women are as physically capable as men may explain some modern high shooting averages. A less-than-centered shot with the smaller, slightly lighter ball is more likely to bounce through the hoop. Joan Crawford scoffed that the modern sphere was too small for her hands. Commenting on a Nike commercial that asserted that "Basketball is basketball, athletes are athletes," Nera White wondered, "then why do women play with a smaller ball?"[20]

Though still concentrated in mid-America, the AAU women's game enjoyed more depth during and after World War II. There were ample industrial sponsors; and colleges, especially Iowa Wesleyan and Wayland, entered the fray. More good teams came to the national tourney. Except in small locales where teams were located though, publicity of women's basketball remained scant. Even when Nashville teams began winning championships, newspaper sports pages would feature baseball spring training as the AAU tournament was being contested. Nationally recognized columnists Raymond Johnson of the *Nashville Tennessean* and Fred Russell of the *Nashville Banner* never wrote about the unique local excellence of women's basketball, and the newspapers only sporadically assigned a writer to their sport. It was thus hard for Alline Banks, Hazel Walker, Nera White, and others to achieve "star"quality and attract more girls to play the game.

International competition toughened the AAU game. The increasingly shallow AAU field in the 1960s meant that the good teams played only a few challenging opponents each year. Carla Lowry lauded the competitive pleasure gotten from scrimmaging the tough Cuban team in New York in 1961 as the USA team prepared for a trip to the USSR.[21] American women learned to run the full court and absorb the blows of opponents unfettered by reliable officiating. Initially enjoying dominance because of their historic head start, U.S. players had to respond to the rapid improvement of foreign players of this most popular women's team game in the world. When politics abetted the development of powerful international teams from the 1950s forward, the United States lost its dominance relative to the rest of the world. The belated institution of national training camps late in the 1960s and implementation of Title IX began the return of U.S. women's international basketball competitiveness.

U.S. women's participation in organized basketball after college, however, has almost halted. The demise of AAU women's basketball, industrial basketball leagues, and touring teams (e.g., Hazel Walker's Travelers) means there is little women's competition beyond college except for the professional leagues. The viability of such leagues has been uncertain, and there are slots for only a very few outstanding players. Unlike softball, there are few opportunities for recreational basketball. In the vicinity of Nashville, a city historically synonymous with female basketball, there are multiple manufacturing plants employing thousands of people. Women make up almost half of that work force. These plants provide ample on-site exercise and recreation facilities, but none regularly sends a women's basketball team to play municipal basketball in an obscure league of eight to ten teams. There is no available national competition analogous to the defunct AAU tournament.

The Women

Who were these women AAU basketball players? Generalizations always fail in the instance, and no blanket characterization can be made of them. Any statistical conclusions based on a nonsystematic oral history should be suspect. One would expect some heterogeneity since their forty-year era was more disruptive, dangerous, and volatile than any other similar span in United States history, excepting possibly the Revolution and the War between the States. However, certain common geographical and personal features of these women and their experiences characterized them and caused them to stand out from the general herd. They were from a large but discretely located part of the nation; they were outstanding and dedicated athletes; they were white; and they were independent people.

Demographics

Most AAU women's basketball excellence sprang from the Midwest, Southeast, and Southwest. That female basketball belt can be cartographically depicted by drawing a broad vertical line from Iowa through

Kansas, Oklahoma, and Texas and then adding a perpendicular right tangent through Arkansas, Tennessee, Georgia, and North Carolina. In terms of the Interstate Highway System, think of the areas along and at the intersections of north–south highways I-35 and I-55 and east–west highways I-40 and I-30. Though there were other pockets of strong independent basketball such as industrial New England and the upper-midwest metropolitan areas (Chicago, Cleveland, Milwaukee), the vast majority of players and champions came from states within the area beneath this imaginary horizontal "T" on the map. Especially productive were the states of Arkansas, Iowa, Oklahoma, Tennessee, and Texas. In contrast to the mythical status that states such as Indiana and Kentucky have achieved as boys' basketball hotbeds, most of the good girl players came from these five states—a virtual basketball belt for females.

These states were similar in regards other than that they produced good women basketball players. They were mostly rural states whose economies were until the last half of the twentieth century agriculture based. In 1930 at the start of the AAU era, the national urban to rural population ratio was 51 percent to 49 percent, while the averages in these five states were reversed, 34 percent to 66 percent. After three decades of urban immigration, the 1960 national averages were 63 percent to 37 percent. Skewed by the marked urbanization of Texas and Oklahoma, the five-state 1960 ratio had tilted urban, 55 percent to 44 percent; but these states were still more rural than the rest of the nation.[22]

The people in the five strong women's basketball states were also poorer and less educated than those elsewhere in the United States. Though the disparities were not great, only Iowa families' incomes were similar to the mean realized around the country. In 1949, the mean family income in the United States was $3,083. Family incomes in the five big AAU states were 76 percent of that, $2,351. Twenty years later, as the AAU era neared an end, the differential had closed somewhat. The five-state median, $7,788, was 81 percent of the U.S. family median income. Similarly, the general level of education among these five states lagged behind the nation. As late as 1960, only Iowa women age twenty-five or older had attended school longer than the U.S. mean of 10.9 years.[23]

The great AAU players did not come from the metropolitan areas in these states. Though they may have represented teams from Dallas, Des

Moines, Little Rock, or Nashville, the women were rarely from those cities. Instead they were raised, educated, and first taught basketball in truly tiny towns. The sizes of several representative players' high school graduation classes is illustrative: Lynn Suter Hickey, Welch, Oklahoma—twenty-four; Dixie Woodall, Kiefer, Oklahoma—twenty-one; Lurlyne Greer, Des Arc, Arkansas—twenty; Pauline Lunn, Sheldahl, Iowa—seventeen; Ann Matlock, Salina, Oklahoma—fifteen; Jill Upton, Walnut Grove, Mississippi—thirteen; Betty Murphy, Cross Plains, Tennessee—eleven; and Carolyn Miller of Woodhouse, Texas, and Mary Link Winslow of Farrar, Iowa, both with eight students in their graduating classes. (Mary Winslow has been married to one of the two boys in her class for almost sixty years.) Any AAU player whose graduation class approached fifty was considered to have matriculated at a big school.

The locations and populations of hometowns of a couple of outstanding teams also reflect the rural origin of the players. The 1953 (first) World Championship team members were exclusively from Iowa and Tennessee. Five of the women were from two little Tennessee high schools.

PLAYER	HOMETOWN (POPULATION, 1950)
Agnes Baldwin	Cross Plains, Tennessee (400)
Pauline Lunn Bowden	Sheldahl, Iowa (200)
Betty Clark	LeClaire, Iowa (1,124)
Fern Gregory Nash	Cross Plains, Tennessee (400)
Agnes Cagle Loyd	Ashland City, Tennessee (1,024)
Betty Murphy	Cross Plains, Tennessee (400)
Mildred Sanders	Ashland City, Tennessee (1,024)
Janet Thompson	Elliot, Iowa (450)
Katherine Washington	Murfreesboro, Tennessee (13,052)

All but two of the players on the 1963 NBC team, its dynastic status well established and with several more championships to go, were from small- to medium-sized, rural towns—nothing resembling a metropolis.

PLAYER	HOMETOWN (POPULATION, 1960)
Beth Adkins	Springfield, Tennessee (9,221)
Doris Barding	Morristown, Tennessee (21,267)
Doris Blackwelder	Kosciusko, Mississippi (6,800)

Judy Coble	Greensboro, North Carolina (119,574)
Joan Crawford	Van Buren, Arkansas (6,787)
Sally Nerren	Cleveland, Tennessee (16,196)
Shannon Osborne	Nashville, Tennessee (170,874)
Doris Rogers	Seymour, Tennessee (2,427)
Linda Singleton	Crab Orchard, Tennessee (3,211)
Nera White	Lafayette, Tennessee (1,590)

Erskine Caldwell could not have based his *Tobacco Road* on such dry, marginally significant data. Neither could he have mined any dissolute characteristics like those he portrayed in that book from the players' families. To the contrary, based on player interviews, most were apparently lower middle class. None described coming from a truly downtrodden background. The players recognized their economic stratum but were never ashamed of or felt deprived by their parents' incomes. Generally their families were intact, supportive, industrious, and virtuous. Those families believed in work, education, and (obviously) athletics.[24]

Playing Games

The busy ballplayers had no feeling of privation as they played their games and went about their full lives. Most of the women recognized no motivation for putting so much work and so many years into basketball competition other than a love for the game and a general enjoyment of sport. They enjoyed athletics and thrived on competition. They just loved to play.

Lucille (Ludy) Davidson was archetypal. Ludy played six-on-six basketball during her Lee's Summit, Missouri, high school years. There was no women's basketball at Kansas University where she was enticed to enroll by a family friend, the famous basketball coach Forrest (Phog) Allen. So Ludy played tennis and field hockey, a team sport long considered appropriate for women. After graduating from KU in 1946, she taught physical education. She did not even begin serious AAU basketball competition until the mid-1950s, when she played for some of Alberta Cox's teams in the Kansas City area. She represented the United States internationally well into her late thirties. Along the way she maintained her tennis, winning more than two hundred Missouri Valley

Tennis Association titles and twenty-three national titles. After her knees gave out, the inveterate athlete began playing golf.

When basketball was still their prime sport, most players indulged in an off-season sport as well. Whether intended for it or not, such year-round athletics maintained a level of aerobic conditioning that likely was comparable to that achieved by modern athletes using specialized programs featuring weight lifting and running. Sue Gunter, Mary Jane Marshall, Barbara Sipes, Nera White, and Dixie Woodall were outstanding softball players. Alberta Cox trained and showed horses. There were water skiers (Barbara Sipes), tennis players (Eckie Jordan, Phyllis Lockwood, Katherine Washington), bowlers (Blanche McPherson), outdoors types (Eunies Futch, Lurlyne Greer, Nera White), and numerous golfers (Becky Harris Hartman, Katherine Washington, Colleen Bowser Edwards, Missouri Arledge Morris).

Those still healthy enough enjoyed sports participation throughout life. Even when no longer able to compete or even physically recreate, the ladies maintained an interest in viewing, cheering, and arguing many sports, but especially basketball.[25]

Race

There were very few black ballplayers or teams during the AAU era. From the Arkansas-Tennessee latitude southward, society was segregated for most of that time. The AAU, itself, did not seem opposed to blacks competing. As early as 1934, one of the spate of exhibition games played after the tournament finals was one "between two local colored teams." It is uncertain whether this gesture was to provide an opening for inclusion of black teams into competition or to provide tournament fans some athletic exotica. Any further groundbreaking pursuit of integration by either the organization or team sponsors was *sub rosa*. George Sherman believed that the AAU was put into a bind between pressures from tournament hosts and southern attitudes. He claimed that anytime a strong black team from metropolitan areas such as Chicago or Cleveland made it to the tournament, seeders put them opposite one of the strongest white northern teams, thereby minimizing the likelihood of their meeting a southern team. There is no documentation of any racial problems stemming from such a set-up, and

Sherman did not give the particulars of his assertion. Perhaps one reason there were such rare appearances of black teams was the expense of traveling to the Midwest or further for the tournament; they just could not afford it.[26]

There was no disturbance when a team from an all-black college, Philander Smith of Little Rock, Arkansas, came to the tournament in 1955. This small, liberal arts college was founded as part of the effort to educate freedmen after the War between the States. Historically associated with the Methodist Episcopal and then the United Methodist Church, it had never had an auspicious reputation in athletics. The 1954–1955 women's basketball team provided an unaccustomed spot in the limelight.

Missouri ("Big Mo") Arledge, a talented 5' 10" pivot player from Durham, North Carolina, led the team to a regular-season record of 19–3 and the tournament championship of the South Central Athletic Conference. That conference consisted of black colleges such as Dillard and Alcorn from Arkansas and adjoining states. Because they played no AAU teams, it is unclear why they were asked to the tournament. Missouri Arledge Morris opined that their coach, Bob Green Jr., was well known in AAU track circles and may have thereby had the influence to garner an invitation. The Pantherette players detected no racism at the competition. They were just thrilled to be there and upset the fourth-seeded Denver Viners, 39–36, before losing to Midland Jewelry in the quarterfinals.

Then and later, various publications said Philander Smith's was the first black team to have played in the AAU tournament. They were not. In 1953 NBC won a forfeit game from a black team, the Lane Askine AC of Columbus, Ohio. If George Sherman's incomplete depiction of black teams' tournament participation was correct, there may have been more before this. Philander Smith apparently was the first team from a black college, and Missouri Arledge was the first black AAU All-American.[27]

In the late 1960s, more blacks were showing up in lineups, mainly on teams above the Mason-Dixon Line. Colleen Bowser (Edwards) became one of the first two blacks, along with Marian Washington, to be on the USA team in 1969. The easy solo integration of her high school in Des Moines had been no big deal to her. She was usually the

The 1954–1955 Philander Smith Pantherettes. *Front row:* Bessie Hanson, Barbara Jackson, Missouri Arledge, Perlie Kendrick; *back row:* Geraldine Taylor, Olawease Benjamin, Billie Johnson, Mollie Gwynn, Elizabeth Hinnant, Patsy Willis, Naomi Pemberton. *Photograph by Tommie W. Taylor, courtesy of Philander Smith College Office of Alumni Affairs.*

only black player on her various college and AAU teams—Midwestern, Look Magazine (Des Moines), Parsons. Marian Washington joined her on the Raytown team in the early 1970s.

Sally Smith, on the other hand, had not received a universally hospitable reception during her record-breaking high school career in Waverly, Tennessee. She and a couple of black teammates had experienced the occasional hurling of racial epithets and spittle but observed that such behavior just about disappeared as her team progressed inexorably toward a state championship. H. O. Balls had once vowed he would never have a "nigger" on his team and had been upset when a black family attended his downtown Nashville church. His hostility began to wane when he evaluated Smith's huge ability. He consulted Nera White about the advisability of having her on the team. Nera, who knew Sally's ability and had met her replied, "I'd rather be playing with her than against her." Sally Smith spurned Wayland among others who had recruited her to play with the NBC players she had admired up close.

The father of Smith's traveling roommate said he did not want his daughter "roomin' with no nigger." Well, she did. Sally encountered a few problems on the road, recalling specifically one restaurant in Arkansas that refused to wait on her; so NBC did not patronize the eatery. The team warmly received and nurtured her. In turn she admired and loved them and became the AAU Rookie of the Year. Some NBC players were fifteen years older than Smith, but she did not recall their having any of the racist prejudice prevalent in their southern childhoods. They were her pals as well as teammates.

Minority players recognized they might be held to a more rigid standard of behavior. Once when Sally Smith's NBC and Colleen Bowser's Midwestern teams were having at it, a fight broke out involving players and fans. Typically such combat does not compare in intensity or quality to the game the teams are playing. Such was the case in this instance. The two black players found themselves in a tussle on the floor. As they ineffectually grappled, they quietly agreed that in their conspicuous positions as a couple of the few black players, they had best stay out of the thick of things. They stayed far on the periphery, mimed hostility, and were never implicated as instigating combatants. As Sally Smith said, they had to "know their place."

Both Smith and Bowser noted that athletic competition was a very democratizing experience. Perhaps their AAU and college playing experiences were not universal, but in their cases individual and team performances trumped everything else. Colleen Bowser Edwards said it best, "Athletics transcended all that other stuff." Besides, she noted, everyone wanted to win; and teams would have to accept blacks to keep up with others who already had. Longtime AAU official Laurine Mickelsen concurred. As she watched black players gradually being assimilated into the waning AAU women's basketball program, she never saw racial acrimony among the players. She also felt that had the black players

The NBC rookie Sally Smith looks up to her All-American teammates, Nera White and Doris Rogers. *Photograph courtesy of Doris Rogers.*

been accepted earlier, the AAU would have been able to compete with colleges longer and stronger for players and its own survival.[28]

Character

A feature possessed by most interviewed AAU players was personal insight into their capabilities and limitations, usually resulting in life-fulfilling self-confidence or, to use a readily understood psychological descriptor, strong egos. These women were different. Most came to see that as better.

Until the full-blown feminist movement, public recognition of the superior athletic accomplishments of the AAU players was muted by the perception that their talents were, as then socially defined, unlady-like. The general social dictum against athletics as a hobby or avocation for women prevailed. This was before the twenty-first century by which time many fans came to admire physical strength in successful women athletes. In the AAU era, the dominant esthete still favored sleekness and grace over strength. To have the latter was to be known as a "muscle moll," a designation with perverse sexual as well as athletic connotations.[29]

Many players physically stood out. Some of the better ones were euphemistically described, even by their teammates, as "boyish" or "mannish." Though always an attractive woman, Mary Jane (Janie) Marshall Ingram remembered her and some teammates worrying over their relatively big hands and feet. Janie noted that there were not many "china dolls" successfully playing basketball and softball. Some players were heavy. Most were taller than their female peers. Many were better athletes than their male peers. Players were not usually as outsized as now, but seeing an AAU team enter a restaurant would not have elicited confusion with the local gymnastics team.[30]

Then there was the sexuality issue. Contemporary chroniclers of women's sports have noted a high incidence of lesbianism among athletes, a proportion allegedly more prominent in team sports, especially softball. Regardless their appearances or off-court behaviors, the AAU women frequently heard or perceived repetitive tittering about their sexual orientations. Margie McDonald observed that even if one were "all girl," the sexuality of anyone playing major competitive sports was suspect. There was an unequivocal general societal disapproval of homosexuality. The incidence of that among AAU basketball teams is undocumented. During the era depicted, there was no "outing" of lesbian basketball players because of the stigma associated with homosexuality.[31]

The obverse of the sometimes degrading, seemingly inevitable social approval of femininity above all else is that many women's lives were absolutely made by their athletic accomplishments. Barbara Sipes's basketball experience was typical of this salutary effect of playing basketball. Growing up in the Topeka, Kansas, area, Sipes stuck out from the crowd, being described as "big and athletic." She preferred sitting in the back of her classrooms. Then she found basketball. There was no girls' basketball at her high school, but regional AAU teams were immediately interested in her. After learning the game in AAU competition, she played

A group of Vultee Bomberettes relaxing at the pool: Margaret Sexton Petty, Blanche McPherson, Margie Cooper, Mary Jane Marshall, Nora Marshall, Dora McPherson, Mildred Johnson, Alline Banks. *Photograph courtesy of Jane Marshall Ingram.*

for Iowa Wesleyan, choosing that school over Wayland. As she succeeded on the court, she became more relaxed and outgoing off it. A woman of definite opinions, she developed a liberal political philosophy and was not shy in arguing it. Along the way, she was a several time AAU All-American, became one of the first good, truly "big" (6' 3") U.S. players, and enjoyed a long career in education after competition.[32]

Joan Crawford (yes, her parents admired the movie actress) was born with cleft lip and cleft palate. Two operations before she was ten years old provided a good cosmetic result. Modern speech therapy was unavailable though, and she retained a marked speech impediment. Typically cruel children mocked her when she talked, so she just stopped talking. However, for her there was both peace and pleasure on the basketball court. It was not necessary to talk in order to rebound or ease in an unblockable hook shot. Crawford became a handsome woman with a beautiful smile but remained taciturn her entire life except with close friends, especially teammates at all levels from high school onward. Whatever communication problems she suffered off the court were assuaged by basketball and the self-confidence she gained through her huge accomplishments in the game.[33]

Times Change

There are some indications why the USA's best players came from such a unique locus and demographic. Many of the players were farm girls and were used to physical activity. No one was excused from chores that toughened their bodies and wills. Hay bales and feed sacks are as heavy as dead weights in a gym, and necessity compelled they be lifted. Having proved their physical mettle at home, there was little doubt about whether basketball would be too strenuous for them. The sophisticated perception of woman as ornament was a nonstarter down on the farm.

Much of their recreation, including basketball, was out of doors. As depicted by Betty Ann Murphy Willis of Cross Plains, Tennessee, and the 1953 World Championship team, there was "always a goal on front of the smokehouse." In rural, isolated home places, a girl could solitarily work on her shot or scrimmage with her brothers, who might teach her some moves and accustom her to rough play. In the opening of the 1987 movie, "Hoosiers," Coach Norman Dale (Gene Hackman) drives through flat, rural Indiana on his way to a new job in a basketball-crazy burg. In addition to lots of corn fields, he sees country lads shooting balls at misshapen hoops on the sides of farm outbuildings. A scene set in rural Iowa or Tennessee showing a tanned, jean-clad, leggy girl doing the same would have been just as accurate.

Living away from urban areas and not a part of the later global village tied together by television and freeways, there was little to no stigma in participating in public sports competition. Additionally, their fans during high school (extracurricular athletic leagues were yet to come) approved of the activity. Communities cohere through support of a local champion. In small towns, that champion was usually the high school athletic team; and, especially if they were successful, that could just as well be the girls' team as the boys'.

Besides, there was little other social recreation. How many times could one patronize the single movie theater? In the hinterlands television satellite discs had not yet scarred the hillsides like so many monstrous, metallic mushrooms. The school likely had no significant music program, cheerleader squad, or Scout troop. "The team," therefore, provided both recreation and cause for kids and townsfolk. As Jill Upton said, the only things available (in Walnut Grove, Mississippi) were the "church and athletics."[34]

Of course there had to be a high school girls' team in order to play on it, and that availability in the United States was patchy. The same misgivings about participation in vigorous interscholastic athletics that dogged development of college women's programs affected girls in high schools. In tune with the times, there was more high school girls' basketball during the 1920s than afterward for many years. During that looser decade, the old stigma that sports were masculinizing and unladylike was less a concern to the athletes and their society. After the 1920s, however, high school girls' programs were cut back for social and (occasionally) budgetary reasons. Perennially pessimistic physical educators continued to squelch any girls' sports activity that seemed to be approaching those of the boys in style or intensity.

The cases of Kentucky and Illinois are instructive. In Kentucky, a state whose name is synonymous with modern basketball, the first girls' state tournament was held in 1920. After a decade of enthusiastic growth, physical educators became alarmed at "the fever of interscholastic basketball for girls." Based on the premises that anything like the boys' game would be harmful to girls and that girls' sport should not be used for popular entertainment (i.e., tournaments), the Kentucky High School Athletic Association ended basketball for high school girls in 1932. It would not be renewed until 1973.[35]

The Illinois experience reflects the more rapid adoption of women's basketball in urban areas after its invention and its more rapid suppres-

State Champions of Ky. 20

Clark County (Kentucky) High School girls' basketball team, 1920. The caption on the picture is incorrect. Paris High School won the first Kentucky Girls' State Championship that year. *Photograph courtesy of Katherine Everman (Vivion), the author's wife's great-aunt, second from left, front row.*

sion there after misgivings about femininity arose. Spreading outward from Cook County, Illinois, girls were playing interscholastic basketball from the late nineteenth century. A rapid maturity and devolution occurred, and the Illinois version of girls' high school ball was ended by 1908. The women's physical education lobby invoked an argument in Illinois that they also used in Kentucky. They believed only women

Looking Back and Ahead

should coach girls' teams. Regardless the value of that argument, no effort was made to train more women coaches; and the men resented the double duty of coaching both the boys and the girls. In the 1920s Illinois state educators again had some trouble with girls' basketball springing up like pesky weeds, this time in rural schools. They did not allow its official reemergence until 1977.[36]

Yet just to the west of both Kentucky and Illinois is Iowa, where girls' basketball has been more popular and has thrived longer than in almost any other state. Opposite attitudes and different politics allowed the girls to play ball. In her book on Iowa women's basketball, Janice Beran listed several reasons why the game has been so enduringly strong in the Hawkeye State. Politically, Iowa girls' basketball was governed by a private agency, the Iowa Girls' High School Athletic Union. The IGHSAU was not controlled by the American Physical Education Association and thus not influenced by that organization's noncompetitive philosophy. Social conditions in this rural state were like those in the other states that came to dominate the AAU. There were no prejudices against male coaches. Country girls did not consider basketball taxing. Neither did they think it made them masculine. School consolidation was successfully fought in rural states such as Iowa. Thus, familiar neighbor players remained the local heroines. Finally, the sport provided warm community entertainment during cold winter nights.

The best AAU players and teams came from states that promoted girls' basketball in their high schools. Data from Beran's book and a tabulation done for this one show that the states that have offered the sport longest lie along the Central–Southeast locus of AAU excellence. A sanctioned girls' state tournament was started in Iowa in 1920 and has continued uninterrupted. Using 2004 as an endpoint, Oklahoma has held a tournament even more years, ninety-three. Other states that have had long experience with state tournaments (sporadically discontinued for various reasons) until 2004 are South Carolina (84 years), Mississippi (74), Georgia (69), Texas (60), Arkansas (58), and Tennessee (53). In contrast, more metropolitan states began tournaments only under pressure after Title IX passage, for example, California (1973), Maryland (1973), Pennsylvania (1973), Michigan (1974), and Ohio (1976).[37]

A thesis of this book is that AAU women's basketball perpetuated the sport between the founding years and the advent of Title IX. The

AAU teams would not have had players, however, were it not for the school systems that provided basketball for girls and the coaches who taught them the game. Some coaches in those rural, basketball-loving states established amazing records for longevity as well as competitive success. The three high school coaches with the most wins came from those girls' basketball hotbeds. Bertha Teague (1928–1970) coached 1,152 wins at Ada Byng, Oklahoma. Coach Jim Smiddy (1949–1987) recorded 1,072 victories at Cleveland, Tennessee; Sally Nerren, one of his players, was on NBC's great 1960s teams. Thednall Hill's teams (1952–1986) won 1,063 games in Hardy Highland, Arkansas.[38]

There is still an emphasis on girls' basketball in these relatively rural states, but the dominance of its players and coaches has been usurped by wider acceptance of their sport. Inner-city girls have emulated their brothers in pursuing college scholarships, thus grasping at opportunities for pleasure, fame, education, and perhaps an occupation. Coaches look as often for these urban stars as they do the farmers' daughters they previously pursued. Foreign players who play club ball in their countries or matriculate at U.S. high schools are an increasingly fertile source of good, dedicated players. In the early twenty-first century, the Wayland Queens team, formerly consisting mainly of sunburned women from the Texas panhandle, included players from Lithuania.

Because of continued urban immigration and school consolidation, there are fewer small schools. USA international teams loaded with women from teeny towns are unlikely to recur. Proud fans still rally around the local squad, but the girls are probably attending a bigger high school than their parents. Dedicated "programs" in medium-sized towns can produce consistent state and occasional national success. In Shelbyville, Tennessee, a town of sixteen thousand, Coach Rick Insell and his Eaglettes had by the end of the 2004 season won almost eight hundred games. Numerous players had earned college athletic scholarships, some at prestigious schools with prestigious teams. Shelbyville teams had won twelve state championships (ten since 1986) in the highest competition division and mythical *USA Today* national championships in 1989 and 1991.

The Shelbyville team's accomplishments were surely mostly due to outstanding coaching and team tradition with all the impetus that obtains from fan support and expectations. However, over the years there have been frequent rumors of promising girl players' fathers suddenly getting jobs in Shelbyville as their high school years approached. Whatever the verity of specific allegations and regardless stricter rules, the practice of fudging on players' eligibilities at all levels of sport, even high school, has remained an option for boosting a team. Such shenanigans had been around when Alline Banks went across the county line to play interscholastic ball, and they still are. The maxim applies; the more things change, perhaps especially in sport, the more they stay the same.

In no way does the high school athletic experience of these girls compare to the less structured one lived by AAU players, c. 1930–1970. Such current success comes only with pressured year-round training, including summer league competition, weight lifting, and possibly playing for local "travel" teams rather than for the school's varsity. Coaches now often put public pressure on the players. Commenting on such an occurrence she had recently seen between a coach and a player, Alline Sprouse said, "The first time she put her fist in my face, I think I would have put a fist in hers." Coaches and parents now urge very young athletes to specialize in one sport, depriving them of the opportunity to learn and enjoy others. Whether one of these starkly different experiences is better than the other is an unanswered question.[39]

An occasional country girl still dominates. Perhaps the contemporary player most like the best of the AAU is Jackie Stiles. She came from a wee town, played at a less than major college, and labored in obscurity until her superiority was undeniable. At 5' 8", the Claflin, Kansas (population 616), native played at Southwest Missouri State, established a career NCAA scoring record of 3,371 points, led her team to the NCAA Final Four, and was an immediate success in professional basketball. In her youth far from the madding crowd there was little else to do for recreation but shoot a thousand baskets a day. The best AAU players would have recognized and approved of her experience.[40]

The earlier AAU players did differ in a few ways from later ones, largely because of changing societal attitudes and economic and educational opportunities. A look at a couple of outstanding Nashville teams, the 1947 Goldblume and the 1963 NBC squads, highlights these differences that transpired in less than one generation. This snapshot does not represent a statistically significant album but is suggestive of bona fide changes in AAU ballplayers who were taking advantage of different economic times for women.

Looking Back and Ahead

The 1947 Goldblumes were part of a dominant AAU basketball force from 1944 to 1949. The players graduated from high school before or during World War II. Not one attended college. They could not afford it. All needed jobs and wanted to continue playing basketball. In addition to these economic and recreational stimuli, there was another compelling social motivation for these women—getting married. At least eleven members of the twelve-player 1947 squad married.[41]

The members of the 1963 NBC team were from the same area and socioeconomic stratum as the 1947 Goldblumes. Their life directions were different. From the mid-1950s forward, several NBC players attended Nashville's George Peabody College, a school that featured an education curriculum. Four members of the 1963 team somehow went to college between basketball and work responsibilities. Shannon Osborne and Doris Rogers earned graduate degrees. Whether due to coincidence or greater economic opportunities in their era, only half the 1963 team married.

Their differences from the conforming herd dramatized their integrity. There was some fame; but it was little, fleeting, and diluted by sparse, sometimes skeptical public support. Members of noncollegiate teams had jobs while they played. Benefactors such as Leroy Cox and Glenn Martin financially aided many women who pursued higher education while they played. H. O. Balls would *loan* a woman some money or give her a job, but his basketball operation was not a charity. As Nera White sadly learned, there was no lasting security in playing semipro basketball, no matter how good one was.

Few of the industrial or collegiate AAU players were involved in anything beyond their domestic, employment, athletic, or educational endeavors. The time they spent working, practicing, studying, traveling, and playing left little time for other activities. The collegians were matriculating at out-of-the-way, small, often church-affiliated schools. With their busy schedules and generally conservative backgrounds, they did not participate in trendy activities, even in a decade as chaotic as the 1960s. Though far from dull, AAU women seemed to be straight arrows socially.

Doris Rogers recalled her playing and Peabody College days as a busy continuum. After practicing basketball a couple of hours in the early morning, she would take the city bus out to Peabody College. During the evenings she would work at one of Mr. Balls's enterprises.

If not working on the weekends, she was playing basketball for NBC, perhaps at a distant site. The several women who attended the still bustling Business College to attain "high-grade secretarial training," pursued essentially the same dedicated schedules. Neither Doris nor any of her NBC peers had a normal college existence—no frat parties, bridge games in the student union, or schmoozing with fellow students. Their chockablock lives only allowed them to concentrate on their tasks and the pleasure of playing basketball. Because Rogers and her teammates had such focused lives, they were in a sense insulated from the societal chaos around them.[42]

Their motivations to continue training and competing were first and foremost their love of playing sport in general and basketball in particular—the running, jumping, pushing, shooting game orchestrated with pals. Joan Crawford opined that she and her teammates enjoyed the game more than today's players. Patsy Neal certainly lost money when she organized a team in Denver as she pursued a graduate degree; she just wanted to keep playing. Agnes Baldwin spoke for a couple of generations of players when she said they all enjoyed the traveling and broadening experiences, but they mainly played ball "just for fun."[43]

Their integrity and independence served AAU players quite well after basketball. People still being imperfect, there were surely alcoholics, cheaters, and crooks among the group; but such miscreants are hard to identify. On balance, AAU players seem to have led gainful and reasonably happy lives. If fewer of the latter generation of players married, they landed on their own economic feet and cashed in on the increasing opportunities for women in the job market.

Most of their jobs were more predictable than that of farmer (Nera White) or cemetery director (Lurlyne Greer). Taking advantage of their educational opportunities, many AAU players after 1960 got college degrees. Scores of them attained graduate degrees, often beyond the master's level. Their graduate emphases were usually in education or health- and fitness-related fields, for example, physical education/ kinesiology. Many became educators, a traditional "woman's job" with which they were familiar. Lots of those jobs entailed coaching, including sports other than basketball. In addition to the many basketball coaching jobs in secondary schools and colleges, some women took jobs in the officiating and administrative aspects of the sport, often

ascending to impressive heights of responsibility. A few examples typ-
ify their high and satisfying accomplishments.

Lynn Hickey Suter and Jill Upton rose in athletic administration
posts after successful coaching careers. Sylvia Nadler became athletic
director at Wayland, her alma mater. Faye Garmes officiated most of the
first girls' high school championships in Colorado and became supervi-
sor of officials in the Western Athletic Conference. Judy Coble began
teaching and regulating softball officials, eventually providing umps for
scores of (Nashville) regional high schools and numerous major colleges
and conferences. Laura Switzer was women's athletics coordinator
at Southwestern Oklahoma State University. After coaching at the
University of Wyoming, Margie McDonald held high administrative
posts in three conferences, the High Country, Western Athletic, and
Mountain West. Following several coaching stops and the earning of a
Ph.D., Carla Lowry became athletic director at Southwestern University
in Georgetown, Texas. In 2003 Patsy Neal became executive director of
the Women's Basketball Hall of Fame.[44]

In summary, the typical AAU woman basketball player grew up in
a rural setting, was (on average) physically larger than most of her peers,
pursued an athletic avocation in spite of low public recognition, maintained a lifelong devotion to sport, and was emotionally and economically independent. In addition to the pleasure derived from basketball,
many had their educations enhanced by significant travel and interchange with athletes from other nations and cultures. Judging from the
investigative effort used to tell their story, they were also very strong
and interesting people. To know them is to admire them. They were
and are characters with character.

However they lived the balance of their lives, these women remained
part of a big sisterhood established during their playing days. Their strong
bonds as teammates or opponents have been nourished by lifelong contact and caring, especially among the unmarried players. Perhaps this was
because of the unique public obscurity of their sport. Perhaps they
responded to a feminine inclination to nourish friendships. Objective psychological analysis as well as nonprofessional observation support the conclusion that women are superior to men in trust, tender-mindedness and
nurturance.[45] Whatever the reason, the AAU players (and their coaches)
have maintained joyful and supportive contact over the years. Whether

by letter, telephone, or electronic mail, they know each other's whereabouts and are ready to share joy or bring succor when needed.

Though getting really big, the NCAA Women's Final Four is still smaller and more clubby than its men's equivalent. The basketball sorority (men coaches accepted) eagerly convenes wherever the tournament is held. The gathering includes participants from the AAU through the AIAW to the NCAA eras. There they rehash former tourneys in St. Joe and Gallup, international competition against the Russians and gastroenteritis, and stories of individual exploits that inevitably grow with time. (Did Nera really . . . ?) In viewing the big tournament and admiring the fields stocked with fast, strong, well-financed squads, the AAU gang confidently asserts that they started it all and voices no doubt that, given current opportunities, they could beat the current teams. That is probably true.

APPENDIX A

AAU WOMEN'S BASKETBALL ALL-AMERICANS*

1929

Agnes Iori—(Dallas) Golden Cyclones
Quinnie Hamm—Sparkman (Arkansas)
Louise Milam—(Dallas) Schepps Aces
Verna Montgomery—Golden Cyclones
Alma Russell—Randolph (Texas) College Kittens
Gypsie Williams—Schepps Aces

1930

Babe Didrikson—Golden Cyclones
Fulford—Randolph
Haden—(Dallas) Sunoco Oilers
Quinnie Hamm—Sparkman
Agnes Iori—Golden Cyclones
Leonard—Sparkman
Lipman—Sunoco Oilers
McElvey—Sunoco Oilers
Patterson—Randolph
Russell—Randolph

1931**

1932

Babe Didrikson—Cyclones
Doll Harris*—Oklahoma Presbyterian College (OPC)

---

* The asterisk designates the Most Valuable Player, when that player could be identified. The AAU used various methods of selecting teams over the years. Sometimes
more than one team was chosen; only the first is listed here. Identification of these
All-Americans was done mainly through newspapers and issues of the *Amateur
Athlete*. I stopped with 1969 because of the increasing irrelevance of AAU women's
basketball after that date.

** The 1931 team consisted of twenty-four players. I chose not to list them.

Bonnie Harwood—(Wichita) Southern Stage Lines
Correne Jaax—Southern Stage Lines
Isla Rhea Leister—Cyclones
Agnes Robertson—Cyclones
Lucy Stratton—Cyclones
Lucille Thurman—OPC
Hazel Vickers—OPC
Coral Worley—OPC

1933

Alberta Harris—Cyclones
Doll Harris—OPC
Correne Jaax—Wichita Thurstons
Ernestine Lampson—OPC
Lucille Thurman★—OPC
Frances Williams—Fort Worth Lucas

1934

Troy Azlam—Tulsa Business College Stenos
Floy Maxey—El Dorado (Arkansas) Oilers
Lucille Thurman—Oklahoma City Cardinals
Hazel Vickers—Oklahoma City
Hazel Walker—Tulsa
Alberta Williams★—Tulsa

1935

Alberta Williams Beck★—Tulsa
Ruth Dean—Shreveport
Myrtle Fisher—Des Moines AIB
Irene Hamm—Shreveport
Martha Hickman—Tulsa
Ernestine Lampson—Holdenville Oilers
Peggy Lawson—Holdenville
Gladys Lommier—Chicago Baby Ruths
Madge Sennett—Chicago
Correne Jaax Smith—Wichita Merchantettes

Lucille Thurman—El Dorado
Hazel Walker—El Dorado
Frances Williams—Holdenville

1936

Nora Cain—Tulsa
Frances (Sonny) Dunlap–Tulsa
Jo Langerman—AIB
Peggy Lawson—Tulsa
Lucille Thurman—El Dorado
Frances Williams*—El Dorado

1937

Leota Barham—Little Rock Travelers
Nora Cain—Galveston Anicos
Frances Dunlap—Tulsa
Correne Jaax Smith—Wichita Thurstons
Lucille Thurman—Travelers
Frances Williams*—Galveston

1938

Leota Barham—Little Rock
Nora Cain—Galveston
Lillian Justice—Galveston
Myrtle Shiever—Wichita
Correne Jaax Smith—Wichita
Frances Williams—Galveston

1939

Leota Barham—Little Rock
Glennis Birket—Galveston
Lottie Jackson—Galveston
Lucille Thurman—Little Rock
Hazel Walker—Little Rock
Frances Williams—Galveston

1940

Alline Banks*—NBC

Leota Barham—Little Rock

Hazel Walker Crutcher—Little Rock

Margaret Sexton—NBC

Myrtle Shiever—Little Rock

Mary Winslow—NBC

1941

Alline Banks*—NBC

Leota Barham—Little Rock

Loretta Blann—Little Rock

Mary Parker—Little Rock

Margaret Sexton Petty—NBC

Myrtle Shiever—Little Rock

LaVerne Simpson—Little Rock

Monica Ward—(Davenport, Iowa) American Institute of
    Commerce (AIC)

Mary Winslow—NBC

Dorothy Wirds—AIB

1942

Alline Banks—NBC

Loretta Blann—Little Rock Motor Coaches

Ruth Campbell—AIC

Hazel Walker Crutcher*—Little Rock

Jeannette Haas—AIB

Marcille Kaufman—AIB

Margaret Macomber—AIC

Viola Meyer—AIC

Jimmie Vaughn—NBC

Mary Winslow—NBC

1943

Alline Banks—(Nashville) Vultee

Loretta Blann—Little Rock

Jeannette Haas—AIB

Helen Joura*—AIC
Ann Lineback—Chatham Blanketeers
Mary Link—AIB
Chloe McCray—Little Rock
Jennie Sherrill—Chatham
Frances Stansberry—AIC
Mary Winslow—NBC
Florence Woodman—AIB

1944

Mary Winslow Hoffay—NBC
Annie Lineback—Chatham
Mary Link—Des Moines Pepsi-Cola
Alline Banks Pate*—Vultee
Margaret Sexton Petty—Vultee
Marjorie Polar—AIB
Bertha Smith—Dallas Hornets
Correne Jaax Smith—Wichita Boeings
Hazel Walker—Little Rock
Florence Woodman—AIB

1945

Loretta Blann—Little Rock
Dorothy Bruce—NBC
Ann Cramer—Pittsburgh Westinghouse
Mary Winslow Hoffay—NBC
Mary Jane Marshall—Vultee
Alline Banks Pate*—Vultee
Margaret Sexton Petty—Vultee
Hazel Reynolds—Wichita Boeings
Correne Jaax Smith*—Boeings
Hazel Walker—Little Rock

1946

Alline Banks*—(Nashville) Goldblumes
Elizabeth Brinkema—(Des Moines) Dr. Swett's
Juanita Coleman—Okmulgee (Oklahoma)

Oleta Coleman—Okmulgee
Mary Link—Dr. Swett's
Pauline Lunn—Dr. Swett's
Mary Jane Marshall—Goldblumes
Margaret Sexton—Goldblumes
Doris Weems—Goldblumes
Florence Woodman—Dr. Swett's

1947

Alline Banks★—Atlanta Blues
Joy Crowell—AIB
Lurlyne Greer—Goldblumes
Mary Hoffay—NBC
Lottie Jackson—(New Orleans) Jax Beer
Mary Jane Marshall—Goldblumes
Anne Paradise—Atlanta
Margaret Sexton—Goldblumes
Doris Weems—Atlanta

1948

Agnes Baldwin—NBC
Alline Banks—Atlanta
Elizabeth Brinkema—Chatham
Pat Carney—Atlanta
Margaret Sexton★—Goldblumes
Lurlyne Greer—Goldblumes
Mary Jane Marshall–Goldblumes
Anne Paradise—Atlanta
Janice Sherrill—Chatham
Doris Weems—Atlanta

1949

Dorothy Bruce—Goldblumes
Margie Cooper—Goldblumes
Margaret Sexton Gleaves—Goldblumes
Lurlyne Greer—Goldblumes

Fern Gregory—NBC

Phyllis Lockwood—Denver Dry Goods

Mary Jane Marshall★—Goldblumes

Anne Paradise—Chatham

Alline Banks Sprouse—NBC

Jackie Swaim Fagg—(Winston-Salem, North Carolina)
    Hanes Hosiery

1950

Beckman—Denver Viners

Cleo Brooks—Wayland

Dorothy Bruce—Goldblumes

Joy Crowell—AIB

Lurlyne Greer—Goldblumes

Evelyn Jordan—Hanes

Doris Weems Light—NBC

Agnes Loyd—Nashville Generals

Alline Banks Sprouse★—NBC

Jimmie Vaughn—Hanes

1951

Pauline Lunn Bowden—Goldblumes

Juanita Clepper—Wayland

Helen Corrick—AIB

Joy Cummings—AIB

Jackie Swaim Fagg—Hanes

Lurlyne Greer—Goldblumes

Evelyn Jordan★—Hanes

Peggy Ryan—Atlanta

Pat Tate—Wayland

Marie Wales—Wayland

1952

Betty Clark—AIC

Eunies Futch—Hanes

Lurlyne Greer★—Hanes

Evelyn Jordan—Hanes
Louise Lowry—Dallas Hornets
Sarah Parker—Hanes
Norma Schoute—AIC
Janet Thompson—Iowa Wesleyan
Katherine Washington—NBC
Dorothy Welp—Iowa Wesleyan

1953

Ruth Cannon—Wayland
Eunies Futch—Hanes
Cristine Hurtado—Chihuahua (Mexico)
Lurlyne Greer★—Hanes
Evelyn Jordan—Hanes
Dorothy Major—Denver Viners
Lometa Odom—Wayland
Barbara Sipes—Topeka
Marie Wales—Wayland
Helen Jo White—Amarillo

1954

Ruth Cannon—Wayland
Eunies Futch—Hanes
Norma Lee Johnston—(St. Joseph) Goetz Country Club
Evelyn Jordan—Hanes
Edith Kline—Kansas City Dons
Jean McAndrews—Denver Viners
Lurlyne Greer Mealhouse★—Hanes
Lometa Odom—Wayland
Barbara Sipes—Kansas City
Betty Spears—NBC

1955

Missouri Arledge—Philander Smith
Ruth Cannon★—Wayland
Alberta Cox—Kansas City Midland Jewelry
Janette Engel—Omaha Commercial Extension (OCE)

Shirley Martin—Milwaukee Real Refrigeration
Toby Martin—Jackson (Mississppi) Pine Sol Queens
Lometa Odom—Wayland
Norma Rowland—Goetz Country Club
Louise Short—Clarendon (Texas) Jr. College
Alice Van Dyke—OCE
Nera White—NBC
Fay Wilson—Wayland

1956

Rita Alexander—Wayland
Janice Armstrong—Iowa Wesleyan
Jannette Engel—OCE
Kaye Garms—Wayland
Barbara Johnson—Iowa Wesleyan
Barbara Kelley—OCE
Doris Murley—NBC
Lometa Odom★—Wayland
Katherine Washington—NBC
Nera White—NBC
Faye Wilson—Wayland
Raye Wilson—Wayland

1957

Rita Alexander—Wayland
Alice Barron—Wayland
Alberta Cox—(Kansas City) Midland Jewelry
Joan Crawford—Clarendon Jr. College
Lucille (Ludy) Davidson—Midland Jewelry
Carroll Dierks—Denver Viner Chevrolet
Sandra (Sandy) Fiete—Iowa Wesleyan
Kaye Garms—Wayland
Doris Scoggins—NBC
Barbara Sipes—Iowa Wesleyan
Katherine Washington—NBC
Nera White★—NBC

1958

Joan Crawford—NBC
Ludy Davidson—Midland Jewelry
Sandy Fiete—Iowa Wesleyan
Barbara Johnson—Iowa Wesleyan
Edith Keaton—Midland Jewelry
Glenda Nicholson—Iowa Wesleyan
Shirley Peterson—(St. Joseph) Platt College
Barbara Sipes—Iowa Wesleyan
Peggy Tate—NBC
Katherine Washington—Wayland
Nera White★—NBC

1959

Joan Crawford—NBC
Sandy Fiete—Iowa Wesleyan
Margaret Halloran—NBC
Rita Horky—Iowa Wesleyan
Karen Jones—OCE
Carolyn Miller—Wayland
Patsy Neal—Wayland
Glenda Nicholson—Iowa Wesleyan
Margaret Odom—Wayland
Eloise Turner—Atlanta Tomboys
Katherine Washington★—Wayland
Nera White★—NBC

1960

Alberta Cox—Platt College
Joan Crawford—NBC
Sue Gunter—NBC
Marilyn Heckler—Defiance (Ohio)
Judy Hodson—Iowa Wesleyan
Rita Horky—Iowa Wesleyan
Sue Lett—Platt College
Carolyn Miller—Wayland

Patsy Neal—Wayland
Jill Upton—NBC
Katherine Washington—Wayland
Nera White★—NBC

1961

Joan Crawford—NBC
Ludy Davidson—Platt College
Sandy Fiete—Platt College
Judy Hodson—Iowa Wesleyan
Rita Horky—(Topeka) Ransom's Boosters
Joan Joyce—Worcester (Massachusetts)
Carla Lowry—Wayland
Glenda Masten—Wayland
Norma Schwarz—Sioux City (Iowa)
Laura Switzer★—Wayland
Jill Upton—NBC
Nera White—NBC

1962

Philis Bothwell—OCE
Joan Crawford—NBC
Diane Frieden—(Des Moines) Look Magazine
Rita Horky—NBC
Karen Jones—OCE
Glyna Masten—Wayland
Dixie Ramsbottom—Iowa Wesleyan
Norma Schwang—Sioux City
Betty Scott—Wayland
Laura Switzer—Wayland
Nera White★—NBC
Lori Williams—Iowa Wesleyan

1963

Joan Crawford★—NBC
Sandy Fiete—St. Joseph Pepsi Cola

Deanna Grindle—Omaha Wrights
Rita Horky—NBC
Glyna Masten—Wayland
Doris Rogers—NBC
Betty Scott—Wayland
Barbara Sipes—Iowa Wesleyan
Laura Switzer—Wayland
Linda Wagner—T F & R (Silverton, Texas)
Nera White—NBC
Lori Williams—Iowa Wesleyan

1964

Opal Bogard—Wayland
Alberta Cox—Ransom's Boosters
Joan Crawford★—NBC
Dianne Frieden—Iowa Wesleyan
Margie Hunt—Wayland
Peg Peterson—Iowa Wesleyan
Carole Phillips—Ransom's Boosters
Doris Rogers—NBC
Dixie Southard—Ransom's Boosters
Judy Wallek—Wayland
Nera White—NBC
Cindy Wiginton—Wayland

1965

Betty Bansom—Wayland
Alberta Cox—Raytown (Missouri)
Joan Crawford—NBC
Carolyn James—Wayland
Joan Joyce—Orange (California)
Patsy Neal—Utah Lakers
Carole Phillips—Raytown
Doris Rogers—NBC
Marie Rogers—NBC
Diane Schliegel—OCE

Nera White★—NBC
Cindy Wiginton—Wayland

1966

Joan Crawford—NBC
Lois Finley—Wayland
Loi Hamm—Wayland
Myran Hauschildt—OCE
Carolyn Miller—Pasadena (Texas)
Carole Phillips—Raytown
Betty Ransom—Wayland
Doris Rogers—NBC
Loretta Smith—NBC
Judy Wallek—Wayland
Nera White★—NBC
Dixie Woodall—Raytown

1967

Carole Phillips Aspedon—Raytown
Joan Crawford—NBC
Myrna DeBerry—Ouachita College (Arkansas)
Lois Finley—Wayland
Doris Rogers—NBC
Barbara Sipes—Raytown
Loretta Smith—NBC
Maurice Smith—Raytown
Marie Rogers Thomas—NBC
Nera White★—NBC
Carol Wolfe—John F. Kennedy College (Nebraska)
Dixie Woodall—Raytown

1968

Carole Aspedon—Raytown
Joan Crawford—NBC
Myrna DeBerry—Ouachita College
Mildred Endsley—Anamill (Long Beach, California)

Patty Hill—Ouachita College
Ann Matlock—Raytown
Marbaret Propst—Raytown
Doris Rogers—NBC
Barbara Sipes—Raytown
Loretta Smith—NBC
Marie Thomas—NBC
Nera White★—NBC

1969

Joan Crawford—NBC
Ann Matlock—Wayland
Pam Mindemann—Wayland
Ellen Mosher—Midwestern (Iowa)
Linda Price—Hutcherson (Kansas)
Kay Roberson—John F. Kennedy
Doris Rogers—NBC
Katy Smith—NBC
Sally Smith—NBC
Lois Stuflick—John F. Kennedy
Marie Thomas—NBC
Nera White★—NBC

APPENDIX B

TOP-FOUR FINISHERS IN AAU TOURNAMENTS*

YEAR	FIRST PLACE	SECOND PLACE	THIRD PLACE	FOURTH PLACE
1926	Pasadena Athletic & Country Club	Anaheim		
1929	Schepp's Aces (Dallas)	Employer's Casualty Company Golden Cyclones (Dallas)	Sparkman (AR) Sparks	Wallenstein-Raffman (Wichita)
1930	Sunoco Oilers (Dallas)	Sparkman	Randolph College (Cisco, TX)	Golden Cyclones
1931	Golden Cyclones	Wichita Thurstons	Sunoco Oilers	Crescent College (Eureka Springs, AR)
1932	Oklahoma Presbyterian College Cardinals (OPC, Durant, OK)	Golden Cyclones	Southern Kansas Stage Lines (Wichita)	Crescent College
1933	OPC	Golden Cyclones	Wichita Thurstons	Kansas City Steubens
1934	Tulsa (OK) Business College Stenos	Oklahoma City	El Dorado (AR) Oilers/ Lions	Shreveport (LA) Meadows-Draghon
1935	Tulsa Stenos	Holdenville (OK) Flyers	El Dorado	Shreveport
1936	Tulsa Stenos	El Dorado	American Institute of Business (AIB, Des Moines, IA)	Wichita Thurstons

*Just as with the AAU All-Americans, these rankings were obtained mostly from reports in newspapers and in *Amateur Athlete*. I identified the top-four finishers through 1969, after which the AAU tournament rapidly waned and coverage was very skimpy. The emphasis in this book was through that year. Thus, the four top teams were not identified for all the few subsequent years of AAU competition.

1937	Little Rock (AR) Flyers	Galveston (TX) Anicos	Wichita	Tulsa Stenos
1938	Anicos	Wichita	Tulsa	Little Rock
1939	Anicos	Little Rock Flyers	Wichita	AIB
1940	Little Rock	Nashville Business College (NBC)	Anicos	AIB
1941	Little Rock Flyers	NBC	AIB	American Institute of Commerce (AIC, Davenport, IA)
1942	AIC	Little Rock Flyers	NBC	AIB
1943	AIC	AIB	Little Rock Motor Coaches	Lenox, Iowa
1944	Vultee Bomberettes (Nashville)	AIB	Chatham Blanketeers (Elkin, NC)	Dallas Hornets
1945	Bomberettes	Little Rock Dr. Pepper	Wichita Boeings	NBC
1946	Cook's Goldblumes (Nashville)	Dr. Swett's (Des Moines)	Little Rock Dr. Pepper	Chatham Blanketeers
1947	Atlanta Sports Arena Blues	Goldblumes	AIB	Des Moines Home Federal
1948	Goldblumes	Atlanta Blues	Chatham Blanketeers	NBC
1949	Goldblumes	NBC	Hanes Hosiery (Winston-Salem, NC)	Chatham
1950	NBC	Goldblumes	Hanes Hosiery	AIB
1951	Hanes Hosiery	Wayland Baptist College	Goldblumes	AIB
1952	Hanes Hosiery	AIC	NBC	Iowa Wesleyan
1953	Hanes Hosiery	Wayland	Chihuahua (Mexico)	Denver Viners

Appendix B

1954	Wayland	Kansas City Dons	Hanes Hosiery	Denver Viners
1955	Wayland	Omaha Commercial Extension (OCE)	St. Joseph Goetz	Midland Jewelry (Kansas City)
1956	Wayland	NBC	Iowa Wesleyan	OCE
1957	Wayland	Iowa Wesleyan	Midland Jewelry	NBC
1958	NBC	Iowa Wesleyan	Wayland	Midland Jewelry
1959	Wayland	NBC	Iowa Wesleyan	OCE
1960	NBC	Wayland	Iowa Wesleyan	Platt College
1961	Wayland	NBC	Iowa Wesleyan	Platt College
1962	NBC	Wayland	Iowa Wesleyan	Sioux City (IA)
1963	NBC	Wayland	Iowa Wesleyan	T F & R
1964	NBC	Wayland	Ransom's Boosters (Topeka, KS)	Iowa Wesleyan
1965	NBC	Wayland	Raytown	OCE
1966	NBC	Wayland	Raytown	Pasadena
1967	NBC	Raytown	Wayland	Anamill (Long Beach, CA)
1968	NBC	Wayland	Anamill	Ouachita College
1969	NBC	John F. Kennedy College (JFK)	Wayland	Midwestern
1970	Wayland	Ouachita		
1971	Wayland	Raytown		
1972	JFK	Ouachita	Raytown	Wayland
1973	JFK	Raytown	Parsons College	Allentown (PA) Crestettes
1974	Wayland			
1975	Wayland	General West (Fullerton, CA)	Allentown Crestettes	Marion-Kay Peppers (Brownstown, IN)

1976	General West	Wayland	Darlington (SC) Recreationals	New York City Planters
1977	Anna's Bananas (Los Angeles, CA)	Adidas (formerly National General)	Sharman's Shooters (Long Beach, CA)	Darlington
1978	Anna's Bananas	Washington, D.C., Sophisticated Ladies	Allentown Crestettes	New York City Planters
1979	Anna's Bananas	Allentown Crestettes		

APPENDIX C

THE MYTHICAL ALL-STAR TEAMS

There is no more controversial, unscientific, or fun activity than choosing the "best" at anything. Team sports particularly lend themselves to that activity. Advocates' opinions are strongly taken and rarely subject to reason, that is, others' opinions. Unanimity is impossible.

Over this forty-year span of AAU women's basketball, the game and its players changed. We have few films, and statistics were kept inconsistently. Such objective impedimenta do not discourage a devoted fan. Selecting six-women teams, paying token credence to positions, assuming the best athletes could adjust to the game's evolution, weighing their contemporary honors and their teams' records, and eliciting numerous opinions, here are the author's AAU all-timers. Let the arguments begin:

First Team

Rita Alexander—Floor leader in 101 Wayland wins.

Alline Banks—Offensive skills ahead of her time. Winner with champion's *hauteur*.

Joan Crawford—Consistent, strong, part of a dynamic championship duo.

Margaret Sexton—A defensive snake. Could stop anyone.

Hazel Walker—All-round skills, outstanding team player, basketball pioneer.

Nera White—Any questions? See above.

Second Team

Lurlyne Greer—A scoring hoss. Good team player

Rita Horky—Among the more powerful of "power forwards."

Eckie Jordan—A pepperpot "quarterback" who could run the show.

Mary Jane Marshall—Tough, very fast. Could score but loved to defend.

Doris Rogers—Tall, fast scorer. No better team player. Way underrated.

Lucille Thurman—Seven-time All-American for four Midwest teams.

Third Team

Babe Didrikson—Her ink helped get the ball rolling. Passing interest in basketball.

Barbara Sipes—Pure pivot player. Much international success.

Correne Jaax Smith—Enduring defensive star and rebounder for 1930s Wichita teams.

Lometa Odom—Inevitable Wayland All-American pivot player.

Katherine Washington—All-round skills. Experienced internationally.

Frances Williams—Multiple All-American for four 1930s teams. Coached Galveston.

Coach

John Head or Harley Redin—"pick 'em."

Sponsors

1. The Coxes

   Alberta Cox was a good AAU player and a tireless visionary after she took off team silks. At a time when U.S. women's basketball had hit the skids, she worked hard to return it to the forefront—coaching national teams, creating training camps, goading national officials about obvious reasons for Team USA's fall. The outspoken Cox was not universally adored by those she was spurring, whether players or basketball organizational leaders. For the love of the game though, she never quit and was a catalyst for the modernization of women's basketball in the United States. She remains mostly unrecognized for this lonely, persistent work.

   Alberta's parents, Lee and Alberta Cox, financially underwrote her teams and its players. Many of the numerous women who attended Midwest colleges at Mr. Cox's expense became important coaches and executive leaders in women's basketball when it burgeoned after Title IX.

2. Claude Hutcherson

   As much as Redin and his players, this Wayland alumnus put his school and its women's basketball team on the map and into sports history. In the current age of tight bureaucratic control of college athletics, his largesse would have been illegal. In a simpler time, his support jump-started women's college basketball. He and his wife, Wilda, assured that this pioneering effort was done with class in accouterments, coaching, and comportment.

3. H. O. Balls

This dour, distant businessman did not disperse money as lavishly as did Leroy Cox or Claude Hutcherson; but he was also not as tightfisted as some claimed. Several of his star players on his 1960s teams were given board and an apartment at his Auto-Diesel College. He provided spending money for trips, including the foreign sojourns. He was probably more generous with such expenditures than most AAU sponsors. Much more important, he underwrote an AAU basketball team longer, three and one-half decades, than anyone else. That team became a very important one—ultimately the best in AAU history.

NOTES

Introduction

1. Bob Duncan, telephone interview by author, Columbia, TN, 16 July 2000. Duncan is the Maury County historian.

2. Cecil Whiteside, telephone interview by author, Hampshire, TN, 30 May 2000.

3. Sam Kennedy, telephone interview by author, Columbia, TN, 2 August 2000. My mother told me the dire tale of drowning many times. It was independently offered by Margaret Dean Akin, longtime Hampshire teacher—telephone interview with author, Millington, TN, 25 May 2000.

4. Bettye Patton, ed., *Hampshire Then and Now* (Hampshire, TN, 1993), 130.

5. Ibid., 288.

6. Newspaper clippings in Hampshire museum; Harold Huggins, "Two Thousand Points a Long Way from Sidewalk Dribbling," *The Tennessean* (hereinafter cited *TT*), 11 February 1999, 7C.

7. Akin telephone interview; Tennie Cathey Chaffin, telephone interview, Columbia, TN, 26 May 2000.

8. "Hampshire and C.M.A. Winners," *Maury Democrat,* 20 February 1936, 3; (Columbia, TN) *Daily Herald,* 6 March 1938, 1, 6.

9. Sometime in the mid-twentieth century, publications began eliminating periods after organizational abbreviations. Unless in a quote or reference, I will for the sake of consistency do that in the manuscript.

10. The quote of Harley Redin was conveyed by Carolyn Moffatt, telephone interview, Hot Springs, AR, 29 June 2000; Zander Hollander, ed., *The Modern Encyclopedia of Basketball* (Garden City, NY: Doubleday & Company, Inc., 1979), 267; Neal Ellis, "World capital of Women's Basketball," *The Nashville Tennessean Magazine,* 16 March 1952, 6–7.

Chapter One: A Forgotten Era

1. Scottie Rodgers, assistant director for the Division I Woman's Basketball Championship, srodgers@ncaa.org; bweesies@ncaa.org; Jo.LaVerde@NielsenMedia.com; Carl Bialik, "Narrowing the Gender Gap," *Wall Street Journal* (hereinafter cited *WSJ*), 14 March 2004, R9.

2. nfhs.org.Participation/SportsPart01_files/sheet001.htm; www.ncaabasketball.net/.

3. For an overview of the history of women's athletics, see Allen Guttmann, *Women's Sports: A History* (New York: Columbia University Press, 1991); Joseph B. Oxendine, *American Indian Sports Heritage* (Champaign, IL, 1988), 22–26; Stewart Culin, *Games of North American Indians* (Lincoln: University of Nebraksa Press, 1992), 708.

4. Guttman, *Women's Sports,* 97, 103–4; Victoria Sherrow, *Encyclopedia of Women and Sports* (Santa Barbara, CA: ABC-CLIO, Inc., 1996), xi–xii; Ruth M. Sparhawk and others, *American Women in Sport, 1887–1987: A One-Hundred-Year Chronology* (Metuchen, NJ: Scarecrow Press, 1989), xv.

5. There is probably a yet unidentified human gene that makes people enjoy competition, and women surely carry such a trait.

6. Guttmann, "From Swedish Drill to Field Hockey," *Women's Sports*, 106–34.

7. Senda Berenson Papers, 1875–1996, http://clio.fivecolleges.edu/smith/berenson/; Betty Spears, "Senda Berenson Abbott," in *A Century of Women's Basketball: From Frailty to Final Four* (Reston, VA: American Alliance for Health, Physical Education, Recreation and Dance, 1991), 19–23. Senda is probably not the best-known person in her family. Her older brother was Bernard Berenson, an important art critic, connoisseur, and collector.

8. The sport was originally designated by the two-word term, sometimes with a hyphen. The word "basketball" was not generally accepted until the mid-1920s. See J. A. Simpson and E. S. C. Weiner, eds., *The Oxford English Dictionary*, vol. 1 (Oxford: Clarendon Press, 1989), 987. Unless used in a quotation or title, for uniformity I will use the single compound word, basketball.

9. Bernice Larson Webb, *The Basketball Man: James Naismith* (Lawrence: University Press of Kansas, 1973), 1–45. Naismith and Stagg were close friends, and their careers had many parallels. Naismith played on a highly competitive YMCA football team organized by Stagg called "Stagg's Stubby Christians." See James Naismith, *Basketball: Its Origins and Development* (New York: Associated Press, 1941), 13–28.

10. Ibid., 29–61; Webb, *The Basketball Man*, 62–67. Despite Naismith's emphasizing that physical contact was not part of his new game, men's competition was extremely rough in the first few decades of the sport. Players became known as "cagers" because cages were put around the court in order to protect players from fans and to minimize collisions between players scrambling for out-of-bounds balls. The latter problem was solved by ruling that such a ball went to the team that did not make it go out.

11. Biographical Note, Senda Berenson Papers, 1875–1996, Smith College Collections Online, http://clio.fivecolleges.edu/smith/berenson; Edith Naomi Hill, "Senda Berenson: Director of Physical Education at Smith College, 1892–1911," *Research Quarterly* (October 1941): 658–65; Spears, "Senda Berenson Abbott," 24.

12. Ibid.; Senda Berenson Abbott, "Basket Ball at Smith College," *Spalding's Athletic Library*, 1914, 69–74, from the Smith College Archive web site: clio.fivecolleges.edu/smith/berenson/Spubs/bball_smith/index.shtml?

13. Lynne Fauley Emery and Margaret Toohey-Costa, "Hoops and Skirts: Women's Basketball on the West Coast, 1892–1930s," in *A Century of Women's Basketball*, 137–54.

14. Joan Paul, "Clara Gregory Baer: Catalyst for Women's Basketball," in *A Century of Women's Basketball*, 37–52; Senda Berenson, "Basket Ball for Women," *Physical Education* (September 1894): 106–9.

15. My father coached the three-division game for most of his career at Hampshire High School. Films at the Naismith Basketball Hall of Fame in Springfield, Massachusetts, of a contest between teams at Mt. Holyoke College show a graceful, almost balletic game that, because of the limited dribble and emphasis on passing, moves faster than anticipated by those who have never seen such a game.

16. Joanna Davenport, "The Tides of Change in Women's Basketball Rules," in *A Century of Women's Basketball*, 83–108.

17. Jill Hutchison, "Women's Intercollegiate Basketball: AIAW/NCAA," *A Century of Women's Basketball*, 309–10.

18. "Title IX," Sherrow, *Encyclopedia of Women and Sports*, 307–8; "Where the Boys Are," *WSJ*, 25 January 2002, W15; Stefan Fatsis, "911 for Title IX?" *WSJ*, 17 May 2002, W4. The quotation is by George Will on ABC's "Sunday Morning with George Stephanopolous," 5 January 2003.

19. Jackson Anderson, *Industrial Recreation: A Guide to Its Organization and Administration* (New York: McGraw-Hill, 1955), 47–48, 62–63.

20. Robert Korsgaard, "A History of the Amateur Athletic Union of the United States" (D.Ed. diss., Teachers College, Columbia University, 1952); Joan S. Hult, "The Governance of Athletics for Girls and Women," in *A Century of Women and Sports*, 53–82; Guttmann, *Women's Sports*, 142–46; Sherrow, Amateur Athletic Union (AAU) in *Encyclopedia of Women and Sports*, 9, 10; Hollander, *The Modern Encyclopedia of Basketball*, 264–67; Frank Callahan, "Industrial athletics," *Amateur Athlete* 9 (June 1938): 6, 14.

21. "Anaheim Girls Cop in First Casaba Game," *Los Angeles Times*, 9 April 1926, 9; "A.A.U. Champions, 1926," *A.A.U. Bulletin* 3 (December 1926): 12. Much of the story of the initial AAU women's basketball champions from Pasadena came from newspaper clippings provided by Dr. Lynne Emery. These included articles in the *Los Angeles Times*, the PAAC newspaper, and the *Mercury*, the club newspaper of the Los Angeles Athletic Club.

22. Roxanne M. Albertson, "Basketball Texas Style, 1910–1933: School to Industrial League Competition," in *A Century of Women's Basketball*, 155–66.

23. Gary Newton, "Hazel Walker: Miss Basketball," unpublished. Newton of Los Angeles, CA, via Mountain Home and the University of Arkansas, has done extensive research on Hazel Walker and has written a screenplay of her life. I am indebted to him for his generosity in sharing his knowledge of her.

24. Albertson, "Basketball Texas Style," 155–66; Susan E. Cayleff, *Babe* (Urbana: University of Illinois Press, 1995), 50–77; Sherrow, *Encyclopedia of Women and Sports*, 28–30.

25. Carolyn Miller, telephone interview, Hockley, TX, 10 June 2000.

Chapter Two: Basketball in the Oil Patch

1. James R. McGovern, "Small Worlds Sustained," chap. in *And a Time for Hope: Americans in the Great Depression* (Westport, CT: Prager Publishers, 2000), 83–104; Lorraine Garkovich, *Population and Community in Rural America* (New York: Greenwood Press, 1989), 85, 98. For an overview of the Great Depression, see Donald M. Kennedy, *Freedom from Fear: The American People in Depression and War, 1929–1943* (New York: Oxford University Press, 1999). For an overview of the 1930s, see Victor Bondi, *American Decades, 1930–1939* (Detroit, MI: Gale Research, Inc., 1995).

2. Doris Rogers, telephone interview, Nashville, 5 April 2000.

3. Newton, "Hazel Walker: Miss Basketball."

4. Named for its early, groundbreaking president, the AAU Sullivan Award is given annually to the amateur athlete who advanced the "cause of sportsmanship." Because the AAU sponsored women's basketball, the women players at least had a

shot at a nomination. None ever won the award. In 1944, a swimmer, Ann Curtis, became the first woman to win the Sullivan Award. With the progressive prevalence of professionalism in sports, the award has lost much of its importance.

5. John Kord Lagemann, "Red Heads, You Kill Me," *Colliers* 119 (8 February 1947): 64–66; Sherrow, "All-American World's Champion Girls Basketball Club," in *Encyclopedia of Women and Sports,* 9; Linda Ford, "'Red Heads, You Kill Me'— Women's Professional Basketball, 1930–1970," in *Lady Hoopsters: A History of Women's Basketball in America* (Northampton, MA: Half Moon Books, 1999), 95–104.

6. Gary Newton, telephone interview, Los Angeles, 4 October 2001; Francies Garroute, telephone interviews, Cabot, AR, 24 January 2002, 12 August 2002; Newton, "Hazel Walker: Miss Basketball."

7. Ibid.; "The Fifty Greatest Sports Figures from Arkansas," *Sports Illustrated* 91 (27 December 1999): 74.

8. "Cage Stars Off for Kansas," *Amateur Athlete* 1 (May 1930): 5; J. Lyman Bingham , "'A Basketball Man Applauds 'The Ladies'"; ibid.; "Girls Basketball," *Amateur Athlete* 3 (April 1933): 7.

9. "Kansas and Sooners to Wage Battle for National Cage Title," *Wichita Beacon* (hereinafter cited *WB*), 25 March 1927, 14; "Sooner Girls Win Basket Title," *WB,* 27 March 1927, 1; "Cook Paint Company Wins National A.A.U. Basketball Meet in Close Game," *WB,* 18 March 1928, 15; "Dallas to Win Title in Tourney," *WB,* 1 April 1928, 1.

10. Bill Singleton, "Aces and Cyclones Pull Through with Close Decisions," *Dallas Morning News* (hereinafter cited *DMN*), 31 March 1929, Sports-4; Singleton, "Three Texas Teams in Semifinal Girls' National Meet," *DMN,* 28 March 1930, 17; Singleton, "Sun Oilers Win Third Consecutive National Basket Ball Title," *DMN,* 30 March 1930, Sports-3; "Ten of Dallas Cagers Placed on All-Stars," *DMN,* 30 March 1930; Singleton, "Golden Cyclones Capture National Women's Basket Ball Championship," *DMN,* 29 March 1931, Sports-2.

11. Anne Semple, *Ties That Bind: The Story of Oklahoma Presbyterian College* (Durant, OK); Henry MacCready, "Oklahoma Presbyterian College for Girls," in *Queen of Three Valleys: A Story of Durant* (Durant, OK: Democrat Printing Company), 94–98; Ibid., "Biographical Sketch of Dixon Durant," 3–5; Lahoma Lassiter Carlton, telephone interview, Houston, TX, 4 December 2002; Virginia Childers, telephone interview, Durant, OK, 8 October 2002. Mrs. Childers is one of the three Hamilton sisters who played for the OPC Cardinals. Lee Reeder, electronic mail, 27 October 2002. Mrs. Reeder is Sam Babb's niece. Her daughter is working on a book on Babb and his Cardinals.

12. Raymond Sage, "Oklahoma Presbyterian College Girls Win National A.A.U. Basket Ball Championship," *Shreveport Times,* 26 March 1932, 13, 14; "Shreveport Girl Crowned Queen of Goal Makers," *Shreveport Times,* 25 March 1932, 11; "The Ladies of the Court Were Champions," *Bryan County* (OK) *Star,* 22 May 1975, 1, 2.

13. "Durant Teachers Defend National Championship Against Dallas Cyclones Here Tonight," *WB,* 24 March 33, 14; "Durant Teachers Flash Brilliant Attack to Win National Basketball Championship," *WB,* 25 March 33, 5; "Oklahoma Sextet Wins Girls Title," *Nashville Banner* (hereinafter cited *NB*), 25 March 1933, 8.

14. Lahoma Lassiter Carlton, telephone interview, Houston, TX, 4 December 2002; Lucille Thurman Berry, "About Sam F. Babb, Coach of the 'Cardinals,'" speech made at induction of Babb into Oklahoma Athletic Hall of Fame, 7 January

1979; "The Ladies of the Court Were Champions," *Bryan County Star*, 22 May 75, 1, 2; "Victor Murdock Learns How Babb Can Direct Winning Cage Team," interview in unknown Wichita newspaper after 1933 AAU tournament; 2003 Oklahoma Sports Hall of Fame Induction Ceremony program. These clippings, etc., were provided by Virginia Hamilton Childers of Durant, OK; Virginia Hamilton Childers, "History of the Oklahoma Presbyterian College National and North American Basketball Championship Teams," in *The History of Bryan County* (Durant, OK: Bryan County Heritage Association, Inc., 1983), 69–72. For a discussion of the France-Oklahoma City game, see Basketball across Borders section.

15. "Tulsa Wins over Cardinals," *Amateur Athlete* 4 (April 1934): 14; "Father of Basketball Pleased with Rules for Girls," *WB*, 30 March 1934, 13; "Stenos Score Big Upset to Defeat Oklahoma City," *WB*, 31 March 1934, 5; "Tulsa Wins over Chicago in Exhibition Basketball Game," *WB*, 1 April 1934, 11A; "Stenos Beat Cards, 32–22, to Win National Cage Title," *Tulsa Daily World*, 30 March 1934, 14.

16. Jack Copeland, "Looking 'Em Over," *WB*, 25 March 1935, 11; Copeland, "Tulsa Favored to Retain U.S. A.A.U. Crown," *WB*, 29 March 1935, 1, 12; "Tulsa Stenos Retain Girls' National Basketball Title with Smashing Win over Holdenville," *WB*, 30 March 1935, 5; P. A. Lightner, "Women's Basketball," *Amateur Athlete* 6 (June 1935): 11.

17. "Father of Basketball Pleased with Rules for Girls," *WB*, 30 March 1934, 13; Lightner, *Amateur Athlete* 7 (November 1936): 5; Harold Reynolds, "Teaching Girls' Basketball," *Amateur Athlete* 7 (December 1936): 2.

18. "Tulsa Stenos Hope to Make It Three Straight Girls' Titles Here Tonight," *WB*, 27 March 1936, 1, 20; "Stenos and Lions Battle for Title," *Tulsa Daily World*, 27 March 1936, 16; "Tulsa Stenos Win Cage Title Third Straight Time," *Tulsa Daily World*, 28 March 1936, 16.

19. "Anicos Beat Tulsa in Opener, 24 to 14," *Galveston Daily News* (hereinafter cited *GDN*), 9 March 1937, 6; "Anicos Defeated in Championship Finals by Flyers, 17–10," *GDN*, 27 March 1937, 7; Handley Cross, "Six Girls and a Basket," *Street and Smith's Sport Story Magazine* 62 (March 1939): 45–52; Mrs. Irvin Van Blarcom, "Women's Basketball," *Amateur Athlete* 8 (April 1937): 7; Jack Copeland, "Women's Basketball," *Amateur Athlete* (May 1937): 9, 16.

20. "Anicos Leave for National Meet," *GDN*, 18 March 1938, 10; "Thurstons to Battle Galveston Anicos in Finals of Girls' National Cage Tournament," *WB*, 36 March 1938, 8; "Little Rock Star Wins Free Throw Title at Wichita," *GDN*, 25 March 1938, 10; "NABUCO Wins," *NB*, 26 March 1938, 5; "Anicos Win National Championship," *GDN*, 27 March 1938, 16; Jack Copeland, "Witchita Awaits Tenth Annual Women's Tourney," *Amateur Athlete* 9 (March 1938); 35; Jack Copeland, "Women's Basketball," *Amateur Athlete* (May 1938): 4, 17; Jack Copeland, "Women's Basketball," *Amateur Athlete* (May 1939): 9; "NaBuCo Wins Fifth Place in National A.A.U. Tourney," *Nashville Tennessean* (hereinafter cited *NT*), 27 March 1938, 2-B; "Galveston Wins Title in Close Game," *NT*, 27 March 1938.

21. "Anicos, With Nashville Girl in Lineup, Bid for National Title Tonight," *NB*, 25 March 1939, 6; "Galveston Holds A.A.U. Net Title, Smears Flyers," *NT*, 26 March 1939, 1-B; "Anicos Crush Flyers and Keep National Title," *GDN*, 26 March 1939, 17.

22. *Sixteenth Census of the United States: 1940,* part 4. United States Department of Commerce, Government Printing Office, Washington, D.C., 1943; http://www.womensbasketballmuseum.com.

23. "Girl Cagers Are Out to End Southern Reign," *St. Joseph News-Press* (hereafter *SJNP*), 19 March 1940, 12; "All Seeded Teams Reach Semi-Final Round of Tourney," Ibid., 29 March 1940, 18; "Nashville to Face Flyers for Court Supremacy Tonight," *NT*, 30 March 1940, 7; "Little Rock Beats Nashville, 23–13, to Capture Crown," *NT*, 31 March 1940, 16A; Van Blarcom, "Women's Basketball," *Amateur Athlete* 10 (May 1940): 11–12.

24. Newton, "Hazel Walker: Miss Basketball."

25. "NBC Is Seeded No. 2 in Meet," *NB*, 24 March 1941, 11; "Nabucos, Flyers Vie in Women's AAU Finals for Second Straight Year," *NB*, 28 March 1941, 35; "NBC's Alline Banks Again Named Best Woman Cager," *NB*, 29 March 1941, 6; Wilbur C. Johnson, "Second Straight Cage Championship for Little Rock," 29 May 1941 (pagination unavailable on clipping from Little Rock newspaper in Margaret Dunaway scrapbook); undated newspaper article in Jane Marshall Ingram's scrapbook; "Leo Long to Quit Nabucos," undated newspaper clipping in Ingram scrapbook; Jane Marshall Ingram, telephone interview, 11 September 2001.

Chapter Three: Beer Distributors, Business Schools, and Hosiery Girls

1. Janice A. Beran, *From Six-on-Six to Full Court Press* (Ames: Iowa University Press, 1993), 149–67; Beran, "Iowa, the Longtime 'Hot Bed' of Girls Basketball," in *A Century of Women's Basketball*, 181–204; Florence Woodman Krohn, telephone interview, Prairie City, IA, 7 March 2003; Keith Fenton, telephone interview, Scottsdale, AZ, 9 March 2003. Fenton's father was Everett, founder of AIB.

2. "Alline Banks, Mary Winslow Star As Nabucos Crush Des Moines 36 to 14," *NT*, 25 March 1942, 10; "Banks, Vaughn, Winslow on Women's All-American," *NB*, 28 March 1942, 7.

3. "Nabucos Beat Kansas City for Women's A.A.U. Consolation Championship," *NT*, 26 March 1943, 31; "Banks, Winslow All-Americans," *NT*, 27 March 1943, 6; "Des Moines, A.I.B. Drops Vulcanettes out of National Tourney 30–26," *NT*, 25 March 1943, 16; "Nabucos Gain in A.A.U. Consolation; Margaret Turrentine Named Queen," *NT*, 24 March 1943, 10.

4. Robert G. Spinney, *World War II in Nashville* (Knoxville: University of Tennessee Press, 1998), 20–22, 32–34; George Zepp, "Nashville Plant Produced Several Important 'Warbirds' in WWII," *NT*, 4 February 2004, 5B. For geographical and cultural reasons, Tennessee is evenly divided into three distinct areas. The pride and distinctiveness of each has led to the designation of the state's grand divisions—east, middle, and west Tennessee.

5. "Vultee Meets Strong AIB in National AAU Tonight," *NB*, 24 March 1943, 18; "Des Moines A.I.B. Drops Vulcanettes Out of National Tourney 30–26," *NT*, 25 March 1943, 16; clips from 1943 Vultee company newspaper, precise date unknown; Jack Little, telephone interview, Nashville, 16 August 2000.

6. "Bomberettes Rout Dallas, 31–8, to Gain National Final," *NT*, 31 March 1944, 28; "Vultee's Bomberettes Crowned National Cage Champs," *NT*, 1 April 1944, 5; "Nabuco's Nell Seagraves Wins Free Throw Title," *NT*, 1 April 1944; "Basket Queens Return Today," Ibid., 2 April 1944, 10-C; "Convairs Were Just an Entry but Won National AAU Title," *NB*, 1 April 1944, 5.

7. Blackstone Dozier, "Bomberettes Continue U.S. Queens with 22–20 Victory," *NT*, 31 March 1945, 5; "City Girls Make History; Take Five of Ten Spots," Ibid.

8. "John Little, 79, Services Today," *NT*, 15 March 1969, 9; "John Little Services Set Saturday," *NB*, 14 November 1969, 1, 4; telephone interviews with author, Nashville: Sara Jane Byrd Ragsdale, 22 May 2000, 19 September 2001; Jane Marshall Ingram, 29 May 2000; Pauline Bowden, 7 June 2000; Buck Pardue, 25 July 2000; Fred Dettwiller, 15 August 2000. Southern Beer's men's team, sponsored by Budweiser, never made much of an athletic splash.

9. Blackstone Dozier, "Last Half Rally Nets Goldblumes Third Straight Title," *NT* 30 March 1946, 6; Jane Marshall Ingram telephone interviews, Nashville, 29 May 2000, 6 June 2000. In 2001 I saw the trophy in Springfield.

10. Anne Paradise Hansford Langston, telephone interview with author, Isle of Palms, South Carolina, 3 October 2001.

11. Telephone interview with Pauline Bowden, Nashville, 7 June 2000; telephone interview with Lurlyne Greer Rogers, Heber Springs, AR, 20 July 2000.

12. Telephone interview with Alline Sprouse, Manchester, TN, 18 September 2001.

13. "Blumes Swamp Dallas 32–9," *NT*, 26 March 1947, 13; "Nashville Girls Seek Fourth Straight National AAU Title," *NB*, 28 March 1947, 28; Gene Sullivan, "The Wise Owl," *SJNP*, 26 March 1947, 15; "Four Pivot Players to Hold Spotlight in Tonight's Semifinals," *SJNP*, 37 March 1947, 25; "Banks Makes It Personal Triumph," *SJNP*, 29 March 1947.

14. "Goldblumes Top Blues 21–18 to Win AAU Title," *NT*, 20 March 1948, 9; Bill Hiles, "'There's Never Been Anything Like It,'" undated (c. mid-1970s) Nashville newspaper article in Jane Marshall Ingram scrapbook; Pauline Lunn Bowden, telephone interview, 30 October 2001; "Sexton Gets MV Award as Cooks Cop," *NT*, 20 March 1948, 2-B; Blackie Stone, "Blumes Record Breaking Feats Making History in Women's AAU," *NT*, 20 March 1948, 2-B.

15. Telephone interview with Jane Marshall, 29 May 2000; "Blumes Meet NBC for AAU Cage Crown," *NB*, 25 March 1949, 39; Edgar Allen, "AAU Finals Have 'Tennessee Tinge,'" *NB*, 25 March 1949; "Blumes Sport Women's AAU Cage Crown for Second Straight Year," *NB*, 26 March 1949, 6; Edgar Allen, "Just Like Old Times," *NB*, 28 March 1949, 15; Guy Tiller, "Basketball Belles," *Sportfolio* (April 1948): 62. The consensus that Leo Long was the best women's basketball coach in Nashville came from interviews with several players.

16. "NBC-Blumes in AAU Finals," *NT*, 24 March 1950, 55; "Nashville Still Tops in Women's AAU Cage," *NB*, 22 March 1950, 18-A; "Five Locals on Women's All-American," *NB*, 25 March 50, 9.

17. Elva Bishop, "Amateur Athletic Union Women's Basketball, 1950–1971: The Contributions of Hanes Hosiery, Nashville Business College, and Wayland Baptist College" (M.A. thesis, University of North Carolina, Chapel Hill, 1984), 12.

18. Ibid., 14, 15; *Women's AAU Basketball Tournament* (game program), 1951; John Trowbridge, "Wayland Coeds Jolt Champions in Stunning AAU Upset, 40–38," *DMN*, 22 March 1951, I-19; Harry Gage, "Seventeen Former Cage Stars to Hold Reunion at AAU," *DMN*, 23 March 1951, I-27; Trowbridge, "Hutcherson, Hanes Gain Finals in AAU Tourney," *DMN*, 23 March 1951; Van Blarcom, "Hanes Girls Win Court Title," *Amateur Athlete* 22 (May 1951): 7, 28.

19. Bishop, "Amateur Athletic Union Women's Basketball," 16, 17; Bill Isom, "Dreamettes Ramble 55–25," *NT*, 27 March 1952, 26; Isom, "NBC Gains AAU Semifinals," *NT*, 28 March 1952, 48; Isom, "NBC Tumbles in AAU Semis," *NT*, 29 March 1952; Van Blarcom, "Hanes Sextette Repeats," *Amateur Athlete* 23 (May 1952): 23; Jackie Fagg, telephone interview, Winston-Salem, NC, 22 February 2004.

20. Sherman, *The Love and the Lore of Basketball in Missouri*, 127–28; Isom, "Lane Forfeits; NBC Wins, 2 to 0," *NT*, 3 April 1953, 46; Isom, "NBC Well Aware That Tourney Was One of Numerous Upsets," *NT*, 5 April 1953, 2-B; Isom, "NBC Stunned by Sante Fe," *NT*, 31 March 1953, 17.

21. Bob Hampton, "Hanes Girls Style Revolutionizes Basketball," *Amateur Athlete* 24 (April 1953): 17, 25; Jackie Fagg, telephone interview, Winston-Salem, 22 February 2004; Elva Bishop and Katherine Fulton, "Shooting Stars: The Heyday of Industrial Women's Basketball," *Southern Exposure* (Fall 1979): 50–56.

22. Description of lifestyles and travel conditions sustained by mid-1940s Nashville teams came from numerous conversations with players of that era, especially Jane Marshall Ingram. Ridley Wills II provided me a season ticket to the Nashville Generals games of that time.

23. Tiller, "Basketball Belles"; Sherman, *The Lure and the Lore of Basketball in Missouri*, 123; Joe Livingston, "Ann Paradise Is Playing Greatest Ball of Career," *Atlanta Journal*, 2 March 1948; Pauline Bowden, telephone interview 30 October 2001; Anne Paradise Hansford Langston interview, Nashville, 25 August 2002; Langston, telephone interview, Isle of Palms, SC, 11 February 2003; Karen Rosen, "Paradise at last," *Atlanta Journal-Constitution*, 9 February 2003, D4.

24. Lurlyne Greer Rogers, telephone interview, Heber Springs, AR, 20 July 2000. I saw Rogers's scrapbooks in Heber Springs, 6 August 2002. The information on the Arkansas girls' high school tournament came from a telephone interview with the Arkansas Activities Association, 5 August 2002. Des Arc population from 1930 census.

25. Bishop, "Amateur Athletic Union Women's Basketball," 18, 19; "Hanes' Lurlyne Greer Wins Carolinas' Athletic Award," *NT*, 26 March 1953, 26; Lurlyne Greer Rogers telephone interview, Heber Springs, AR, 26 September 2000.

26. This account of Greer's career with the Travelers was from Francies Garroute, telephone interview, Cabot, AR, 12 August 2002.

27. Rogers obituary in newspaper clipping, Rogers's scrapbooks. Mike Gains, "Local Legend to Be Inducted into Hall of Fame," Heber Springs *Sun-Times*, 2 April 2004, 3B.

28. Alline Banks Sprouse, telephone interview, Manchester, TN, 11 September 2001.

29. Lesley Yoder, "Legends Overlooked," *Nashville Sports Weekly*, 3 August 1999, 8, 9; Ed Allen, "'She's the Greatest,'" *Manchester Times*, 1 January 2000, 1, 4A; Alline Banks Sprouse telephone interview with author, Manchester, TN, 13 August 2001; Van Blarcom, "Women's Basketball," *Amateur Athlete* 10 (May 1940): 11, 12.

30. Alline Banks Sprouse interview, Nashville, 4 April 2000.

31. Alline Banks Sprouse and Margaret Sexton Gleaves, personal interview with author, Nashville, 26 April 2000; George Sherman, telephone interview with author, St. Joseph, MO, 18 May 2000. The personal perspectives on Alline Banks were provided by numerous interviews with numerous former teammates.

32. Blackstone Dozier, "Alline Pate Launched Phenomenal Cage Career at Eleven; She's Netted 388 This Year, 41 More Than Rivals," *NT*, 1945. This clipping

was in the scrapbook of Pollye Hudson, Alline's teammate on the Bomberettes and wife of the coach, Billy Hudson.

33. Yoder, "Legends Overlooked"; "Twentieth Century: The Fifty Greatest Sports Figures from Tennessee," *Sports Illustrated* 91 (27 December 99): 68–69. NBC never had any trouble filling out their tournament roster by flying in players who had not competed for the team during the year. Sally Nerren played for NBC in 1962–1963, then retired to get married. Because he was a couple of players short due to injury, Coach John Head flew Sally into St. Joseph in spring 1964. She got little playing time for the champions, who breezed through the tournament—Sally Nerren Phillips, telephone interview, Cleveland, TN, 28 April 2003.

34. Jane Ingram interview, 29 May 2000.

Chapter Four: Expansion and Consolidation

1. Gunter used the automobile metaphors during a discussion session at a Wayland/NBC reunion held at the WBHOF induction ceremonies in May 2003.

2. Handley Cross, "Six Girls and a Basket," *Street & Smith's Sport Story Magazine* 62 (March 1939): 45–52; www. Edmontongrads.com.futuresite.register.com/?.

3. "U.S. Five Loses in World Games at London," *Amateur Athlete* 3 (September 1932): 13; Lahoma Lassiter Carlton, telephone interview, Houston, TX, 4 December 2002.

4. Jane Marshall Ingram, telephone interview, Nashville, 21 July 2000, 18 January 2004; Pollye Hudson interviews, Nashville, 20 July 2000 and 8 May 2002; Anne Paradise Hansford Langston, interview, Nashville, 25 August 2002; Agnes Baldwin Webb, telephone interview, Clarksville, TN, 26 July 2000; Blanche McPherson Malone, telephone interview, Nashville, 26 September 2000; Sara Byrd Ragsdale, telephone interview, Nashville, 22 August 2000.

5. Alline Banks Sprouse, interview, Nashville, 26 April 2000.

6. "Agnes Baldwin, Fern Nash to Visit South America with All-Star Team," *Springfield* (TN) *Herald*, 13 April 1951, 1; Agnes Baldwin, Santiago, Chile, to her parents, 22 June 1951;Virgil Yow, Winston-Salem, NC, to Agnes Baldwin, 11 October 1951; "The Latin Hat That Aggie Bought in South America," *NT*, 5 August 1951, 18-A.

7. 'Heading South to the Tango and Rhumba Country," *NT*, 15 February 1953, 1-B; "Pauline Bowden Leads Americans to World Crown," *NB*, 23 March 1953; Janet Thompson Weston, telephone interview, Elliot, Iowa, 2 August 2002; Written synopsis of trip provided via electronic mail by Janet Weston, 19 August 2002; Betty Murphy Willis, telephone interview, Cross Plains, TN, 19 August 2002; J. Cowling Whitt, "Coach Head's NBC Girls Have That Winning Habit," *Nashville* 7 (February 1969): 33–36; http://www.usabasketball.com/factbook/wwc/wwchisl/htm.

8. Sylvia Fay Nadler, "A Developmental History of the Wayland Hutcherson Flying Queens from 1910 to 1979" (Ed.D. diss., East Texas State University, 1980), 29–32; Ailese Parten, "The Queens Fly High," in *The Queens Fly High* (Plainview, TX, 1958), 9–20; Bishop, "The Hutcherson Flying Queens of Wayland Baptist College, Plainview, Texas," in *Amateur Athletic Union Women's Basketball,* 34–43; Elva Bishop, "Women's Basketball: The Road to Respect," University of North Carolina Television, 1997; Cathy Harasta, "Flying Queens Took Basketball to New Heights," *DMN*, 1 July 2001, 1B; Agnes Baldwin Webb, personal interview,

Nashville, 28 November 2000; Patsy Neal, telephone interview, 1 November 2001; Margie Hunt McDonald, electronic mail, 26 August 2002; Carla Lowry, telephone interview, Georgetown, TX, 6 January 2003; Laura Switzer, telephone interview, Weatherford, OK, 17 January 2003; Katherine Washington interview, Knoxville, TN, 9 May 2003.

9. "Wayland Thumps NBC 38 to 21," *NT*, 25 March 1954, 25; "Kansas City Upsets Hanes Hosiery, 44–41," *NT*, 26 March 1954, 34; "Flying Queens Win National AAU Meet," *NT*, 27 March 1954, 11; "Nera White Stars with NBC in Women's A.A.U. Tourney," *Macon County Times*, 25 March 1954, 1.

10. Bill Scott, "The Wise Owl," *SJNP*, 27 February 1955, 10; "Nera White Named to All-American Squad," *Macon County Times*, 10 March 1955, 1; "Omaha Upsets NBC Six, 34–32," *NT*, 2 March 1955, 27; "Unheralded Omaha Squad Has Chance to Cut Down Champions," *SJNP*, 4 March 1955, 16; "Wayland Retains Title, Goetz Girls Win Third," *SJNP*, 5 March 1955, 9; "Wayland Queens Retain AAU Title," *Amateur Athlete* 26 (April 1955): 5, 24.

11. Tennie McGhee, "Women's Basketball Won by Wayland Flying Queens," *Amateur Athlete* 27 (May 1956): 23; "Wayland Edges NBC in Finals," *NT*, 17 March 1956, 13.

12. Tennie McGhee, "Flying Queens Win Fourth Hoop Crown," *Amateur Athlete* 28 (May 1957): 13; "Wayland, NBC in Semis," *NT*, 21 March 1957, 24; "Iowa Wesleyan Stuns NBC Six," *NT*, 22 March 1957, 48.

13. "NBC Shocks Wayland Six," *NT*, 21 March 1958, 48; Johnny Havlicek, "Six NBC Stars Russia-Bound," *NT* 23 March 1958, 5-C; "NBC Wins National AAU Title—Six Nashville Girls, Coach to Tour Russia," *NB*, 22 March 1958, 8.

14. "NBC to Play Russian Girls Twice; Loses in AAU Final," *NB*, 4 April 1959, 10; Lyle M. Foster, "Missouri Coronation," *Amateur Athlete* 30 (May 1959): 16–17.

15. Bishop, "Amateur Athletic Union Women's Basketball," 36–39; Sherman, *The Lure and the Lore of Basketball in Missouri*, 132; wbhof.com/wbhof/whf_inductees.html; hoophall.com/news/womens_nominees_042302.htm; Nadler, *A Developmental History of the Wayland Hutcherson Flying Queens*, 40–90; Redin, *The Queens Fly High*, 63–142; *Sports Illustrated* 91 (27 December 1999): 90.

16. "NBC's Alline Banks Again Named Best Woman Cager," *NB*, 29 March 1941, 6; http://www.aafla.org/8saa/PanAm/pan.am.history.htm.; http://www.usabasketball.com/factbook/wpanam/wpahisl.htm.

17. http://www.usabasketball.com/factbook/wwc/wwchisl.htm.; Whitt, *Nashville* 7, 33–36; Nera White interview, 28 September 2002; "Trip Diary of Ludy Davidon (*sic*), 1957 Women's World Basketball Championship Games," with permission of the author.

18. http://www.usabasketball.com/factbook/wpanam/wpahisl.htm; Laurine Mickelsen, "We Can Be Proud of the U.S. Women's Basketball Team," summary of 1959 Pan-Am Games by team manager Mickelsen, courtesy of the author; Mickelson, telephone interview, Washington, Utah, 17 January 2004.

19. Shirley Martin, "USA Girls Cage Team in Russia," *Women's National A.A.U. Basketball Championship Program, 1959*, 13; Bishop "Amateur Athletic Union Women's Basketball," 36–38; Martin Manning, electronic mail, Washington, D.C., 17 July 2003. Mr. Manning is with the Bureau of International Information Programs, U.S. Department of State.

Chapter Five: NBC, "the Greatest"

1. John Steen, "End to Recruiting Problems?" *NB*, 19 April 1958, 9; George Barker, "When Gals Go A-Courtin'," *NT Magazine*, 7 February 1960, 10–11, 16; "Organization of National League Proves Boon to Women's A.A.U. Basketball," *Basketball Championship* program 1961, 34; "Nashville B. C. and Nera White Rule Women's Basketball, *Amateur Athlete* 33 (May 1962): 12–13.

2. Tom Reno, "NBC Meets Wayland in AAU Finals," *NB*, 26 March 1960, 10; George Sherman, "Nashville Queen," *Amateur Athlete* 31 (April 1960): 8–9; "NBC Brings AAU Title Home Again," *NB*, 18 March 1960, 20; Johnny Havlicek, "NBC Salutes Stellar Six," *NT*, 29 March 1960, 15.

3. "NBC Faces Wayland in AAU Finals," *NB*, 8 April 1961, 10; "Three NBC Players Are Chosen on AAU All-Tournament Team," *NB*, 10 April 1961, 23; George Sherman, "Women's Basketball Round-up," *Amateur Athlete* 32 (May 1961): 18–19.

4. "NBC, Queens Gain Finals," *NT*, 7 April 62, 14; "NBC Roars to AAU Win," *NT*, 9 April 1962, 16; "Nashville B. C. and Nera White Rule Women's Basketball," *Amateur Athlete* 33 (May 1962): 12–13; "NBC Players to Face Russians," *NB*, 9 April 1962, 21; Chuck Edgley, "The Flying Queens Become Drudges," *Amateur Athlete* 33 (November 1962): 10.

5. Bill Isom, "NBC Stings Bees, Reaches AAU final," *NT*, 6 April 1963, 15; Isom, "NBC Six Wins National Title," *NT*, 7 April 1963, 1-E, 5-E; Lyle Foster, "Nashville Clings to Basketball Crown," *Amateur Athlete* 37 (May 1963): 15, 30; Isom, "Food Supplement Big Aid to NBC," *NT*, 8 April 1963, 18; Harley Redin, telephone interview, Plainview, TX, 10 June 2002; Nera White, telephone interview, Lafayette, TN, 6 October 2002.

6. Bill Isom, "NBC Wins 63–49; In Title Tilt Tonight," *NT*, 13 March 1964, 35; Isom, "NBC Cops AAU Crown," *NT*, 14 March 1964, 14; "NBC Favored for Third Straight National Title," *NB*, 9 March 1964, 27; "Crawford Tops; NBC Cops Sixth AAU Hoop Title," *NB*, 14 March 1964, 10; Charles Edgley, "It's Nashville . . . Again," *Amateur Athlete* 35 (April 1964): 12–13; Cross, "Six Girls and a Basket."

7. Cort Klein Jr., "National Sports Event in Gallup," *Gallup Independent* Souvenir edition, 5 April 1965; Official Program Women's National A.A.U. Basketball Championships, Gallup, NM, 1974; Moffatt telephone interview, Hot Springs, AR, 28 March 2002; Laurine Mickelsen telephone interview, Washington, Utah, 22 April 2002.

8. Sherman, *The Lure and the Lore of Basketball in Missouri*, 115–16.

9. "NBC Meets Omaha in National Semis," *NB*, 9 April 1965, 35; "NBC Adds to Record with Seventh Title," *NB*, 12 April 1965, 30; Bill Isom, "NBC Has Four on AA, White Named MVP," *NT*, 12 April 1965, 22.

10. Howard Graves, "Nera White Called 'Greatest Ever' As NBC Captures Fifth AAU Crown," *NB*, 28 March 1966, 25; Bill Isom, "NBC Cops AAU Title," *NT*, 27 March 1966, 1-E.

11. "NBC Gets 31–0 Lead, Buries Foe by 101–23," *NB*, 16 March 1967, 76; Bill Isom, "NBC Cops AAU Title Again," *NT*, 18 March 1967, 19; Edgar Allen, "Eight Former Nashville Players in Women's Basketball Hall of Fame," *NB* (clipping from Ingram scrapbook, precise date unknown); Sprouse and Gleaves interview, 29 April 2000; Ingram interview, 29 May 2000.

12. Bill Isom, "NBC Eyeing Seventh AAU Crown in Row," *NT*, 31 March 1968, 4-C; Isom, "NBC Rules Again," *NT*, 7 April 1968, 2-E; Larry Jarett, "Nashville Takes Seventh Straight Title," *Gallup Independent*, 8 April 1968, 4.

13. Letter, Jackie Fagg to author, March 2004; Bill Isom, "Helms Foundation Honors Balls, McGhee," *NT*, 5 April 1968, 44.

14. C. B. Fletcher, "Change in Tactics Nets Waverly Win," *NB*, 26 March 1968; Bill Isom, "NBC Opens Title Quest," *NT*, 26 March 1969, 37; Isom, "White Leads NBC Into AAU Finals," *NT*, 29 March 1969, 19; Isom, "NBC Wins Eighth National Crown," *NT*, 30 March 1969, 1-E, 4-E.

15. Bishop, "Shooting Stars," 52.

16. "Nera White Stars with NBC in Women's A.A.U. Tourney," *Macon County Times*, 25 March 1954, 1; "Nera White Named to All-American Squad," *Macon County Times*, 10 March 1955, 1; Sherman, *The Lure and the Lore of Basketball in Missouri*, 123; electronic mail from Bobbie White Holland (Nera White's sister), 18 January 2004. I obtained much information on Nera White's personal history and personality from her teammates, other players, and her family. I also had the pleasure of a multi-hour interview with her.

17. In addition to his business college, H. O. Balls also owned an auto-diesel "college" in Nashville.

18. Bill Isom, "AAU Women's Basketball Queen," *Amateur Athlete* 40 (November 1969): 6–8; "Second World Championship—1957," www.usabasketball.com; Dixie Woodall, telephone interview, Great Lake of the Cherokee, OK, 8 July 2000; Woodall, electronic mail, 30 April 2003.

19. Nera White, telephone interview, Lafayette, TN, 6 October 2002.

20. This compendium of White's skills comes from many conversations with those who saw her play. Among these were Patsy Neal (1 May 2000), Harley Redin (2 May 2000), Margie McDonald (17 May 2000), George Sherman (18 May 2000), Carolyn Moffatt (29 June 2000), Colleen Edwards (6 July 2000), Dixie Woodall (8 July 2000), Vic Varallo (24 July 2001), Carla Lowry (3 January 2003), and, on numerous occasions, Doris Rogers.

21. Margie Hunt McDonald, telephone interview, Laramie, WY, 17 May 2000.

22. Carolyn Moffatt, telephone interviews, Hot Springs, AR, 29 June 2000, 25 June 2002.

23. Bob Spencer, telephone interview, Bella Vista, Arkansas, 10 April 2002.

24. Nera White, personal interview, Lafayette, TN, 28 September 2002; Ann Matlock, telephone interview, Highlands Ranch, CO, 26 June 2000.

25. Jeff White, telephone interview, Bryan, TX, 22 May 2002.

26. *Amateur Athlete*, November 1969; Nera White file, Naismith Basketball Hall of Fame, Springfield, MA. This preliminary refusal of White's to attend her induction is akin to William Faulkner's alleged response to the Swedish ambassador who informed him he had won the Nobel Prize in literature. Faulkner was said to have expressed his gratitude but regretted his inability to go to Sweden as he was a farmer and could not leave his crops. Well, he and Nera both went.

27. Carla Lowry, telephone interview, Georgetown, TX, 6 January 2003; Larry Taft, "Hall of Fame Courting, but She Cries Foul," *TT*, 10 May 1992, 2; Taft, "AAU Programs Paved Way," *TT*, 7-C; Taft, "Coping with the Cruelty," *TT*; Taft, "Hall Commits to Women," *TT*; Taft, "At Home, Alone," *TT*, 6-C; Steve Marantz, "A Good Life Regretted," *Sporting News*, 4 March 1996, 32–35.

28. "Twentieth Century: The Fifty Greatest Sports Figures from Tennessee," *Sports Illustrated* 91 (27 December 1999): 68–69. Women fared well in this ranking. Ahead of White were Wilma Rudolph (1st), Pat Summitt (2d), and the swimmer Tracy Caulkins (4th). Alline Sprouse was listed #20. Coach John Head was #17. Expressing contempt for the selection process and saying she did not have time for such stuff, Nera White did not attend her induction into the WBHOF.

29. Hal Brock, "They Got Game Too," www.canoe.com/Hockey/oct17-women-sports.html. This account has a teenage Lieberman calling White. In conversations with me (9/28, 10/6/02), Nera depicted the exchange as here recorded. The connection between Lieberman and White was highlighted in Mike Lupica's fantastic book, *Full-Court Press*, for which Lieberman was a consultant. In this modern fable about the first woman to successfully play in the NBA, the protagonist meets an old NBC point guard who had supposedly fed White the ball during games. They discuss whether White was the greatest. When told this tale, White reminded that no one would be feeding her the ball, as she usually led the offense out front. See Mike Lupica, *Full-Court Press* (New York: G. P. Putnam's Sons, 2001).

30. Sue Gunter, telephone interview, Baton Rouge, LA, 9 July 2002; Sally Smith, telephone interview, Ft. Pierce, FL, 29 August 2002; Nera White, personal interview, Lafayette, TN, 28 September 2002; Carla Lowry, telephone interview, Georgetown, TX, 6 January 2003. I did not see the "Coldslaw" story in the newspaper. Doris Rogers first related it to me. Margie McDonald confirmed it via electronic mail, 5 May 2000. Margie thought that, in general, players today were better than the AAU players—except for Nera that is.

31. Isom, "Cage Hall of Fame Honors Head," *NT*, 18 March 1970, 30; "Basketball Mentor John L. Head Dies," *NT*, 9 May 1980, 30; "Legendary Coach John Head Dies," *NT*, 9 May 1980, 25, 31; Patsy Neal, *At the Rim*, 23; material from Head papers obtained from Verna Head, his wife.

32. http://www.usabasketball.com/factbook/wpanam/wpahisl.htm.

33. Shirley Martin, "USA Girls Cage Team in Russia," *Women's National A.A.U. Basketball Championship* program, 1959, 13; Bishop, "Amateur Athletic Union Women's Basketball," 36–38.

34. Ibid.; http://www.usabasketball.com/factbook/wpanam/wpahiisl.htm.

35. Joan Crawford, telephone interview, Tulsa, OK, 14 May 2002; Alberta Cox, telephone interview, Raytown, MO, 15 May 2002. The Loretta Young story and a copy of her letter were provided by Laurine Mickelsen, January 2004.

36. Hult, "The Saga of Competition: Basketball Battles and Governance War," in *A Century of Women's Basketball*, 229–35.

Chapter Six: Looking Back and Ahead

1. Korsgaard, "A History of the Amateur Athletic Union of the United States" (D.Ed. Diss., Teachers College, Columbia University, 1952); "Durant Teachers defend National Championship against Dallas Cyclones Here Tonight," *WB*, 24 March 1933, 14; Alberta Cox telephone interview, Raytown, 16 June 2001; www.aaujrogames.org/; Laurine Mickelsen telephone interviews, Washington, Utah, 24 July 2000, 11 October 2002; Mary Jane Ingram, telephone interview, Nashville, 29 May 2000; Agnes Baldwin Webb, telephone interview, Clarksville, TN, 26 July 2000; Patsy Neal, telephone interview, Bybee, TN, 1 May 2000; Patsy Neal, *Basketball Techniques for Women* (New York: Ronald Press Co., 1966).

2. Hollander, *The Modern Encyclopedia of Basketball*, 267–68; Tom Harmon, "Generals Dethrone Queens," *AAU News* 46 (May 1976): 3, 4; Peg Morrell, "Ripe Bananas Peel off 1977 Crown," *AAU News* 48 (July 1977): 8; Marc Markowitz, "Bananas Peel off Second Straight," *AAU News* 49 (May 1978): 3, 4; Markowitz, "Bananas: Three Makes It 'A Bunch,'" *AAU News* 50 (May 1979): 3, 4.

3. Jill Hutchison, "Women's Intercollegiate Basketball: AIAW/NCAA," in *A Century of Women's Basketball*, 309–26; Fran M. Hoogestrant, "A Portraiture of the Female Intercollegiate Athletic Experience in Four Elite Women's Basketball Programs" (Ed.D. diss., Peabody College of Vanderbilt University, 1997).

4. www.geocities.com/Collosseum; www.womensbasketballmuseum.com; Bob Spencer, telephone interviews, BellaVista, AR, 10 April 2002, 28 May 2002. Material provided by Lynn Ellsworth, archivist, Iowa Wesleyan College, 1 August 2001; Beran, *From Six-on-Six to Full-Court Press*, 149–67.

5. Alberta Cox, telephone interview, Raytown, 26 June 2002.

6. George Leonard, "Hudson's Girl Cagers Win 304 of 316 Games," *NB*, 20 January 1947, 9; "Former Basketball Coach Billy Hudson Services Held," *NB*, 7 November 1977, 9. Opinions on the relative merits of the Nashville coaches were obtained from multiple interviews with women who played for them.

7. Buck Turnbull, "Ruble's Cagers Are Now Grandmothers," *Des Moines Register Peach*, D-1, 1974 (clipping supplied by Janet Weston, precise date unknown); information provided by Keith Kohorst, Iowa Wesleyan sports information director.

8. Colleen Edwards, telephone interview, Augusta, KS, 6 July 2000; Connie Dillow (widow of the president of JFK College), telephone interview, Wahoo, NE, 9 April 2002; Bob Spencer, telephone interviews, Bella Vista, Arkansas, 10 April 2002, 28 May 2002; Kristen Miller, WBCA manager of Office Administration and Awards, electronic mail, 2 July 2002. Other AAU-associated people who have won the Jostens–Berenson award are Alberta Cox (1991), Harley Redin (1992), and Patsy Neal (1993).

9. Lynn Hickey, telephone interview, San Antonio, TX, 25 September 2002; goutsa.com/player_bios/staff/hickey.htm; "Changing the Game," *Sports Illustrated* 98 (5 May 2003): 46.

10. esu.edu/athletics/simpson.htm.

11. http://texastech.ocsn.com/sports/w-baskbl/mtt/sharp_marsha00.html.

12. kuathletics.com/womensbsketball/coaches/wbbwashington.html; Jill Hutchison, "Women's Intercollegiate Basketball: AIAW/NCAA," *A Century of Women's Basketball*, 309–10; Sparhawk, *American Women in Sport*, 45, 55, 62, 69; Chris Law, "Hall of Famers Rogers Hatchell Have Local Ties," *TT*, 11 June 2004, 6C.

13. lsusports.net/bio.cfm.; LSU Sports Information Department.

14. Patsy Neal, "Basketballs, Goldfish, and World Championships," in *A Century of Women's Basketball*, 345–53; Margie McDonald, electronic mail, 19 January 2004.

15. www.usabasketball.com/history/wpag_affil_roster.html; www.usabasketball.com/history/wwc_coaches.html.

16. Trudy Tynan, "Public Fickle in Support of Sports Halls of Fame," *TT*, 12 October 2000, 3C; Jane Ingram, telephone interview, Nashville, 29 May 2000; Alline Banks Sprouse, telephone interview, Manchester, TN, 12 June 2000; Michael Salmon (research librarian AAFLA), telephone interview, Los Angeles, CA, 14 July 2000; "Chronology of the Helms Athletic Foundation"; "Bank Adopts Athletic Foundation; Inherits Employee of Yesteryear." The latter two documents were pro-

vided by Michael Salmon. The Naismith Hall of Fame opened its new building in September 2002.

17. hoophall.com/halloffamers/Category.htm; hoophall.com/halloffamers/enshrinement_process.htm.

18. www.wbhof.com/menu.htm. Opinions on the hall come from many former AAU basketball players. I visited the hall in December 2001 and May 2003.

19. Gene Sullivan, "Wise Owl," *SJNP*, 28 March 1940, 15.

20. Joan Crawford, telephone interview, Evanston, IL, 28 March 2000; Marantz, "A Good Life Regretted."

21. Carla Lowry, telephone interview, Georgetown, TX, 6 January 2003.

22. U.S. Bureau of the Census. *Fifteenth Census of the United States: 1930*. U.S. Department of Commerce. Vol. 3, Pt. 1. U.S. Government Printing Office, Washington, D.C., 1932; U.S. Bureau of the Census. *Census of the Population: 1960*. Vol. I, Part 27. U.S. Department of Commerce, U.S. Government Printing Office, Washington, D.C., 1963.

23. U.S. Bureau of the Census. *Historical Statistics of the United States, Colonial Times to 1970, Bicentennial Edition, Part 2*, Washington, D.C., 1975; Ibid., *U.S. population: 1960*. Vol. 1, *Characteristics of the Population*. Part 1, United States Summary. U.S. Government Printing Office, Washington, D.C., 1994.

24. The graduating class sizes were obtained from interviews of these and other players. U.S. Bureau of the Census. *U.S. Census of Population: 1950*. Vol. 1, *Number of Inhabitants*, U.S. Government Printing Office, Washington, D.C., 1952; U.S. Bureau of the Census. *U.S. Census of Population: 1960*, Vol. 1, Part A. U.S. Department of Commerce. U.S. Government Printing Office, Washington, D.C., 1961.

25. This information on the players' sports interests beyond basketball came from interviews of each of them.

26. "Tulsa Wins over Chicago in Exhibition," *WB*, 1 April 1934, 11 A; Sherman, *The Lure and the Lore of Basketball in Missouri*, 125–26.

27. *The College Catalog: Philander Smith College*, 2001–2002, 15–19; "Ark. Coed First Negro Girls' Cage All-American," *Jet* 7 (24 March 55): 53; Isom, "Lane Forfeits; NBC Wins, 2 to 0," *NT*, 3 April 1953, 46; Missouri Arledge Morris, telephone interview, Durham, NC, 2 September 2002; Clippings from the *Arkansas Press* electronically mailed to Missouri Morris, 25 November 2002. Missouri Morris's son, Cliff, had an interesting basketball experience. He "walked on" the basketball team at the University of North Carolina at the behest of then assistant basketball coach, Roy Williams. He then won a scholarship, largely by guarding the great Michael Jordan in practice; Missouri Morris telephone interview, 19 March 2004.

28. Telephone interviews, Sally Smith, Ft. Pierce, FL, 18 January 2001, 29 August 2002; telephone interviews, Colleen Edwards, Augusta, KS, 6 July 2000, 2 September 2002, 23 December 2002; Nera White interview, Lafayette, TN, 28 September 2002; telephone interview, Laurine Mickelson, 17 January 2004. Contemporaneous with Sally Smith's integration of the NBC team, a notably similar event was occurring across town in Nashville. Perry Wallace, from Nashville, became the first black basketball player in the Southeastern Conference when he signed a scholarship with Vanderbilt University in 1966. The experience was rough, but the talented, introspective athlete prevailed. See Jack Hurst, "The Other Guys on the Court Played basketball. Perry Wallace played for history," *Nashville Scene*, 19 February 2004, 21–23.

29. Tunku Varadarajan, "Rectus Abdominis: The Bulking Up of Women's Tennis," *WSJ*, 29 August 2002, D10.

30. Jane Ingram interview, Nashville, 7 September 2000.

31. Susan K. Cahn, *Coming on Strong* (New York: Free Press, 1994); Margie McDonald, telephone interview, Laramie, WY, 17 May 2000. As noted in the preface, the author did not study the sexuality of AAU players. For elaboration on this topic, see also Mariah Burton Nelson, *Are We Winning Yet?* (New York: Random House, 1991); Lissa Smith, ed., *Nike Is a Goddess* (New York: Atlantic Monthly Press, 1998); Stephanie L. Twin, *Out of the Bleachers: Writing on Women and Sport* (Old Westbury, NY: Feminist Press, 1979); Pat Griffin, *Strong Women, Deep Closets: Lesbians and Homophobia in Sport* (Champaign, IL: Human Kinetics, 1998).

32. Barbara Sipes, telephone interview, Dexter, IA, 26 June 2000.

33. Electronic-mail correspondence from Joan Crawford, 9 August 2002. Joan played with the less-than-loquacious Nera White for over a decade. There was little chatter or trash-talking by the NBC team. They established their dominance by beating the other team, not talking.

34. Jill Upton, telephone interview, Dallas, TX, 18 July 2002.

35. Peggy Stanaland, "The Early Years of Basketball in Kentucky," in *A Century of Women's Basketball*, 167–79.

36. Scott Johnson, "Not Altogether Ladylike," www.ihsa.org/feature/hstoric/earlybkg.htm. Johnson is an official of the Illinois High School Association.

37. Beran, *From Six-on-Six to Full-Court Press*, 100. Like Beran, I obtained my data by canvassing state high school athletic associations.

38. Bob Hill and Randall Barron, *The Amazing Basketball Book: The First One Hundred Years* (Louisville, KY: Full Court Press, 1988), 55.

39. Paul Kuharsky, "Playing the Eaglette Way," *TT*, 10 February 2002, 7C; Jessica Hopp, "Shelbyville's dandy dozen," *TT*, 14 March 2004, 10C; Alexander Wolff, "The High School Athlete," *Sports Illustrated* 97 (18 November 2002): 74–92; Michelle Hickey, "Athletes and Ladies," *Atlanta Journal Constitution,* 17 August 2003.

40. "Sleep has to wait for top women's scorer," *NT*, 29 March 2001, 7C; Kelli Anderson, "Jackie O," *Sports Illustrated*, 23 July 2001, 46–47.

41. Jane Marshall Ingram, telephone interview, Nashville, 14 August 2002, 15 August 2002. Mary Henry of Little Rock was with the Goldblumes only in 1947. She was not married at that time, and her subsequent life story could not be determined.

42. Doris Rogers, personal interview, Nashville, 12 April 2000; telephone interview, 26 July 2002; Bill Parker, "Nashville Business College Team City's Most Successful Sports Story?" *NB*, 30 March 1962, 19.

43. Telephone interviews with Joan Crawford, 28 March 2000; Patsy Neal, 1 May 2000; and Agnes Baldwin Webb, 19 September 2000.

44. Margie McDonald, electronic mail, Laramie, WY, 26 December 2002; Lowry telephone interview, Georgetown, TX, 6 January 2003; Switzer telephone interview, Weatherford, OK, 17 January 2003.

45. Gerald Matthews, Ian J. Deary, and Martha C. Whiteman, *Personality Traits,* 2nd ed. (Cambridge: Cambridge University Press, 2003), 54.

BIBLIOGRAPHY

Interviews

Margaret Dean Akin (Millington, Tennessee)

Edgar Allen (Nashville, Tennessee)

Alice Barron (Lakewood, Colorado)

Janice Beran (Ames, Iowa)

Doris McPherson Bingham (Nashville)

Elva Bishop (Chapel Hill, North Carolina)

Pauline Lunn Bowden (Nashville)

Lahoma Lassiter Carlton (Houston, Texas)

Lera Dunford Chadwick (Des Arc, Arkansas)

Tennie Cathey Chaffin (Columbia, Tennessee)

Virginia Hamilton Childers (Durant, Oklahoma)

Mae Sharp Chitwood (Helenwood, Tennessee)

Judy Coble (Nashville)

Bea Baldwin Covington (Cross Plains, Tennessee)

Alberta Cox (Liberty, Missouri)

Joan Crawford (Evanston, Illinois; Tulsa, Oklahoma)

Lucille Davidson (Independence, Missouri)

Fred Dettwiller (Nashville)

Connie Dillow (Wahoo, Nebraska)

Margaret Dunaway (Conway, Arkansas)

Robert Duncan (Columbia, Tennessee)

Colleen Edwards (Augusta, Kansas)

Lynne Emery (Pasadena, California)

Jackie Swaim Fagg (Winston-Salem, North Carolina)

Janet Fairchild (Adams, Tennessee)

Keith Fenton (Scottsdale, Arizona)

Eunies Futch (Winston-Salem, North Carolina)

Fran Garmon (Moody, Texas)

Francies Garroute (Cabot, Arkansas)

Margaret Sexton Gleaves (Nashville)

Sue Gunter (Baton Rouge, Louisiana)

Diane Hall (Heber Springs, Arkansas)

Elner Hamner (Nashville)

Becky Harris Hartman (Knoxville, Tennessee)

Verna Head (Hendersonville, Tennessee)

Lynn Hickey (San Antonio, Texas)

Bobbie White Holland (Lafayette, Tennessee)

Pollye Hudson (Brentwood, Tennessee)

Joan Hult (Greenbelt, Maryland)

Mary Jane Marshall Ingram (Nashville)

Cheryl Irby (Murfreesboro, Tennessee)

Evelyn Jordan (Winston-Salem, North Carolina)

Sam Kennedy (Columbia, Tennessee)

Florence Woodman Krohn (Prairie City, Iowa)

Anne Paradise Hansford Langston (Isle of Palms, South Carolina; Nashville)

Jack Little (Nashville)

Joe Livingston (Jacksonville, Florida)

Carla Lowry (Georgetown, Texas)

Alice Cagle Loyd (Whites Creek, Tennessee)

Margie Hunt McDonald (Laramie, Wyoming)

Blanche McPherson Malone (Nashville)

Ann Matlock (Highlands Ranch, Colorado)

Laurine Mickelsen (Washington, Utah)

Carolyn Miller (Hockley, Texas)

Carolyn Moffatt (Hot Springs, Arkansas)

Missouri Arledge Morris (Durham, North Carolina)

Rebecca Brown Morrison (Columbia, Tennessee)

Kathleen Whiteside Morton (Hampshire, Tennessee)

Sylvia Nadler (Liberty, Missouri)

Judy Robinson Nance (Paris, Tennessee)

Patsy Neal (Bybee, Tennessee)

Gary Newton (Los Angeles, California)

George Nicodemus (Hereford, Arizona)

Bettye Patton (Hampshire, Tennessee)

Sally Nerren Phillips (Cleveland, Tennessee)

Buck Pardue (Nashville)

Joe Provence (Plainview, Texas)

Sarah Jane Byrd Ragsdale (Nashville)

Harley Redin (Plainview, Texas)

Lee Reeder (Edmond, Oklahoma)

Doris Rogers (Nashville)

Lurlyne Greer Rogers (Heber Springs, Arkansas)

Sissy Rogers (Nashville)

Fred Russell (Nashville)

Michael Salmon (Los Angeles, California)
George Sherman (St. Joseph, Missouri)
Barbara Sipes (Dexter, Iowa)
Kermit Smith (Pulaski, Tennessee)
Sally Smith (Fort Pierce, Florida)
Wendy Smith (Nashville)
Bob Spencer (Bella Vista, Arkansas)
Alline Banks Sprouse (Nashville; Manchester, Tennessee)
Laura Switzer (Weatherford, Oklahoma)
Larry Taft (Nashville)
Edward Temple (Nashville)
Jill Upton (Dallas, Texas)
Vic Varallo (Nashville)
Katherine Washington (Murfreesboro, Tennessee)
Marian Washington (Lawrence, Kansas)
Agnes Baldwin Webb (Clarksville, Tennessee; Nashville)
Charles S. Wells Jr. (Nashville)
Janet Thompson Weston (Elliot, Iowa)
Jeff White (Bryan, Texas)
Nera White (Lafayette, Tennessee)
Cecil Whiteside (Hampshire, Tennessee)
Jimmie Vaughn Williams (Winston-Salem, North Carolina)
Betty Murphy Willis (Cross Plains, Tennessee)
Mary Link Winslow (Altoona, Iowa)
Dixie Woodall (Jenks, Oklahoma)

Newspapers

Arkansas Press
Atlanta Journal
Atlanta Journal-Constitution
Bryan County (Oklahoma) *Star*
Daily Herald (Columbia, Tennessee)
Dallas Morning News
Des Moines Register Peach
Gallup Independent
Galveston Daily News
Los Angeles Times
Macon County (Tennessee) *Times*
Manchester (Tennessee) *Times*
Maury Democrat (Columbia, Tennessee)

Nashville Banner
Nashville Scene
Nashville Sports Weekly
Nashville Tennessean (from 1972, *The Tennessean*)
Robertson County (Tennessee) *Times*
Saint Joseph Gazette
Saint Joseph News-Press
Shreveport Times
Springfield (Tennessee) *Herald*
Tulsa Daily World
Wall Street Journal
Wichita Beacon

Magazines

Amateur Athlete
AAU News
Colliers
Sports Illustrated

Books

Anderson, Jackson M. *Industrial Recreation: A Guide to Its Organization and Administration*. New York: McGraw-Hill, 1955.

Beran, Janice A. *From Six-on-Six to Full Court Press*. Ames: Iowa University Press, 1993.

Bondi, Victor, ed. *American Decades 1930–1939*. Detroit, MI: Gale Research, Inc., 1995.

Bondi, Victor, ed. *American Decades 1940–1949*. Detroit, MI: Gale Research, Inc., 1995.

Brinkley, Alan. *Culture and Politics in the Great Depression*. Waco, TX: Markham Press Fund, 1998.

Cahn, Susan K. *Coming on Strong*. New York: Free Press, 1994.

Cayleff, Susan E. *Babe*. Urbana: University of Illinois Press, 1995.

Childers, Virginia Hamilton. "History of the Oklahoma Presbyterian College Cardinal National and North American Basketball Championship Teams." In *The History of Bryan County*. Durant, OK: Bryan County Heritage Association, Inc., 1983.

Culin, Stewart. *Games of the North American Indians,* vol. 2, *Games of Skill*. Lincoln, University of Nebraska Press, 1992.

Doyle, Don. *Nashville since the 1920s*. Knoxville: University of Tennessee Press, 1985.

Ebert, Frances H., and Billye Ann Cheatum. *Basketball: Five Player*. Philadelphia, PA: W. B. Saunders Company, 1972.

Ford, Linda. *Lady Hoopsters: A History of Women's Basketball in America*. Northampton, MA: Half Moon Books, 2000.

Garkovich, Lorraine. *Population and Community in Rural America*. New York: Greenwood Press, 1989.

Griffin, Pat. *Strong Women, Deep Closets*. Champaign, IL: Human Kinetics, 1998.

Guttman, Allen. *Women's Sports: A History*. New York: Columbia University Press, 1991.

Halberstam, David. *The Fifties*. New York: Villard Books, 1993.

Hill, Bob, and Randall Baron. *The Amazing Basketball Book: The First One Hundred Years*. Louisville, KY: Full Court Press, 1988.

Hollander, Zander, ed. *The Modern Encyclopedia of Basketball*. Garden City, NY: Doubleday & Company, Inc., 1979.

Howell, Reet, ed. *Her Story in Sport*. West Point, NY: Leisure Press, 1982.

Hult, Joan S., and Marianna Trekell, eds. *A Century of Women's Basketball: From Frailty to Final Four*. Reston, VA: American Alliance for Health, Physical Education, Recreation and Dance, 1991.

Kennedy, David M. *Freedom from Fear: The American People in Depression and War, 1929–1945*. New York: Oxford University Press, 1999.

Lannin, Joanne. *A History of Basketball for Girls and Women: From Bloomers to Big Leagues*. Minneapolis, MN: Lerner Sports, 2000.

Layman, Richard, ed. *American Decades 1950–1959*. Detroit, MI: Gale Research, Inc., 1994.

Layman, Richard, ed. *American Decades 1960–1969*. Detroit, MI: Gale Research, Inc., 1995.

Lupica, Mike. *Full-Court Press*. New York: G. P. Putnam's Sons, 2001.

MacCready, Henry. *Queen of Three Valleys: A Story of Durant*. Durant, OK: Democrat Printing Company, 1946.

Matthews, Gerald, Ian J. Deary, and Martha C. Whiteman, *Personality Traits*. 2nd ed. Cambridge: Cambridge University Press, 2003.

McGovern, James R. *And a Time for Hope: Americans in the Great Depression*. Westport, CT: Prager Publishers, 2000.

Naismith, James. *Basketball: Its Origins and Development*. New York: Associated Press, 1941.

Nashville City Directory. Nashville: Marshall-Bruce-Polk, 1924.

Neal, Patsy. *Basketball Techniques for Women*. New York: Ronald Press Company, 1966.

Nelson, Mariah Burton. *Are We Winning Yet?* New York: Random House, 1991.

Oxendine, Joseph B. *American Indian Sports Heritage*. Champaign, IL: Human Kinetics, 1988.

Patton, Bettye, ed. *Hampshire Then and Now*. Printed for Hampshire's Tennessee 2000 Bicentennial Committee.

Redin, Harley J. *The Queens Fly High*. Plainview, TX: Wayland Baptist College, 1958.

Rush, Cathy, with Laurie Mifflin. *Women's Basketball*. New York: Hawthorn Books, Inc., 1976.

Sherman, George. *The Lure and the Lore of Basketball in Missouri*. Virginia Beach, VA: Donning Company Publishers, 1994.

Sherrow, Victoria. *Encyclopedia of Women and Sports*. Santa Barbara, CA: ABC-CLIO, Inc., 1996.

Simpson, J. A., and E. S. C. Weiner, eds. *The Oxford English Dictionary*, 2d ed., vol. 1. Oxford: Clarendon Press, 1989.

Smith, Lissa, ed. *Nike Is a Goddess*. New York: Atlantic Monthly Press, 1998.

Spalding Athletic Library, 1914. Web address: clio.fivecolleges.edu/smith/berenson/5pubs/bball_smith/index.shtml?

Sparhawk, Ruth M., Mary E. Leslie, Phyllis Y. Turbow, Phyllis and Zina R. Rose. *American Women in Sport, 1887–1987: A One-Hundred-Year Chronology*. Metuchen, NJ: Scarecrow Press, Inc., 1989.

Spinney, Robert G. *World War II in Nashville*. Knoxville: University of Tennessee Press, 1998.

Twin, Stephanie L., ed. *Out of the Bleachers: Writing on Women and Sport*. Old Westbury, NY: Feminist Press, 1979.

Very Special Arkansas Women. Little Rock, AR: First Commercial Bank, 1986.

Webb, Bernice Larson. *The Basketball Man: James Naismith*. Lawrence: University of Kansas Press, 1973.

Wilson, R. Jackson, James Gilbert, Stephen Nissenbaum, Karen Kupperman, and Donald Scott, eds. *The Pursuit of Liberty*, 2d ed. Belmont, CA: Wadsworth Publishing Company, 1990.

Articles

Berenson, Senda. "Basketball for Women." *Physical Education* 3 (September 1894): 106–9.

Bishop, Elva, and Katherine Fulton. "Shooting Stars: The Heyday of Industrial Women's Basketball." *Southern Exposure* 8 (Fall 1979): 50–56.

Cross, Handley. "Six Girls and a Basket." *Street and Smith's Sport Magazine* 62 (March 1939): 45–52.

Hill, Edith Naomi. "Senda Berenson: Director of Physical Education at Smith College, 1892–1911." *Research Quarterly* (October 1941): 658–65.

"Arkansas Coed First Negro Girls' Cage All-American." *Jet* 7 (24 March 1955): 53.

Jokl, Ernst. "The Athletic Status of Women." *Amateur Athlete* 33 (May 1962): 14–15, 23.

Lagemann, John Kord. "Red Heads, You Kill Me." *Colliers* 119 (8 February 1947): 64–66.

Marantz, Steve. "A Good Life Regretted." *Sporting News* (4 March 1996): 32–35.

Neal, Patsy. "Introduction." In *At the Rim*. Charlottesville, VA: Thomasson-Grant, Inc., and Eastman Kodak Company, 1991.

Ogilvie, Bruce C. "Psychological Consistencies within the Personality of High-Level Competitors." *Journal of the American Medical Association* 205 (9 September 1968): 156–62.

Tiller, Guy. "Basketball Belles." *Sportfolio* (April 1948).

"Twentieth Century: The Fifty Greatest Sports Figures from Arkansas." 91
(27 December 1999), 74.

"Twentieth Century: The Fifty Greatest Sports Figures from Tennessee." 91
(27 December 1999), 68–69.

"Twentieth Century: The Fifty Greatest Sports Figures from Texas." 91
(27 December 1999), 90.

Videorecording

Bishop, Elva. *Women's Basketball: The Road to Respect*. University of North Carolina
Television, 1997.

Dissertations/Theses

Bishop, Elva Elisabeth. "Amateur Athletic Union Women's Basketball, 1950–1971:
The Contributions of Hanes Hosiery, Nashville Business College, and
Wayland Baptist College." Master's thesis, University of North Carolina,
Chapel Hill, 1984.

Hoogestraat, Fran M. "Qualitative Portraiture of the Female Intercollegiate Athlete
Experience in Four Elite Women's Basketball Programs." Ed.D. diss.,
Peabody College of Vanderbilt University, 1997.

Koenig, Frances Becker. "Comparative Analysis of Selected Personal and Social
Background Characteristics of High School Girls at Three Levels of
Participation in Basketball." Ph.D. diss., Michigan State University, 1969.

Korsgaard, Robert. "A History of the Amateur Athletic Union of the United States."
Ed.D. diss., Teachers College, Columbia University, 1952.

McCray, Mary Elizabeth. "A Documented Analysis of Rule Changes in Women's
Basketball from 1935 to 1970." Master's thesis, Springfield College, 1971.

Nadler, Sylvia Faye. "A Developmental History of the Wayland Hutcherson Flying
Queens from 1910 to 1979." Ed.D. diss., East Texas State University, 1980.

Semple, Anne. "Ties That Bind: The Story of Oklahoma Presbyterian College."
Ed.D. diss., Oklahoma State University, date unavailable.

Government Publications

U.S. Bureau of the Census. *U.S. Population: 1960*. Vol. 1, *Characteristics of the
Population*. Part 1, United States Summary. Washington, D.C.: U.S.
Government Printing Office, 1964.

U.S. Bureau of the Census. *U.S. Census of Population: 1960*. Vol. 1, *Characteristics of
the Population*. Part 26, Mississippi. Washington, D.C.: U.S. Government
Printing Office, 1963.

U.S. Bureau of the Census. *U.S. Population: 1960* Vol. 1, *Characteristics of the
Population*. Part 1, United States Summary. Washington, D.C.: U.S.
Government Printing Office, 1964.

U.S. Bureau of the Census. *Fifteenth Census of the United States: 1930*. U.S. Department of Commerce. Vol. 3, Part 1. Washhington, D.C.: U.S.Government Printing Office, 1932.

U.S. Bureau of the Census. *Sixteenth Census of the United States: 1940*. U.S. Department of Commerce. Vol. 2, Part 4. Washington, D.C.: U.S. Government Printing Office, 1943.

INDEX

AAU Hall of Fame, 91, 127, 144
Ada Teachers College, 32
Adkins, Beth, 182
Agee, Gene, Jr., 122
AIB. *See* American Institute of
   Business Secretaries
AIC. *See* American Institute of
   Commerce Stenos
Alexander, Rita, 112, 118
All-American teams: in 1929, 32, 201;
   of 1931, 33; of 1932, 36; of 1933,
   36; of 1935, 40; of 1937, 43; of
   1941, 49–50; of 1942–43, 52, 53; of
   1944–45, 55–56; of 1946, 58; of
   1949, 65; of 1950, 66; of 1955, 111;
   of 1958, 112; of 1961–62, 125; in
   1963, 126–27; in 1965, 130; in
   1968, 132; of 1969, 134; Banks on,
   87, 88; Crawford/Rogers on, 136;
   first black player, 185; first for
   women's basketball, 32; Hickey on,
   168; Neal on, 108–9; OPC players
   on, 38–39; player on by year,
   201–14; players from Iowa
   Wesleyan, 161; players from
   Wayland Flying Queens, 161; Sipes
   on, 190; Texas players on, 46;
   Walker on, 24; White on, 143
Allen, Allean, 16
Allen, Howard, 33
Allen, Sam, 105
Allentown team, 158
All-Star Team (author choices),
   219–21
Amarillo Dowell's Dolls, 117
Amateur Athletic Foundation of Los
   Angeles (AAFLA), 174
Amateur Athletic Union (AAU), 32;
   coaches of/from, 164–70 (*see also
   specific coach*); demise of, 114; eligi-
   bility of players, 64–65, 85, 86, 91,
   195; encouragement of interna-
   tional competitions, 96–104;

epicenter of women's basketball,
   29–30, 46, 51; filling historical gap,
   13; game governance by, 177–80;
   geographic distribution of teams,
   69; history of, 155–58; inclusion of
   Mexican teams, 97; national teams
   populated by, 95, 170–73; organizational changes, 156; overview of
   the game under, 177–80; players of,
   180–91, 194–95 (*see also specific
   player*); portrayal of women's
   basketball in 1930s, 30; promulga-
   tion of rules, 14; provision for public athletic competitions, 15;
   publicity for, xiii, 15–17, 20, 30,
   46, 76, 92, 131, 153, 179, 197;
   recognition by halls of fame,
   174–77; rules changes, 40–41, 63,
   69; success of, xiii–xv. *See also* All-
   American teams; beauty contest;
   championship tournaments; free-
   throw champions; *specific teams*
American Association for Health,
   Physical Education, and Recreation
   (AAHPER), 158
American Institute of Business
   Secretaries: in 1936 tournament,
   42; in 1939 tournament, 45; in
   1941 tournament, 48; in 1943–44
   tournament, 54; in 1946 tourna-
   ment, 24; at 1947 tournament, 61;
   at 1951 tournament, 69; back-
   ground of, 51, 52; coach of, 165;
   sponsor, xiii
American Institute of Commerce
   Stenos, 51, 52, 70, 72, 102, 165
American Medical Association, 153
American Physical Education
   Association (APEA), 11
Anna's Bananas, 158
Arkansas girls' basketball, 194
Arkansas Sports Hall of Fame, 29
Arkansas Tech team, 110

NOTE: Page numbers in *italic* type indicate a photograph.

Arkansas Travelers, 26, 28, 85, 98
Arledge, Missouri, *186*
Aspedon, Carole Phillips, 152
Association for Intercollegiate Athletics
for Women (AIAW), 159–60,
162–63
athletic clubs, 3, 14
Atlanta Blues: at 1947 tournament,
60, 61, *62*, 165; background of, 59;
Banks as player for, 91; big three at
practice, *60;* coaches of, 165; exhibition game with new rules, 69; at
photo ops 1948 tournament, 63;
players of, 77, *78*
Auriemma, Geno, 1, 2

Babb, Sam F.: as best of AAU coaches,
165; as coach of Galveston team, 43;
as coach of OPC Cardinals, 34–35;
as coach of Shreveport team, 40; as
coach of U.S. team in London, 97;
disbanding of Cardinals, 38–39; in
Oklahoma Hall of Fame, 39
Baer, Clara, 10
Baldwin, Agnes, 101–2, *104*, 157,
182, 198
Baldwin, Bea, 63
Balls, Angie, 57
Balls, H. O.: as coach of NBC team,
42; financial support of players,
197; Helms Foundation honoree,
132; help for Banks continued
AAU play, 64, 91; Naismith Hall
of Fame and, 175; racial attitudes
of, 186–87; recruitment of Head,
63, 146; view of full-court play,
132–33; view of international
competitions, 152; withdrawal
of NBC, 134
ball size, 11, 178–79
Banks, Alline: in 1940–41 tournaments,
47, 48; at 1944–45 tournaments, *56;*
at 1946 tournament, 58; at 1947
tournament, 61, 165; at 1949–50
tournament, 64–65; as All-
American, 55; as Atlanta Blues
player, *62, 78;* attitude of, 77, 92;

awards of, *90,* 91; background of,
87; basketball career of, xiii, 87; eligibility of, 195; Helms Hall of Fame
induction, 131; marriage to Sprouse,
64; move to Atlanta Blues, 59, 82;
move to Cook's Goldblumes,
57–58; Naismith Hall of Fame and,
175; Olympic cancellation and, 101;
at practice for Atlanta, *60;* publicity
and, *179;* relaxing, *190;* retirement
of, 91; on *Sports Illustrated* list of
sport figures, 235n28; sportswriters'
interest in, 47, 60; Sullivan Award
nomination, 144; supremacy of play
of, 53, 54, 55; teammate's feelings
toward, 89; teams played for, 90;
Tiller's description of, 77; as trophy
presenter, 111; on Vultee
Bomberettes, 54, *88;* Women's
Basketball Hall of Fame and, 176
Barding, Doris, 182
Barham, Leota, 42–43, *44*, 131
Barnard College, 4–5
Barron, Alice (Cookie), 112
basketball, 5, 6–7, 224n8
Basketball Techniques for Women
(Neal), 157
Basquette (Baer), 10
beauty contest, 30, *31*, 53, 55, 126
Bechtel, Rueben, 48, 165
Benjamin, Olawease, *186*
Beran, Janice, 194
Berenson, Bernard, 224n7
Berenson, Senda (nee Valvrojenski):
at 1901 basketball game, *9;* adjust-
ments to basketball for women, 7–8;
background of, 5; codification of
rules, 10–12; founding of women's
basketball, 4, 7–8; rule on snatching,
10; view of women's sports, 10,
127, 133
Berenson's rules, 10–11
Berry, Lucille (nee Thurman).
See Thurman, Lucille
Bingham, J. Lyman, 30
Bingham, Ruth, *70*
Bishop, Elva, 67, 135

black players/coaches: Colleen
    Bowser, 166, 183–84, 185; Lane
    Askine AC team, 185; Perry
    Wallace, 237n28; Philander Smith
    team, 110, 111, 185; Sally Smith,
    133–34, 168, 186–87; Southern
    attitudes and, 184–85; standards for,
    187; Marian Washington, 169, 185
Blackwelder, Doris, 182
Blann, Loretta, 48
Blazejowski, Carol, 158
Bloomer, Amelia, 3
Booker, Betty, x
Boston Normal School of Gymnastics
    (BNSG), 5
Bowden, Pauline Lunn. See Lunn,
    Pauline
Bowser, Colleen, 166, 183–84, 185
Bradley, Bill, 144
Bruce, Dot, 61, 65, 66
Bryn Mawr College, 4–5
Bulgarian team, 148
business leagues. See industrial leagues

cagers, 224n10
Caledonian Society of New York, 14
Campbell, Ruth, 52
Canadian-American competitions, 36,
    96–97
Cannon, Ruth, 111
Carlton, Lahoma Lassiter, 35
Carney, Pat, 59, 64, 65, 78
Carol Eckman Award, 169, 170
Cathey, Tennie, xi
Catholic Youth Organization
    (CYO), 13
Caulkins, Tracy, 235n28
championship tournaments: in
    1929–31, 32–33; in 1932–33,
    35–36; in 1934–35, 39–40; in 1936,
    41–42; in 1937, 42–43; in 1938–39,
    43–45; in 1940–41, 47, 47; in
    1942–43, 52, 54; in 1944, 54–55; in
    1946, 58; in 1947, 59–63; in 1948,
    63–64; in 1949, 64–65; in 1950,
    65–66; in 1951, 69; in 1952–53,
    70–72; in 1954, 72, 74; in 1955,

110; in 1956–57, 111; in 1958–59,
    112; in 1960, 124–25; in 1962, 125;
    in 1963, 126; in 1964, 127; in
    1965–68, 128, 130–31; in 1969,
    134; changes in flavor of, 129; first
    for women's basket ball, 15–16;
    Gallup, New Mexico as site for,
    128, 158; held by NCAA/AIAW,
    159–60; St. Joseph as site for, 46,
    128; top four finishers by year,
    215–18; Wichita as site for, 30
championship tournaments (WGBL),
    124–25
Chatham Mills Blanketeers, 58, 64, 65
Chattanooga Central, x
cheating, avoidance of, 15
Cheyney State, 160
Chicago Spencer Coals, 40
Chihuahua Adelitas, 72
Childers, Virginia, 226n11
Chilean Basketball Federation, 101
Clarendon Junior College team,
    110, 118
Clark, Betty, 102, 104, 182
clothing, 3, 17, 35, 106
coaches: best in AAU, 165–67; charac-
    teristics of, 164; current trends in
    attitudes of, 196; demographics of,
    195; migration of in 1930s, 33;
    recognition by halls of fame, 175;
    respect for in small towns, x; retired
    players as, 167–68, 197–98. See also
    specific coach
Coach of the Year Award, 169, 170
Coble, Judy, 183, 199
Cockerill, Kansas, 32
Cockerill Robins (Pittsburgh,
    Kansas), 32
collegiate teams: AAU encouragement
    of, 14; current status of, xiii; at
    early AAU tournaments, 32; early
    recruiting efforts, 16; first game of,
    8; history of, 160–64; increasing
    numbers of, 134, 158; interest in
    rising, 110; pioneering colleges, 4.
    See also collegiate competition;
    specific college

Commercial Graduates' Club teams, 96
commercialization, avoidance of, 15
commercial team sports, 3
Commission on Intercollegiate
    Athletics for Women (CIAW),
    154, 159
Commission on the Status of
    Women, 153
communist bloc countries, 95
competition, 6
competitive spirit, xiv, 4, 76, 224n5
conditioning, 76–77
consolation tournaments, 52, 62, 126
Consolidated Vultee Aircraft team.
    See Vultee Bomberettes
Convair Bomberettes, 99
Cook, Johnny, 84
Cook's Goldblumes: in 1946 tourna-
    ment, 58; at 1947 tournament, 61,
    61; at 1948 tournament, 63; at 1949
    tournament, 65; in 1950 tourna-
    ment, 66; Banks as player for, 91;
    championship streak, 72; coach of,
    165; competition with Mexico, 98,
    99, 101; disbanding of, 84; domina-
    tion of AAU, 125; Greer as replace-
    ment player, 82; Henry as player on,
    238n41; modern teams vs., 196–97;
    NBC ancestor, xii–xiii; players of
    Vultee Bomberettes as, 57–58;
    record of, 66; replacement players
    in 1946, 59; swan song of, 69
Cooper, Margie: at 1944–45 tourna-
    ments, 56; at 1949 tournament, 65;
    move to Cook's Goldblume team,
    57; relaxing, 190; on Vultee
    Bomberettes, 54
court divisions, 8, 10, 11, 36
Cox, Alberta: background of, 129, 150;
    as coach of Piperettes, 164; as coach
    of U.S. team, 149–50; Helms Hall
    of Fame induction, 131; Jostens-
    Berenson Service Award for, 236n8;
    Naismith Hall of Fame and, 175; as
    Olympic coach, 147; other sports
    played by, 183–84; push for U.S.
    team training camps, 152

Cox, Leroy, 129, 175, 197
Crawford, Joan: at 1957 World
    Championship, 112; in 1959 tour-
    nament, 112; accomplishments of,
    136; as All-American, 125, 127;
    experiences with White, 141–42;
    Helms Hall of Fame induction,
    131; hometown population, 183;
    motivation to play, 198; as MVP,
    125, 127; Naismith Hall of Fame
    induction, 175; as NBC player, 116;
    on Pan-American games, 148; pres-
    sure to work, 152; retirement of,
    133; salutary effect of playing ball,
    190–91; skills of, 121, 123; on
    smaller ball size, 179; on U.S.
    World Championship team, 118;
    WBHF induction, 144; on WGBL
    All-American team, 125
Crescent College team, 33
Crowell, Joy, 61
Crutcher, Gene, 28
Crutcher, Hazel Walker. See Walker,
    Hazel
Curtis, Ann, 226n4
Czechoslovakian team, 118, 148

Dallas, Texas teams, 17, 32, 40, 69.
    See also Employer's Casualty Life
    Insurance Company Golden
    Cyclones
Dallas Trezevant & Cochran team,
    32, 33
Davidson, Lucille, 118, 119, 183–84
Davis, Bette, 99
Delta State, 163
demographics, xii, 17, 22, 29–30, 32,
    180–83, 191–95
Denver Viners Chevrolet team, 69,
    165, 185
Department of Girl's and Women's
    Sports (DGWS), 158
Des Moines Home Federal, 61
Didrikson, Mildred (Babe): awards
    of, 174; exhibition stunt refusal,
    157; farewell game, 36; financial
    support of, 18; Helms Hall of Fame

induction, 132; as member of
Golden Cyclones, 17–18, *18*, 33;
national fame of, xiii; rooting for
Cyclones, 36; turn to professional
sports, 18–20; Walker vs., 22–23
diplomacy, 120
Division of Girl's and Women's Sports
(DGWS), 132, 148, 153–54
dribbling: 1966 continuous dribble rule,
154; change in rules on, 114; early
rules on, 11; evolution of rules on,
132, 139, 178; two allowed, 63;
unlimited rule, 127
Dr. Swett's team, 58
DuBois, Lee, 132
Dunaway, Bill, 42–43, *44*, 47, 98
Dunaway, Margaret, 98
Dunford, Lera, 38
Dunford, Vera, 38, *44*
Durant, Oklahoma, 34, 36
Durant Young Men's Business
Alliance, 35

ECC. *See* Employer's Casualty Life
Insurance Company Golden
Cyclones
Eckman, Carol, 12, 161, 169
Edmonton Grads, 36, 96
El Dorado (Arkansas) Lions, 42
eligibility rules: of AIAW, 159; of early
years, 86; enforcement of, 64–65,
85, 86, 91
Ellensburg State Normal School, 9–10
Employer's Casualty Life Insurance
Company Golden Cyclones: 1929
tournament, 32; 1930 tournament,
33; in 1931 tournament, 165;
1932–33 tournament, 35–36;
Didrikson signed to, 17; salary for
Didrikson, 18; team photo, *19*
Epps, Patsy, *31*

Fagg, Jackie Swaim. *See* Swaim, Jackie
fans: attempt to entice, 126; in Chile in
1953, 103; of Dallas teams, 17; during Depression era, 22; financial
commitment and, 167; of Flying

Queens, 109; lack of, 16–17, 119; in
Mexico, 99; of NBC, 112; of small
college teams, 164; view of White,
136; of women's basketball, 2
Fay, Carol, *128*
federal legislation, 153
Federation Internationale de Basketball
Amateur (FIBA), 44
Fenton, Everett O., 51
Fenton, Stephen, 51
FIBA, 95
Fiete, Sandy, 111, *128*, 132, 161
five-player game: AAU contemplating
use of, 132; adoption of, 154, 171;
impact on AAU rules, 127; institution of, 134; international competition and, 152, 178; need for rule
changes, 148; played at first AAU
tournament, 15; Redin advocacy
for, 114; rover rule and, 41
Foster, Lyle, 132
free-throw champions: of 1932, 36; in
1938, 45; in 1939, 46; of 1941, 50;
in 1943, 52; of 1944, 55; of 1947,
62–63; of 1952, 72; in 1964, 127;
Greer, 84; Neal, 109; tournaments
contests, 30; Walker, 24
full-court game: at 1926 tournament,
15; adopted in 1969, 154; Cardinals
instruction in, 37; exhibition game
at 1934 tournament, 40–41; experimental for Pan American games,
74; impact on AAU rules, 127;
international competition and, 152;
played by Canadians, 96–97; in
South America, 101
Full Court Press (Lupica), 235n29
funding: for AAU players, 156–57; for
Arkansas Travelers, 26; for Atlanta
Blues, 59; for Flying Queens, 105–7;
for halls of fame, 173, 174; of international competition, 96, 97, 102;
for OPC Cardinals, 36–38; solution
to problems, 160. *See also* sponsors
Futch, Eunies: at 1951 tournament, 69,
70; All-American 1952, 72; as
nucleus of Hanes Hosiery team, 67,

68; other sports played by, 183–84; on Pan-American team, 85; recruitment of, 75; winner of Louis Teague Award, 84

Gallup, New Mexico, 128, 158
Gallup Catholic Indian Center Falcons, 129
Galveston Anicos, 38, 45–46, 47, 87–88, 164
game governance, 14, 157, 171. See also Amateur Athletic Union (AAU); rules
Garmes, Faye, 199
Garms, Kaye, 111, 112
Garroute, Francis (Goose), 28, 85–86
Gentry, Lucille, 56
Georgia girls' basketball, 194
Georgia Sports Hall of Fame, 80, 91
girls' high school basketball: current trends, 195–96; of Dallas, 32; early breeding ground, 17; as farm clubs for AAU, 87; in Illinois, 192–94; in Kentucky, 192, 193; of Lawton, Oklahoma, 32; limitations on, 92; in Mississippi/South Carolina/Georgia, 194; national championships, 30, 32; popularity of, 2; in Tennessee, ix–x, 194
Gleaves, Margaret Sexton. See Sexton, Margaret
Goelzer, Bernice, 44
Golden Cylcones. See Employer's Casualty Life Insurance Company Golden Cyclones
Great Depression, 20, 21–22
Green, Joe, Jr., 185
Greer, Lurlyne: in 1945, 83; at 1947 tournament, 61; at 1949 tournament, 65; at 1950 tournament, 66; in 1952 tournament, 71, 72; attitude of, 77; background of, 82; basketball career of, 82–86; eligibility refused, 111; as featured player, xiii; as Goldblume player, 61; graduating class size, 182; Helms Hall of Fame induction, 131; job

after basketball, 198; marriage of, 84; move to Goldblumes, 59; move to Hanes Hosiery, 70, 75; Naismith Hall of Fame and, 175; other sports played by, 183–84; on Pan-American team, 84, 85, 117; personality of, 86; post-basketball career, 86; skills of, 80, 82; winner of Louis Teague Award, 84; Women's Basketball Hall of Fame and, 176
Gregory, Fern, 63, 65, 182
Gregory, Loretta Blann, 131
Grindle, Deanna, 127
Gulick, Luther, Jr., 6
Gunter, Sue: on All-American team, 125; education of, 136; other sports played by, 183–84; professional longevity of, 170; on quality of Wayland/NBC, 96; view of White, 139, 144–45; Women's Basketball Hall of Fame and, 176
Gwynn, Mollie, 186

Halford, Betty, 115
halls of fame, 173–74. See also specific hall of fame
Hamlen, Virginia, 56
Hampshire, Tennessee team, ix–xi, xi
Hampton, Hugh, 72
Hanes Hosiery team: at 1949 tournament, 65; at 1951 tournament, 69, 70; in 1953 tournament, 72; in 1954 tournament, 72, 110; defeat of Goldblumes, 59; disbanding of, 74–75, 84, 103; domination of AAU, 66, 67, 112, 125; end of winning streak, 104; exhibition game in 1954, 74; Greer as player for, 84; Pan-American qualifying tournament, 117; philosophy of, 74–75; replacement of players in 1952, 70; sponsor of, xiii; Vaughn as member of, 65
Hanson, Bessie, 186
Harris, Doll, 35–36, 38
Harris, Lusia, 143

Hartman, Becky Harris, 183–84

Hartness, Julie, *62*

Hays (basketball court builder), ix

Head, John Lyman: on 1958 victory over Wayland, 112; background of, 146; as best of AAU coaches, 165; career of, 146–47; as coach of U.S. World Championship team, 102, *104*, 117, 138; as coach on USSR tour, 120; decline USSR tour, 125; first championship, 66; induction into WBHF, 144; leader of dominant team, 65; Naismith Hall of Fame and, 175; recruiting program of, 121, 135; running duel with Redin, 114; on *Sports Illustrated* list of sport figures, 235n28; use of food supplements, 126; use of outside players, 64, 231n33

Head, Verna, 110

Hedgecock, Irma, *70*

Heiss, Tara, 158

Helms, Paul, 174

Helms Athletic Hall of Fame: 1968 inductees, 132; Banks selected for, 91; first class of inductees, 131; Greer's induction, 86; Head's induction, 147; history of, 174; Hudson selected for, 166; Redin selected for, 114; Walker's induction, 28; White's induction, 144; Yow's induction, 75

Helms Foundation Athlete award, 91, 132

Henry, Mary, 238n41

Hickey, Lynn Suter, 168, 182, 199

Hill, Thednall, 195

Hinnant, Elizabeth, *186*

Hodson, Judy, *128*

Hoeppner, Shirley, *128*

Hoffay, Mary, 55, 62, 131

Holdenville Flyers, 40

holding, 11

Holdsclaw, Chamique, 2, 145

Holt, Peggy, 126

Hood, Alberta Williams. *See* Williams, Alberta

Hoover, Lou, 15

Horky, Rita: in 1958 tournament, *128;* as All-American, 125; as coach, 168; Helms Hall of Fame induction, 131; as player from Iowa Wesleyan, 161; on World Championship team, 119, 150

Hudson, Billy: at 1944–45 tournaments, *56;* assembly of Vultee Bomberettes, 54; as best of AAU coaches, 165–66; recommendations for laxer rules, 63; retirement as coach, 64; as Vultee Bomberettes coach, 53

Hudson, Pollye, 54, 98

Hungarian team, 118

Hutcherson, Claude, 105–6, *108, 115*, 175

Hutcherson, Wilda, 106, *108, 115*

Hutcherson Flying Queens. *See* Wayland Flying Queens

Ikard, Robert Edwin, x–xii, *xi,* 224n15

Illinois girls' basketball, 192–94

Immaculata College, 163

industrial leagues: AAU encouragement of, 14; amateur standing of, 18; of Dallas, 32; decreasing popularity, 95–96, 129, 134, 158; demise of, 180; Hanes Hosiery as last of, 67; inception of, 13; intercompany competition of, 16, 17; stars of, xiii. *See also specific team*

Ingram, Jane Marshall. *See* Marshall, Mary Jane

Insell, Rick, 195

Intercollegiate Athletic Association, 14

intercollegiate competition, 8–9, 12, 105

international competition: AAU encouragement of, 96–104; with AAU players, xiii, 95; adjustments needed for, 152–53, 178; development camp for, 138, 150, 152, 179–80; Head as coach for U.S. teams, 147; history of, 170–73; impact on AAU rules, 127, 179;

with Mexico, 97–99, *99, 100,* 101;
NBC games of, 122; Olympic
games, 101; Pan-American games,
74, 84, 111, 114, 117, 119, 148,
152; Redin as coach of U.S. team,
114; rule changes and, 132; tour in
Lima, Peru, 127, 173; tours of
Mexico, 125, 171; tours of South
America, 101–2, 151, 173; tours
of USSR, 112, 125, 148, *149,* 171;
U.S. decline, 148–49; U.S. vs.
Canadian teams, 36–37, 96–97;
White's view of, 137–38, 147,
152; World Championship
Tournament, 38, 97, 101,
102–3, 112, 117–19, 148–51
International YMCA Training School,
6–7
Iowa, 160, 181–82, 194. *See also* Iowa
Wesleyan Tigerettes
Iowa Girls' High School Athletic
Union, 194
Iowa Wesleyan Tigerettes: in 1952
tournament, 70, *71;* 1953 upset, 72;
in 1955 tournament, 110; in 1956
tournament, 111; in 1957 tournament, 111–12; in 1958 tournament,
112, *128;* in 1961 tournament, 125;
1962 games with USSR, 126; in
1962 tournament, 125; in 1963
tournament, 127; in 1965 tournament, 129; in 1968 tournament,
131; among first collegiate teams,
xiii; coach of, 166; competition
with Flying Queens, 110; competition with NBC, 121; history of
competition, 160–61; in NGBL,
123–24; players of on World
Championship team, 102; school
population, 160

Jaax, Correne, 35, 131
Jackson, Bessie, *186*
Jackson, Lottie, 46, 62
James E. Sullivan Award, 24, 91, 144,
145, 225n4–26n4

Jim Thorpe Memorial Oklahoma
Athletic Hall of Fame, 38
John F. Kennedy College team: in
1969 tournament, 134; AIAW and,
163; championships of, 158; coach
of, 166; financial failure of, 164; in
NWIT, 161
Johnson, Billie, *186*
Johnson, Don, 165
Johnson, Mildred, *190*
Johnson, Raymond, 179
Jordan, Evelyn (Eckie): at 1951 tournament, 69, *70;* in 1952 tournament,
72; All-American 1952, 72; as
nucleus of Hanes Hosiery team, 67,
68; other sports played by, 183–84;
on Pan-American team, *85;* winner
of Louis Teague Award, 84
Jostens-Berenson Service Award, 115,
167, 236n8

Kansas City Dons, 72, 104, 110,
117, 165
Kendrick, Perlie, *186*
Kennedy, John F., 153
Kentucky girls' basketball, 192, *193*
Kirtley, June, *44*
kissing-your-brother award, 53
Kite, Joyce, *115*
Korsgaard, Robert, 155–56
Krzyzewski, Mike, 146

Ladies Professional Golf Association, 20
Lambuth College of Jackson,
Tennessee, 40, 42
Lampson, Ernestine, 42
Lane Askine AC team, 185
Laurenson, Eddie, 16
Lawton, Oklahoma high school
team, 32
Levy, Henry, 26
Lewis-Norwood Insurance
Company, 24
Lieberman, Nancy, 144
Link, Mary, 61, 182
Linville, Lorene, *56*

Lion Oil, xiii, 24
Little, John Wesley, 57, 69
Little Rock Dr. Peppers, 24, 55, 82, 98
Little Rock Flyers: in 1937 tourna-
    ment, 24, 42–43; in 1938–39
    tournaments, 45; in 1940–41 tour-
    naments, 24, 47, 48, 88, 89; in 1958
    tournament, 24; domination of
    early competitions, 125; team pho-
    tograph, 44
Little Rock Motor Coaches, 52, 54.
    See also Little Rock Flyers
Lockwood, Phyllis, 183–84
London Shamrocks, 96
Long, Leo: at 1942–43 tournaments, 52;
    apparent retirement of, 54; as best
    coach, 65, 229n15; as coach of
    Goldblumes, 65; as coach of NBC,
    44; at loss of 1941 championship,
    48–49; provision of gym for work-
    outs, 76; White's jumpshot and, 139
Look Magazine team, 130, 186
Los Angeles Athletic Club, 15–16
Louisiana State University (LSU),
    163, 170
Louisiana Tech, 160, 163
Louis Teague Award, 84
Lowry, Carla: 1959 championship
    photo, 115; as coach, 168; on inter-
    national competition, 179; jobs
    after basketball, 199; try outs for
    Flying Queens, 107–8; view of
    White, 139, 145
Loyd, Agnes, 66, 182
Lunn, Pauline: at 1949 tournament,
    65; in 1952–53 tournaments, 72; on
    1953 World Championship team,
    103, 104; graduating class size, 182;
    hometown population, 182; move
    to Goldblume team, 59, 61

Macomber, Margaret, 52
Mahan (namer of basketball), 7
Majors, Les, 165
marketing. See publicity
Marshall, Kathryn, 54, 56

Marshall, Mary Jane: at 1944–45
    tournaments, 56; at 1946 tourna-
    ment, 58; in 1947 tournament, 49;
    at 1949 tournament, 65; change of
    sports, 66; on conditions in
    Mexico, 98–99; as Goldblumes
    player, 61; Helms Hall of Fame
    induction, 131; knee injury, 66; on
    lack of historic integrity, 93; as
    leader of Goldblumes, 59; at loss of
    1941 championship, 48, 49; on
    Mexican players, 101; move to
    Goldblumes, 57; other sports
    played by, 183–84; on physical
    appearance of players, 189; relax-
    ing, 190; talents of, 48; on Vultee
    Bomberettes, 53–54
Marshall, Nora, 190
Martin, Glenn, 175, 197
Martin, Shirley, 164
Martin Squaws, 100, 160
Mathias, Bob, 91
Matlock, Ann, 142, 168, 182
Matthews, Caddo, 85, 104, 111,
    114, 117
McCarley, John, 59, 165
McCombs, M. J., 17–18
McCrary, Chloe, 44
McDonald, Margie Hunt: on being a
    Flying Queens player, 106; as
    coach, 168; on dangers of interna-
    tional competitions, 173; experi-
    ences with White, 140; jobs after
    basketball, 199; on sexual innuen-
    dos, 189; on today's players,
    235n30; view of White, 145
McGhee, Tennie, 104, 111, 132
McPherson, Blanche, 54, 59, 78,
    183–84, 190
McPherson, Dora, 54, 59, 78, 190
Mealhouse, Lurlyne Greer. See Greer,
    Lurlyne
men's basketball, 101, 224n10
Merrill, Gary, 99
Mesquite (Texas) High School team, 35
Mexican Politas, 98, 99

Mexican teams, 97–99, *99, 100*
Mexico, 125
Mexico City Chihuahuas, *100*
Meyers, Ann, 158
Mickelsen, Laurine (Mickie), 119, 127,
   151, 156, 187–88
Middle Tennessee Teachers College, 32
Midland Jewelry team, 111, 117,
   118, 185
Midwestern College team, 131, 161,
   164, 186
migration of players, 18, 33, 38,
   42–43, 45
Miller, Carolyn, 1, 20, *115*, 182
Miller, Cheryl, 2, 145
Miss Head's School, 9–10
Mississippi girl's basketball, 194
Mississippi State College for Women
   team, 131, 163
Moffatt, Carolyn, 141, 164
Moody, William L., III, 45, 175
Moon, Johnny, 165
Moon, Madge, *62*
Moore, Billie, 176
Moorman, Sheila, 168
Morris, Cliff, 237n27
Morris, Missouri Arledge, 183–84, 185
Mosher, Ellen, 168
Most Valuable Player award: of 1950,
   66; of 1961–62, 125; for Banks, 48,
   50, 88, 89, *90;* for Sexton, 64; for
   Walker, 52; White as ten times, 143
Mt. Holyoke, 4–5
Mueller, Joyce, *70*
municipal leagues, 13
Murphy, Betty, 102, *104,* 182

Nabucos. *See* Nashville Business
   College (NBC) team
Nadler, Sylvia, 199
Naismith, James: background of, 5;
   at first Olympic basketball game,
   101; invention of basketball, 4, 6–7,
   16; view of women's rules, 40–41,
   127, 178
Naismith Award, 2
Naismith Basketball Hall of Fame:

AAU players/coaches in, 174–75;
   AAU players/coaches missing
   from, 29, 147; AAU trophy in, 58;
   Banks selected for, 91; funding for,
   173; Harris/White induction into,
   143; Meyers induction into, 158;
   new building opening, 236–37n16;
   opening of, 174; Redin nomination
   for, 115; White/Crawford in, 136
Nash, Fern, 101, 102, *104*
Nashville, Tennessee: Cook's
   Goldblume team from, 57–58;
   Helms Hall of Fame inductees from
   team of, 131; low point in 1953,
   72; as paramount city for AAU
   women's basketball, 53–56; seventh
   year of championship finals, 66;
   welcome of NBC team in 1958, 112
Nashville Business College (NBC)
   team: at 1936 tournament, 42; in
   1938 tournament, 44; in 1939 tournament, 46; in 1940–41 tournament, 47; in 1943 tournament, 53;
   in 1944 tournament, 55; at 1948–49
   tournament, 64–65; in 1950 tournament, 66; at 1951 tournament,
   69; in 1952 tournament, 71; 1953
   upset, 72; in 1955–57 tournaments,
   111; at 1957 World Championship,
   112; in 1958–59 tournaments, 112;
   in 1961–62 tournaments, 125; 1962
   games with USSR, 126; 1963 team
   demographics, 182; in 1963 tournament, *124,* 126, 127; in 1965–67
   tournaments, 129, 130–31; in
   1968–69 season, 133; in 1968 tournament, 131; in 1969 tournament,
   134; absence of players on 1967
   World Championship team, 151;
   Banks as player for, 87, 89, 91;
   championships of 50s, 66; character
   of players, 238n33; competition
   with Flying Queens, 110, 114, 161;
   competition with Mexico, 98;
   domination of AAU, 96, 121, 125;
   modern teams vs., 196, 197; newspaper articles about, xii–xiii; in

NGBL, 123–24; players on World Championship team, 102, 118; rise of, 53; rivals of, 51; Sally Smith as player for, 187; source of players, 231n33; travel time, 106; withdrawal from AAU, 134–35, 158
Nashville teams, xiv
National Amateur Athletic Federation (NAAF), 14–15
National Association of Intercollegiate Athletics (NAIA), 163
National Basketball Association, xiii
National Coach of the Year, 169
National Collegiate Athletic Association (NCAA): change in standard ball size, 11, 178–79; Division One women's basketball, 1, 2, 22; effect on early prominent teams, 163; former players in administration of, 168; game governance and, 159–60; men's basketball, 2; Women's Final Four, 200
National General West team, 158
National Girls' Basketball League (NGBL), 122–24, 126
National Invitation Tournament (NIT), 22
National Sports Institute, 154
National Women's Invitational Tournament (NWIT), 114, 161–62, 167
Naylor, Hazel, 70
NCAA. See National Collegiate Athletic Association (NCAA)
Neal, Patsy: in 1959 tournament, 112, 115; accomplishments of, 157, 236n8; as coach, 168; international competitions of, 171; jobs after basketball, 199; motivation to play, 198; prayer of, 95; tryouts for Queens, 108–9
Nerren, Sally, 183, 195, 231n33
"A New Game," 7
Newton, Gary, 25–26
New York Athletic Club, 14
NGBL All-American teams, 124
Nichols, Ethel, 16

Nicholson, Glenda, 128
Nicodemus, Karen Williams, 168
North American Amateur Athletic Association, 14
North American championship, 36
Northeastern Oklahoma A&M team, 110, 123

Odom, Lometa, 111, 115, 132
Oklahoma championship, 40
Oklahoma City University Cardinals, 38, 39–40
Oklahoma Presbyterian College for Girls Cardinals, 34–39, 37, 40, 96–97, 160
Oklahoma teams, 33–39, 181–82, 194. See also Tulsa Business College Stenos
Old Dominion College, 162, 163
Olson, C. M., 26
Olson's All-American Red Heads, 25–26, 38
Olympics: 1940 cancellation, 101; 1976 delayed, 147; AAU influence on player choices, 95; consideration of women's' basketball, 44–45; Didrikson as contestant, 18–20; inclusion of men's basketball, 101; inclusion of women's basketball, 166; Meyers on U.S. team, 158; Sharp's contribution to, 169; U.S. team's record, 171; women coaches of U.S. teams, 170
Omaha Aces, 130
Omaha Comets, 130
Omaha Commercial Extension team, 111, 122
OPC. See Oklahoma Presbyterian College for Girls Cardinals
Orange Lionettes, 130
Osborne, Shannon, 183, 197
Osterloh, Elizabeth, 44
Ouachita Baptist College team, 126, 131, 141, 161
out-of-bounds balls, 11, 224n10

Page, Percy, 96, 127
Pan-American games: 1955 team, *85;*
of 1959, 119; in 1963, 148; in 1967,
152; AAU coaches/players, 84, 111,
114, 173; current U.S. team rank-
ing, 171; history of, 114
Paradise, Anne: as Atlanta Blues player,
62, 78, 78–79; attitude of, 77, *79,*
80; on Mexican fans, 98–99; move
to Atlanta Blues, 59; move to
Blanketeers, 64; physical features
of, 77, 80, *81;* at practice for
Atlanta, *60;* skills of, 80; teams
played for, 77–78, 80
Parisi Dreamettes, 62
Parker, Sarah, 72
Parsons, Pam, 168
Parsons College, 164, 166, 186
Pasadena Athletic & Country Club
Flying Rings, 15–16
Pate, Alline Banks. *See* Banks, Alline
Peabody Demonstration School, x
Pemberton, Naomi, *186*
Perón, Eva, 171, *172*
personal fouls, 11
Peruvian tour, 127
Petty, Margaret Sexton. *See* Sexton,
Margaret
Philander Smith Pantherettes, 110,
111, 185, *186*
Phillips, Hazel Starret, *70,* 72
physical education departments, 4
Plainview, Texas, xiv
Platt College Secretaries, 46, 118,
122, 125
players: of AAU era vs. today, 196–98;
characteristics of, 18, 21, 23,
199–200; character of, 188–91, 198;
demographics, 180–83, 191–95; education of, 197, 198; jobs after basketball, 198–99; jobs during basketball
career, 18, 198; motivations of,
183–84, 198; race of, 184–88. *See
also individual players by name*
Poff, Mona, *115*
practice, 76

Prause, Ann, *44*
publicity: in 1960s, 153; for 1968 tournament, 131; AAU era vs. today,
197; for AAU women's basketball,
xiii, 15–17, 20, 46, 92, 179; about
Banks, 47; during Depression era,
22; for industrial leagues, 16; loca-
tion of national tournament and,
30; for NCAA basketball, 1–2;
solution to problems, 160; for
Walker, 22–23

Queens College, 163

Radcliffe University, 4–5
Rainey, Genevieve, *62*
Ramsey, Pat, 168
Randolph College Kittens, 32, 33
Ransom, Chuck, 165
Rapp, Cherri, 168
Raytown Piperettes: in 1965 tournament, 129, 130; in 1967 tournament, 130; in 1968 tournament,
131; Bowser as player for, 186; players on Pan-Am team in 1999, 173;
players on World Championship
team, 150; Marian Washington as
player for, 169, 186
recruitment: AAU as source for, 156;
AIAW limits on, 159; of Babb, 34;
by colleges in early years of AAU,
16; Flying Queens program, 107–9;
NBC's program, 121; of Walker, 24
Redin, Harley: awards of, 114–15,
236n8; as best of AAU coaches,
165; as coach of Flying Queens,
105, 110, 112, 113–15, *115, 116;*
coach of team playing USSR, 120,
125; as coach of U.S. World
Championship team, 119–20; Head
vs., 146, 147; on history of AAU,
xiii; Naismith Hall of Fame and,
175; record of, 114; recruitment
program of, 146–47, 161; on tour
in Peru, 127; on Wayland in collegiate competition, 163

Richardson, Margaret, *62*

Rogers, Doris (Gunner): on AAU country women, 23; accomplishments of, 136; as All-American, *125, 188;* on daily schedule, 197–98; education of, 136, 197; hometown population, 183

Rogers, Frank W., 86

Rogers, Lurlyne Greer. *See* Greer, Lurlyne

rover rule, 41, *123,* 132, 154, 177, 178

Ruble, Olan, 102, *128,* 132, 161, 166

Rudolph, Wilma, 235n28

rules: changes in, 40–41, 92, 127, 177–78; codification of, 10–12; on dribbling, 11, 63, 114, 127, 132, 139, 154, 178; five-player game and, 127, 134, 148, 154, 171; governing bodies, 14; gradual relaxation of, 63; liberalization of, 75; need for changes, 148; on rovers, 41

Rupp, Adolph, 146

Russell, Fred, 179

Russell, Virginia, *44*

Rutgers team, 160

Ryden, Alice, 16

Sanders, Mildred, *104,* 182

Sante Fe Streamliners, 72

Schepp's Aces, 32, 33

Schmidlin, Father Dunstan, 128–29

school-related activities, ix, 16

Schroeder, Bill, 174

Schultz, Leo, 165

Scoggin, Marsha, *115*

Seagraves, Nell, 55

season tickets, 76

Selle, Lu Nell, 109

Seminole Junior College, 160

semiprofessional status, 18, 42–43

Seven Sisters, 4–5

Sexton, Margaret: at 1944–45 tournaments, *56;* at 1946 tournament, 58; at 1948 tournament, 64; at 1949 tournament, 65; on All-American team, 55; Helms Hall of Fame

induction, 131; as leader of Goldblumes, 59, *61, 190;* move to Goldblumes, 57–58; retirement of, 66; on Vultee Bomberettes, 54

sexual orientation, 189

Sharp, Martha, 169, 176

Sherman, George: on 1953 upset, 72; on AAU coaches, 165; on Bank's star quality, 89; creation of conference, 122; on integration of teams, 184–85; view of White, 136, 139

Shoute, Norma, 70–71

Simpson, Juliene Brazinski, 168

Singleton, Linda, 183

Sioux City, Iowa team, 125

Sipes, Barbara: in 1957 tournament, 111; in 1958 tournament, 112; at 1967 Pan-American games, 152; in 1968 tournament, 132; AAU debut of, 110; Helms Hall of Fame induction, 132; other sports played by, 183–84; as player from Iowa Wesleyan, 161; salutary effect of playing ball, 189–90; on U.S. World Championship team, 118, 150

six-player game, xii

Smiddy, Jim, 195

Smith, Correne Jaax, 35, 131

Smith, Dean, 146

Smith, Kermit, 29

Smith, Nelda, *115*

Smith, Sally: 1969 Rookie of the Year, 134; as All-American, *188;* as coach, 168; discrimination of, 186–87; skills of, 133–34; view of White, 145

Smith College, 4–5, 8, *9*

snatching, 10, 11

South Carolina girls' basketball, 194

Southeastern Teachers College Savages, 36

Southern Beer Company, 57, 229n8

Spalding's Official Women's Basket Ball Guide (Berenson), 10–11, 12

Sparkman (Arkansas) Sparks, 32, 33

Spencer, Bob, 141, 166, 167

Spivey, Mildred, 45

sponsors: after World War II, 56–57;
American National Insurance
Company, 45; for Cardinals, 35;
Leroy Cox as, 130; diminution of,
95–96, 129, 134, 158; in early years,
xiii; for Flying Queens, 105–6;
industry/business leagues, 13, 16,
18; oil-related businesses, 29;
recognition by halls of fame, 175;
of Walker's teams, 24. *See also*
funding
sports club, 14
Sports Illustrated list of sports figures,
29, 91, 115, 144, 235n28
sportswriters, 47, 60, 77, 87
Springfield, Massachusetts Young
Men's Christian Association
(YMCA), 7
Sprouse, Alline Banks. *See* Banks,
Alline
Sprouse, H. B., 64
Stagg, Amos Alonzo, 6
Stanford University, 9–10
State Department, 95, 120
Stephen F. Austin College, 170
Stewart, June, *115*
Stiles, Jackie, 196
St. Joseph, Missouri, 46, *47*, 128
St. Joseph Goetz Beer team, 46, 111
St. Joseph Welders, 46
Stroud, Sara Parker, *70*
Suggs, Louise, 91
Sullivan, James E., 14
Summitt, Pat, 1, 146, 235n28
Sunoco Oilers, 33
supporters, 132
Swaim, Jackie: 1949 free-throw cham-
pion, *74;* at 1951 tournament, 69,
70; on Coach Yow, 75; move to
Hanes Hosiery team, 67; view of
Mrs. Van Blarcom, 132
Swedish System, 4
Swigert, Nancy, *70*
Switzer, Laura, 125, 199
Swoops, Sheryl, 2, 145, 169

Taft, Larry, 143
Taurasi, Diana, 2, 145
Taylor, Geraldine, *186*
Teague, Bertha, 195
Temple Junior College team, 131, 160
Tennessee: divisions in, 228n4; girls'
high school basketball, 194; players
from, 181–82; Shelbyville team,
195; strength in 1949 tournament,
65. *See also* Nashville Business
College (NBC) team
Tennessee Hall of Fame, 91
Tennessee Highway Patrol
Dreamettes, 71–72
Tennessee State Hall of Fame, 144, 147
Tennessee State High School
Tournament, xii
testing of instincts, ix–x
Texas, 181–82, 194
Texas team, 160, 162
Texas Tech Red Raiders, 169
T F & R Queen Bees, 161
Thompson, Janet, 102, *104,* 161, 182
Thompson, Neva, x
three-division game, 52, 224n15
Thurman, Lucille: in 1936–37 tourna-
ments, 42, 43; as All-American, 38;
Helms Hall of Fame induction,
131; on Little Rock Flyers, *44;*
migration of, 42–43
Tiller, Guy, 77
Title IX: end of AAU and, 158; girls'
high school basketball and, 194;
implementation of, 12–13; imple-
mentation of training camps,
179–80; influence of, 159, 167, 171
Tobacco Road (Caldwell), 183
training camps, 138, 150, 152, 179–80,
179–80
transportation: in 40s and 50s, 76; for
Arkansas Travelers, 26; of Flying
Queens, 105–6; private vehicles,
98; to South America, 98
Travis, Leslie, x
Tucker, Linda, 168
Tugwell, Susie, 36
Tulsa Business College Stenographers:

in 1933 tournament, 24; 1934–35 tournament, 39–40; in 1936 tournament, 42; in 1937 tournament, 43; in 1938 tournament, 45; awards of, 42; domination of early competitions, 72, 125; marriage of players of, 28; win over Cardinals, 38
Turrentine, Margaret, 53
two-division game, 40–41, 52, 177

Underwood Trophy, 96
uniforms, 17–18, 35, 106. *See also* clothing
United States Information Agency, 120
United States Olympic Committee, 148, 154
University of California, Berkeley team, 9–10
University of California, Los Angeles, 162, 163
University of Connecticut Huskies, 1, 2
University of New Mexico, 129
University of South Carolina, 163
University of Tennessee Volunteers, 1, 163
University of Washington, 9–10
Upton, Jill, 125, 136, 168, 182, 199
USSR: in 1957 World Championship, 117, 118–19, 138; at 1967 World Championship, 151; tours of/by, 120, 125, 126, 148, *149, 171*

Van Blarcom, Mrs. Irvin, 43, *85, 104, 132, 175*
Vassar, 4–5
Vaughn, Cornelia, *70*
Vaughn, Jimmie: in 1942–43 tournaments, 53; as 1944 beauty queen, 55; at 1947 tournament, 62–63; at 1949 tournament, 65; at 1951 tournament, 69, *70;* as Atlanta Blues player, *62, 78;* move to Atlanta Blues, 59; move to Hanes Hosiery team, 67, 75; Tiller's description of, 77
Vickers, Hazel, 38, 42

Victorian concepts: Berenson on, 10; girls' high school basketball and, 192–94; girls' physical education and, 4, 5; influence on Berenson, 10; organizations holding to, 14–15
Vultee Bomberettes: in 1942–43 tournaments, 52; in 1944–45 tournaments, 54–56, *56;* background of, 53–54; Banks as player for, *88,* 91; coach of, 165; domination of AAU, 125; games with Mexican teams, 97–98; NBC ancestor, xii–xiii; players of, *190*

Walker, Hazel: in 1934 tournament, 40; in 1937 tournament, 42; in 1940–41 tournaments, 47, 48, 49; in 1942–43 tournaments, 52–53; at 1944 tournament, 55; amateur career of, 24–25; on amateur/professional status, 18; awards of, 28–29, 52, 174; background of, 23–24; as featured player, xiii; as free-throw champion, 45, 46, 53; as Greer's coach, 82; Helms Hall of Fame induction, 131; on her life as player, 21; on Little Rock Flyers, *44;* Naismith Hall of Fame and, 175; personal life of, *25,* 28, 29; popularity in Mexico, 98; professional career of, 21, 25–26, *27,* 28; publicity and, 179; screenplay of, 225n23; Sullivan Award nomination, 144; teams played on, 53; view of El Dorado Lions, 42
Wallace, Perry, 237n28
Wallenstein-Raffman team (Wichita), 32
Warren, L. D., 59
Washington, Katherine: in 1952 tournament, 71; in 1953 tournament, 72; on 1953 World Championship team, 103, *104;* 1959 championship photo, *115;* Helms Hall of Fame induction, 132; hometown population, 182; other sports played by, 183–84; tryouts for Queens, 109;

on U.S. World Championship team, 118
Washington, Marian, 169, 176, 185
Wayland Baptist College of Plainview, Texas, xiii, 105
Wayland Flying Queens: at 1951 tournament, 69; in 1953 tournament, 72, 104; in 1956 tournament, 111; in 1957–59 tournaments, 112; 1959 team, 115; 1962 games with USSR, 126; in 1962 tournament, 125; in 1963 tournament, 126, 127; in 1965–67 tournaments, 129, 130–31; in 1968 tournament, 131; in 1969 tournament, 134; in 1970s, 158; in collegiate competition, 163; competition with NBC, 114, 121; domination of AAU, 96, 110–13, 125; emergence of, 51, 66–67; exhibition game in 1954, 74; funding for, 105–7; history of competition, 161; naming of, 105; in NGBL, 123–24, 125; in NWIT, 161, 162; Pan-American qualifying tournament, 117; players on tour of USSR, 125; players on U.S. Pan-Am teams, 117, 119, 173; players on U.S. World Championship team, 118; recruitment, 107–8; standards for, 109; style of, 109–10; swan song of AAU era, 125; transportation of, 105–6, 107; winning record of, 114
Wayne State team, 131
WBHOF. See Women's Basketball Hall of Fame
Weems, Doris: at 1944–45 tournaments, 56; at 1946 tournament, 58; at 1950 tournament, 66; as Atlanta Blues player, 62, 78; move to Goldblumes, 57; at practice for Atlanta, 60; Tiller's description of, 77; on Vultee Bomberettes, 54
Wellesley, 4–5
Wells, Lamar, 59
West Chester State Ramettes, 12, 163, 169

West State Teachers College, 32
White, Jeff, 142
White, Linda, 168
White, Nera Dyson: at 1957 World Championship, 112; in 1959 tournament, 112; 1959 World Championship and, 119; in 1961 tournament, 125; in 1968–69 season, 133; in 1968 tournament, 131–32; AAU debut of, 110; as AAU player, xiii, 136–38; after NBC's retirement, 142–43; as All-American, 125, 127, 134, 188; as anchor for NBC, 116, 121; awards and honors, 143–44; background of, 135–36; connection with Lieberman, 235n29; decline of USSR tour, 125; financial status of, 197; Helms Hall of Fame induction, 131; hometown population, 183; job after basketball, 198; as MVP, 125, 134; Naismith Hall of Fame induction, 136, 137, 143, 175, 234n26, 235n28; newspaper articles about, xii; other sports played by, 183–84; physical features of, 136, 138; publicity and, 179; quiet demeanor of, 136, 141–42, 238n33; skills of, 139–40, 140, 144–46; on smaller ball size, 179; on Sally Smith's ability, 187; softball career of, 138; on Sports Illustrated list of sport figures, 235n28; on U.S. World Championship team, 118–19; view of Head, 147; view of international competitions, 137–38, 152; on WGBL All-American team, 125
Wichita, Kansas, 30, 32
Wichita Beacon Trophy, 42
Wichita Centrals, 42
Wichita Thurstons: in 1931 tournament, 33; in 1934 tournament, 24; in 1936 tournament, 42; in 1937 tournament, 43; in 1938–39 tournament, 45; full-court exhibition game, 40

Wiginton, Jan, *115*
William Penn College, 161
Williams, Alberta, 36, 39, 40, 131
Williams, Frances, 42, 45, 164
Williams, Jimmie Vaughn. *See* Vaughn, Jimmie
Williams, Kathryn, *62, 78*
Willis, Patsy, *186*
Wilson, Cathy, 168
Wilson, Macile, *62*
Wilson, Mildred, *62*
Winslow, Mary Link. *See* Link, Mary
Winston-Salem, North Carolina, xiv
women's basketball, 238n41
Women's Basketball Committee, 11
Women's Basketball Hall of Fame: Blazejowski/Heiss/Meyers as inductees, 158; criteria of, 176–77; director of, 199; Greer's induction, 86; Head's induction, 147; nominating body of, 174; Redin selected for, 114; Sharp induction, 169; Walker's induction, 29; Marian Washington induction, 170; White/Head/Crawford induction, 144, 235n28
women's basketball history, 4–16
Women's Division of National Amateur Athletic Federation (WDNAAF), 15
Women's National Basketball Association, 144
women's professional leagues, xiii
women's sports history, xv, 3–4, 13–14
Woodall, Dixie, 136, 150, 168, 182, 183–84
Woodard, Lynette, 169

World Basketball Hall of Fame, 91–92
World Championship Tournament: in 1934 in London, 38, 97; in 1953 in Chile, 72, 101, 102–3, *104;* in 1957, 112, 117–18, 138; in 1964, 148–49; in 1967 tournament, 149–51; AAU coaches/players, 114, 170, 173; Cardinals participation, 38; U.S. participation, 170–71; U.S. team players' demographics, 182
World University Games (1967), 153
World War II, 50, 51, 53, 56
WSM Girls, 165

Young, Loretta, 151–52
Young Men's Christian Association (YMCA), 6–7, 13, 14
Young Men's Hebrew Association (YMCA), 13
Young USA, 150
Young Women's Christian Association (YWCA), 13
Young Women's Hebrew Association (YWHA), 13
Yow, Virgil: at 1951 tournament, *70;* assessment of 1951 win, 69; as best of AAU coaches, 165; as coach of Hanes Hosiery team, 67, 75; on Greer, 84; knowledge of women, 155; methods of, 72; tour of South America, 101–2

Zacharias, Mildred (Babe) Didrikson. *See* Didrikson, Mildred (Babe)
Zimmerman, Mary, 168